W9-BXY-260

The Conservatives
Have No Clothes

The Conservatives Have No Clothes

Why Right-Wing Ideas Keep Failing

GREG ANRIG

John Wiley & Sons, Inc.

WEST HARTFORD PUBLIC LIBRARY

3322

Copyright © 2007 by Greg Anrig. All rights reserved

Published by John Wiley & Sons, Inc., Hoboken, New Jersey
Published simultaneously in Canada

Wiley Bicentennial Logo: Richard J. Pacifico

No part of this publication may be reproduced, stored in a retrieval system, or transmitted in any form or by any means, electronic, mechanical, photocopying, recording, scanning, or otherwise, except as permitted under Section 107 or 108 of the 1976 United States Copyright Act, without either the prior written permission of the Publisher, or authorization through payment of the appropriate per-copy fee to the Copyright Clearance Center, 222 Rosewood Drive, Danvers, MA 01923, (978) 750-8400, fax (978) 646-8600, or on the web at www.copyright.com. Requests to the Publisher for permission should be addressed to the Permissions Department, John Wiley & Sons, Inc., 111 River Street, Hoboken, NJ 07030, (201) 748-6011, fax (201) 748-6008, or online at http://www.wiley.com/go/permissions.

Limit of Liability/Disclaimer of Warranty: While the publisher and the author have used their best efforts in preparing this book, they make no representations or warranties with respect to the accuracy or completeness of the contents of this book and specifically disclaim any implied warranties of merchantability or fitness for a particular purpose. No warranty may be created or extended by sales representatives or written sales materials. The advice and strategies contained herein may not be suitable for your situation. You should consult with a professional where appropriate. Neither the publisher nor the author shall be liable for any loss of profit or any other commercial damages, including but not limited to special, incidental, consequential, or other damages.

For general information about our other products and services, please contact our Customer Care Department within the United States at (800) 762-2974, outside the United States at (317) 572-3993 or fax (317) 572-4002.

Wiley also publishes its books in a variety of electronic formats. Some content that appears in print may not be available in electronic books. For more information about Wiley products, visit our web site at www.wiley.com.

Library of Congress Cataloging-in-Publication Data:

Anrig, Greg, date.
    The conservatives have no clothes : why right-wing ideas keep failing / Greg Anrig.
      p. cm.
    Includes index.
    ISBN 978-0-470-04436-0 (cloth)
    1. Conservatism—United States. 2. United States—Politics and government.
  I. Title.
    JC573.2.U6A57 2007
    320.520973—dc22

                      2006100245

Printed in the United States of America

10 9 8 7 6 5 4 3 2 1

320.5209
Anrig
   B

*To Gregory R. Anrig (1931–1993), a pragmatist
who delivered on his lifelong commitment
to improving educational opportunity for children*

CONTENTS

ACKNOWLEDGMENTS

Like the leading funders of the modern conservative movement, Edward A. Filene was a highly successful Republican businessman who devoted a substantial portion of his wealth toward developing government policy ideas. But Filene's central premises in 1919 when he endowed the Twentieth Century Fund, now known as the Century Foundation, were diametrically opposed to those motivating individuals like Richard Mellon Scaife, David H. and Charles G. Koch, John M. Olin, Joseph Coors, and the other leading funders of movement conservatism. A supporter of old-age pensions and unemployment insurance long before the New Deal, Filene believed that it was in the self-interest of corporate leaders to be what he called "liberal." He wrote in 1923, "I do not know of a better word for describing the sort of business man who, broadly speaking, is the opposite of a reactionary, the sort of business man who faces fresh problems with a fresh mind, who is more interested in creating a better order of things, who realizes that a private business is a public trust, and who has greater reverence for scientific method than for the traditions and majority opinions of his class." Filene argued that business executives should recognize that rising wages and increased purchasing power for all citizens would enable Americans to consume more of their companies' products and services, and that government had a meaningful and legitimate role to play in propelling that virtuous cycle.

Today, the endowment of the Century Foundation (TCF), where I have had the good fortune to work since 1992, amounts to pocket change compared to the riches bestowed on its conservative movement counterparts in recent years. For TCF and most of the other relatively small number of underfunded, center-left think tanks trying to attract attention and support for our progressive arguments about policy in the face of the right's juggernaut has often been something like playing one-against-five basketball. But every now and then we've managed to bat away our opponents' shots while scoring on a few of our own. Those of us who work at the foundation have been highly motivated by a shared commitment to Filene's belief in the possibilities of social and economic progress through the application of hard-headed analysis drawing from real-world experience. His spirit animates this book.

My boss throughout my tenure at TCF has been its president, Richard C. Leone, who over the years presciently anticipated many of the failures arising from right-wing ideas that the book documents. Dick's service in a variety of public sector leadership positions, beginning as New Jersey treasury secretary, as well as an extended period toiling successfully on Wall Street, left him with an unusually nuanced understanding of the complex interplay between the public and private spheres. When he hears the conservative movement's mantras about the inherent superiority of the marketplace over government, anyone within earshot should be prepared for a detailed and impassioned disquisition about the superficiality of those claims and why it is simple-minded to view the two realms as engaged in nothing but zero-sum games. Under Dick's leadership, TCF has always strived to bring together leaders from both political parties and from business and government, to try to reach a consensus about the best course of action. Alas, that has become much harder to do as the Republican Party has become increasingly aligned with the brand of conservatism explored in this book. Dick Leone's insights have been enormously influential on me, and the country could have avoided a great deal of damage if it had had the opportunity to listen to him as closely as I have.

In researching and writing this book, I relied heavily on the input of my colleagues at TCF, who specialize in many of the topics covered, as well as the wide range of policy experts outside of TCF with whom I have had the opportunity to work over the years. I am especially grateful to the observations, advice, and suggestions of each of our policy team members: Morton I. Abramowitz, Alex Baker, Leif Wellington Haase, Richard Kahlenberg, Patrick Radden Keefe, Jeff Laurenti, Carl Robichaud, Michael Shtender-Auerbach, Emerson Sykes, Ruy Teixeira, Tova Andrea Wang, and Bernard Wasow. A number of my other TCF colleagues also provided various forms of moral and other support, including Loretta Ahlrich, Nezam Aziz, Suzanne Chang, Chavon Cox, Beverly Goldberg, Jennifer Grimaldi, Christy Hicks, Cynthia Maertz, Jason Renker, Carol Starmack, Stephanie Theirl, John Williams, and Aly Wolff-Mills.

Among the reviewers of one or more of my draft chapters who saved me from making errors while generously offering their ideas were Tom Baker, Gary Bass, Alan J. Borsuk, Jason Furman, Jeffrey R. Henig, Timothy Stoltzfus Jost, Donald F. Kettl, Iris Lav, David E. Lewis, Karen Lyons, Peter R. Orszag, Patrick S. Roberts, Mark Schmitt, Daniel A. Smith, Steve Weinberg, Amy Stuart Wells, and John Witte. Others who may not be cited directly but whom I have learned much from in connection with sundry Century Foundation–related collaborations include Henry Aaron, Dean Baker, Robert M. Ball, Alan Brinkley, Joseph A. Califano Jr., David Callahan, Brewster C. Denny, John DiIulio, Christopher Edley Jr., James K. Galbraith, Robert Greenstein, Jacob Hacker, Simon Head, Alan B. Krueger, Robert Kuttner, Jeffrey Madrick, Charles R. Morris, Alicia M. Munnell, Gary Orfield, John Podesta, Richard Ravitch, Arnold Relman, David Rusk, Stephen J. Schulhofer, David Smith, Robert Solow, Theodore C. Sorensen, Paul Starr, Kathleen M. Sullivan, Joseph White, and William Julius Wilson.

The book's genesis owes much to one of the leading progressive journalists and thinkers in the increasingly important political blogosphere, Joshua Micah Marshall. In the spring of 2005, Josh launched a spin-off group blog from his own widely read talkingpointsmemo.com called tpmcafe.com and asked me to be a regular contributor. Not long after, John Wiley & Sons editor Eric Nelson, on the prowl for books that could try to compete with conservative best sellers, suggested after reading some of my posts at tpmcafe that we get together to discuss what became this book's main arguments. Given how consistently helpful and enthusiastic Eric has been in the months since our initial lunch, the path I have traveled beginning with Josh's generous invitation to contribute to tpmcafe couldn't have been more serendipitous.

In addition to Eric, others at John Wiley & Sons who helped ferry me skillfully to the book's culmination include Lisa Burstiner, Rachel Meyers, and Constance Santisteban. Also of note was Patti Waldygo's contribution.

I dedicated this book to my late father for many reasons, but two in particular. One was that throughout his career as an educator, he relentlessly focused on the single goal of improving educational opportunities for disadvantaged kids, and he measured his own performance based on the results he achieved in pursuing that mission. That was true in every job he had, traversing from history teacher to principal to superintendent to leading the federal government's efforts to provide technical assistance to desegregating school districts in the south, to Massachusetts Commissioner of Education during the commonwealth's early busing era, to president of the Educational Testing Service. He liked to say that his hero was the lowly paramecium, which keeps pushing against one obstacle after another until it finds its way. More often than not, my father's efforts succeeded. But when he failed, he learned from his mistakes and tried something new while always remaining focused on his central goal. I saw his approach to public and nonprofit sector leadership, which is essentially the inverse of movement conservatism's inattentiveness to the real-world outcomes of its policies, work again and again in big ways and small.

The other main reason for dedicating this book to Dad is that he was a wonderful father who would have been a great grandfather to my three awesome children, Greg, Charlotte, and Henry. Though he never had the chance to meet them, thankfully my mother, Charlotte, remains vibrant in her role as super-grandma. My amazing wife, Jeanne L. Reid, did get to know my father well and shares his easy laugh, love of kids, and commitment to helping those who are less fortunate than us. She also is a great editor in her own right, and her love and support for me and our family make me the luckiest man alive.

Finally, I'd like to thank Jeanne's parents, James and Donna Reid, who spend a lot of time in conservative social circles in Cleveland. Jim, a Republican who created thousands of jobs over decades as he built the family auto-parts business into a major company, is no flaming liberal (whatever you do, don't get him started about labor unions!). But he has come to recognize in recent years how conservatives have taken the country off track. Jim and Donna have been enthusiastic supporters of this project and vowed to make sure that all of their right-of-center friends receive a copy. For that first bulk order, as well, I am grateful.

INTRODUCTION

"We Never Believed in Progress Anyway"

The 2003 annual report of the Heritage Foundation, the conservative movement's flagship purveyor of government policy ideas, is triumphant. Published on the thirtieth anniversary of the think tank's founding, the report, titled "Creating Solutions. Getting Results," is packed with one example after another of the ways in which the foundation influenced the policy making of the Republican administration of George W. Bush and the Republican Congress:

> Armed with Heritage's reality-based analysis of competing tax reform proposals, Congress wisely enacted pro-growth tax cuts last spring; . . . .
>
> In health policy, this year's Medicare bill was a disappointment. . . . But the end product would have been even worse without Heritage's dogged fight for market-based reforms; . . . .
>
> Research fellow Jim Phillips' papers outlining the need to remove Saddam [Hussein from power in Iraq] were so influential, a Japanese television documentary used them to illustrate how think tanks affect American foreign policy; . . . .
>
> As the United Nations dithered, Research Assistant Carrie Satterlee penned the 'Facts on Who Benefits from Keeping Saddam Hussein in Power'. . . . Radio talk show host Sean Hannity's on-air discussion of the paper brought it national attention.

Under the heading "Other Heritage Ideas Adopted in 2003," the list includes U.S. rejection of calls to let the UN take over in postwar Iraq; resistance of pressure to assume a "peacekeeper" role in Liberia; getting Russia to follow America's lead in rejecting the Kyoto Protocol on the environment; congressional funding of studies on developing low-yield nuclear weapons for tactical use; congressional granting of

1

the District of Columbia's request to develop a school voucher program; and the Social Security Administration's decision to add "disclosures" about the system's financial condition (such as, full benefits may be unavailable by 2042) in its annual statements to workers.[1]

It is difficult to overstate the impact of the Heritage Foundation—along with the much broader network of conservative think tanks, foundations, university-based programs, activist organizations, and media affiliates—on U.S. public policy and debates over the role of government in recent years. Under Republican president George W. Bush and, for most of the time between 2001 and 2006, a Republican Congress,[2] and with Republican governors in a majority of the states over a longer period, ideas brewed in those conservative institutions have finally been put into practice after years of being forcefully touted as superior alternatives to a relentlessly derided liberal status quo. Governmental actions have become driven largely by belief systems and policy proposals that percolated from the 1970s through the 1990s in places that initially relied heavily on funding from only a handful of family foundations. Heritage and its collaborators on the right have unequivocally delivered results in transforming public policy and dominating debate across a multitude of fronts: international military interventions, taxes, Social Security, education, health care, regulation, public sector management, executive branch authority, state fiscal policy, and on and on. After Bush's defeat of John Kerry in the 2004 presidential election, Paul Glastris, the editor in chief of the moderate-to-liberal *Washington Monthly*, wrote, "[A]t this point, it requires a willful act of self-deception not to see the deeper problem: conservatives have won the war of ideas."[3]

But what about the results of the conservative movement's ideas, now that they have been put into practice, for the United States and its citizens? This book's central argument is that *those* results have been equally unequivocal: across-the-board failure.

The Flawed Playbook

In the realms of public policy where it is possible to fairly judge how ideas emanating almost exclusively from the conservative movement have played out to date in practice, based on concrete data and the analysis of experts who are widely recognized as authoritative—

including some conservatives—the record couldn't be clearer. In most cases, they made conditions for Americans and the country as a whole considerably worse in measurable ways.

One of the reasons for the conservative movement's rise has been its effectiveness in clearly and simply communicating what it stands for. If there is a single overarching viewpoint that has unified the elaborate conservative enterprise, it is Reagan's famous line from his first inaugural: "Government is not the solution to our problem; government is the problem."[4] Most Americans know that, like Reagan, conservatives say they believe in a strong defense, smaller and more efficient government, and what has come to be called "family values." Values by their nature can't be quantified in any meaningful way, but it is possible to assess the extent to which the conservative movement's policy ideas have delivered on the other promises.

Each of the chapters that follow is devoted to a particular idea that the right espoused, in order to determine whether in practice each idea has indeed left the United States stronger, safer, and with a smaller and more efficient government. As we will see, government in the hands of conservatives who pursued to a tee the ideas promoted by the right's networks have created all kinds of new problems without solving much of anything.

Even prominent conservatives have become deeply dismayed over the direction of the country. The columnist George F. Will, criticizing the Iraq War and the rationale for it, complained about what he called "a spectacularly misnamed radicalism, 'neoconservatism.'"[5] Bruce Bartlett lost his job at the National Center for Policy Analysis, a conservative think tank, because he wrote a book titled *Impostor: How George W. Bush Bankrupted America and Betrayed the Reagan Legacy*.[6] The *National Review*'s Jonah Goldberg chastised Bush over and over for his "big government conservatism." Andrew Sullivan, the author of a new book called *The Conservative Soul: How We Lost It, How to Get It Back*, relentlessly complained on his widely read blog about the Bush administration's "incompetence."[7]

The *Weekly Standard*'s Andrew Ferguson, bemoaning the scandals connected to the lobbyist Jack Abramoff, which embroiled a number of Republican members of Congress, wrote:

> Conservative institutions, conceived for combat, have in power become self-perpetuating, churning their direct-mail lists in pursuit

of cash from the orthodontist in Wichita and the Little Old Lady in Dubuque, so the activists can continue to fund the all-important work of ... churning their direct-mail lists. ... Conservative activists came to Washington to do good and stayed to do well. The grease rubbed off, too. It's a lucky stroke for conservatives that we never believed in progress anyway.[8]

All of the consternation on the right certainly reinforces the case that the country went badly off track under the leadership of a conservative Republican president and a conservative Republican Congress, which together embraced and implemented many ideas emanating from the movement's think tanks. But beware of the efforts by conservatives to try to distance themselves from the bad things that have happened. Saying, as Bartlett or Goldberg do, that Bush is not a "true conservative" or, as Sullivan does, that the administration is simply "incompetent" neglects the fact that they have largely governed in ways completely consistent with conservative ideology. They have cut taxes at every turn. They talked tough, dissed the UN, and invaded Iraq, following the game plan of the widely read conservative manual, *The Weekly Standard*, every step of the way. The president hired dyed-in-the-wool movement conservatives, many of them with close links to Heritage, the Cato Institute, the Reason Foundation, the Federalist Society, and other conservative idea factories, to manage just about every last government agency and most of its programs. Those conservative political appointees have implemented policies and management practices that the movement promised would deliver more bang for the taxpayer's buck but that have demonstrably done the opposite — most vividly in the aftermath of Hurricane Katrina. The entire regulatory system run by the executive branch has basically downshifted to idle, consistent with the movement's agenda, but at a cost to public health and safety largely hidden from Americans.

Any human beings following the conservative playbook for governing, as we will see, will appear to be incompetent because the playbook itself is filled with hopeless Hail Mary passes, ideas that have never worked but remain cherished, and the sort of trickery favored on school playgrounds. The right's coaches noodling in the think tanks and bloviating in the media can blame the players in government all they want, but their ideas above all else have been responsible for the follies.

The unhappiness on the right that the conservative administration and Congress failed to significantly reduce government spending, as chapter 4 will explain, pays insufficient attention to the fact that hardly any conservatives raised alarms when spending constraints that helped to eliminate federal deficits under President Clinton were dropped with dispatch by the Republican Senate and House, with acquiescence from Bush. Moreover, the kind of fiscal austerity that Bartlett, Goldberg, and other disillusioned conservatives want has been in effect for years in Colorado under its Taxpayer's Bill of Rights constitutional amendment. As chapter 5 will show in detail, the results in Colorado have been so painful that voters rebelled against the amendment in 2005, egged on by a Republican governor who had long supported the state's severe tax-and-spending limits. The real-world outcomes that conservatives have joined the public at large in bemoaning are a direct outgrowth of governance arising from a movement predicated on the premise that government is the problem, not part of the solution.

Rick Perlstein, the author of the extraordinary narrative history *Before the Storm: Barry Goldwater and the Unmaking of the American Consensus*, delivered a speech before an assembly of conservatives at Princeton University in which he focused in part on the fleetingness of their allegiances to individuals over time. He said, "In conservative intellectual discourse there is no such thing as a bad conservative. Conservatism never fails. It is only failed."[9] It will be up to the rest of us to recognize that, no, it is conservatism itself that has failed.

Failure's Roots

The challenge for the right was attempting to make the transition from the role of government critic and opponent of change to the activity of governing in a more purposeful and politically sustainable way. Central to that process was the creation of new public-policy think tanks, beginning in the 1970s and proliferating after Reagan's inauguration in 1981, that fundamentally differed from preexisting institutions. Before the Heritage Foundation's creation in 1973, think tanks considered to be conservative, such as the American Enterprise Institute (AEI), the Hoover Institution, and the Hudson Institute, were much like counterparts generally viewed as liberal and moderate, such as the Brookings Institution, the Urban Institute, and the RAND

Corporation. They didn't have a clearly identified agenda aside from supporting the abstraction of "good government," they housed mainly scholars with PhDs who wrote and sounded like inscrutable university professors, they often received public sector contracts to produce analysis about the best course of action to take, they issued highly technical reports sometimes above the heads of even many journalists and congressional staffers, and, with relatively few exceptions, they distanced themselves from the political fray in order to retain the patina of objectivity. It was this aloofness that spurred the creation of Heritage, whose success in turn is largely responsible for spawning the powerful conservative ideas apparatus that exists today.

One of Heritage's founders and the current president, Dr. Edwin J. Feulner Jr., served as an administrative assistant to the arch-conservative congressman Philip Crane (R-Ill.) in the early 1970s, and he often recalls the trigger event for him in recognizing the need for a new kind of institution. In 1971, AEI prepared a compelling publication explaining why the government should not finance the supersonic transport airplane. The problem, Feulner said, was that AEI didn't distribute the brief to members of Congress until after they voted on the matter. As Feulner recalled to Andrew Rich, the author of *Think Tanks, Public Policy, and the Politics of Expertise,* "It defined the debate, but it was one day late. We immediately called up the president [of AEI] to praise him for this thorough piece of research—and ask why we didn't receive it until after the debate and the vote. His answer: they didn't want to influence the vote. That was when the idea for Heritage was born."[10] Feulner and cofounder Paul Weyrich, who was also working on Capitol Hill, as press secretary to conservative senator Gordon Allott (R-Colo.), secured the necessary initial funding from the beer magnate Joseph Coors. Additional support soon followed from the foundation of John M. Olin, who made his fortune building a conglomerate that began primarily as an ammunition company, and Richard Mellon Scaife, a newspaper owner and the great-grandnephew of the Pittsburgh industrialist Andrew W. Mellon.

The Cato Institute, the second most important cog in the conservative movement's ideas machinery, was launched just a few years later, in 1977, by Edward Crane, who was chairman of the Libertarian National Party. Financed largely through support from the Koch conglomerate fortune and originally based in San Francisco before moving to Washington in 1981, Cato was part of the first wave of libertarian research organizations created in the late 1970s. Others included the Reason Foundation, the Pacific Institute, and what is now known as the Manhattan Institute. Many more would follow in the 1980s, a large share of which were charged with promoting ideas for privatizing the activities of various state governments.[11] Although Heritage and Cato have advocated on behalf of many of the same ideas over the years, most especially Social Security privatization, tax cuts, the elimination or slashing of sundry government programs, and school vouchers, the libertarian mind-set is the most hostile on the right toward the public sector and elevates individual liberty and private property rights above all other political concerns.

The individuals involved in giving birth to Heritage and Cato—the names Scaife, Coors, Olin, and Koch, along with the Milwaukee-based Bradley Foundation, appear again and again throughout these pages—were motivated to change just about every aspect of how government operated in the 1970s.[12] Like most archconservatives and libertarians at the time, they disdained the civil rights and antiwar movements about as much as they hated communism. They also shared a deep hostility toward what they perceived to be rampant radicalism and permissiveness on college campuses. But on top of that, the creation in the 1960s and 1970s of numerous federal departments and agencies assigned with writing and enforcing new environmental, public health, and antidiscrimination rules, aimed mainly at employers, particularly infuriated many well-heeled leaders of the business community who had traditionally represented the base of the Republican Party. So their money flowed to the new generation of think tanks, and they demanded results, especially in cutting off the domestic tentacles of government.

Pushing for dramatic change that would reverse the directions that the U.S. government had been moving in for decades under both Democrats and Republicans, deeply disrupting existing arrangements and practices—what Perlstein called "the American consensus"—turned upside down the sort of conservatism that had characterized the stuffy pipe smokers at the *National Review* and other traditionalists like Edmund Burke and Michael Oakeshott.

For all of the elaborate philosophical debates that have enraptured followers of the right for decades, definitions of traditional conservatism at a basic level are rather easy to grasp. As Russell Kirk, one longtime *National Review* editor and the author of the 1953 book *The Conservative Mind*, responded to the question about conservatism's meaning: "Is it not adherence to the old and tried, against the new and untried?"[13] Similarly, Barry Goldwater, who had much to do with lighting the flame under what has become the dominant force in American politics with his 1964 run for the presidency, wrote, "In its simplest terms, conservatism is economic, social, and political practices based on the successes of the past."[14] And William Safire, the former speechwriter for President Richard M. Nixon, who for decades opined from the right as a columnist for the *New York Times*, defined a conservative as "a defender of the status quo who, when change becomes necessary in tested institutions or practices, prefers that it come slowly and in moderation."[15]

The mission of the right's new think tanks was to do the very opposite of adhering "to the old and tried," pursuing "practices based on the successes of the past," "defending the status quo," or ensuring that change to "tested institutions or practices . . . come slowly or in moderation." To abide by those principles would have required sustaining and building on established and largely successful government activities. Social Security, Medicare, civil rights legislation, environmental regulations, food and drug oversight, antitrust laws, transportation safety rules, and other public protections have demonstrably improved conditions in the United States. Poverty among the elderly declined from more than 35 percent before 1960 to about 10 percent today, primarily because of improvements to Social Security and the advent of Medicare. The nation's air and water are vastly cleaner than before the introduction of the 1970s environmental regulations. Crime levels, death rates in automobile and other transportation accidents, racial and gender discrimination, workplace injuries, and cigarette smoking have all significantly declined over recent decades, in no small measure because of governmental efforts. But preserving and enhancing those "successes of the past," as Goldwater put it, necessitates not only acknowledging the usefulness of government but actively supporting it with resources, capable civil servants, and innovation that draws lessons from experience based on attention to reliable data and research.

The sponsors of the right-wing ideas industry simply wanted to roll back government, through any means necessary. In contrast to the intellectuals who reveled in the conservative canon, the central financiers of the modern conservative movement were successful men of action with enormous wealth, in most cases built on inherited assets. Most of them harbored a barely contained sense of fury over their own personal encounters with the government—especially despising taxes and regulation. Not coincidentally, the Coors, Bradley, and Koch families all had roots extending to the John Birch Society, the secretive organization founded in the late 1950s that suspected that communists were taking over the U.S. government, among other conspiracies. Scaife believed that Clinton aide Vince Foster's death was "the Rosetta stone" that would explain what he believed to be untold conspiracies related to a president he abhorred.[16] The leading funders of movement conservatism didn't think twice about what the consequences for the public—intended or unintended—might be of getting rid of this or that program or regulation or tax or policy. Just do whatever it takes to get on the offensive, attack, and beat back the government. Those were the kinds of results they wanted.

That attitude instilled a belligerence into the movement that has come to characterize the right's portrayal of any particular issue, as well as the broader debate about government's role. Listen to Feulner in a 1986 lecture to a group of public relations executives that he titled "Waging and Winning the War of Ideas":

> Unless you understand how to fight [the ongoing war of ideas that shape U.S. and world events], you cannot hope to win. [At the Heritage Foundation] we man the ivory towers as well as the trenches in this war of ideas. We define the objectives, devise the strategies, and manufacture the ammunition. . . . Lenin put it this way: "Ideas are much more fatal things than guns."
>
> Unlike a university, we do not see ourselves merely as a forum for pure research—where competing ideas can be debated. Our role is not to compromise or to consider only what is politically and pragmatically possible. Our role is to study, analyze, and apply innovative solutions to public policy problems and press for change. As the former chief economic adviser to Senator Edward Kennedy told the *Wall Street Journal* recently: "Heritage is a constant ideological presence." To us, that is high praise. Or as one of my colleagues says: "There are no pacifists in the war of ideas."[17]

It is important to underscore that traditional conservatives and the early neoconservatives of the 1960s, who legitimately called attention to the unintended negative consequences of various government initiatives, contributed insights of lasting value. Their critique of the old system of Aid to Families with Dependent Children, for example, created the impetus leading to bipartisan welfare reforms in 1996 that produced significantly more good than harm. The conservative scholar James Q. Wilson's "broken windows" arguments about crime prevention, which encouraged efforts to stop the kinds of minor infractions that create environments in which major felonies are more likely to flourish, inspired policing innovations that have helped to significantly reduce crime. The libertarian Milton Friedman's "negative income tax" proposal evolved into today's earned income tax credit, widely recognized to be an effective antipoverty policy. But those successful ideas, which came to be embraced across the political spectrum, differed in fundamental ways from the main agenda items of today's conservative movement. They were based on careful, honest analysis of history and data. They were pragmatic, as opposed to dogmatic. They were focused on genuinely improving real-world outcomes. And they at least implicitly recognized the importance of energetic, innovative government. Movement conservatism's ideas, which are the focus of this book, share none of those traits.[18]

The Art of Selling

The take-no-prisoners attitude embraced by Heritage and its multitude of conservative emulators left the long-established liberal and centrist think tanks in an utterly flummoxed state of "shock and awe"—a condition that by and large remains to this day. Places like the Brookings Institution, the Urban Institute, and RAND didn't remotely see themselves engaged in anything like a "war of ideas," much less pursuing a strategy designed to win over broad public opinion or participate in trench warfare on Capitol Hill. Overseen by boards that include more than a token number of Republicans and business executives, in contrast to the single-mindedness to be found on the boards of the much younger right-wing think tanks, the Brookings Institutions and RANDs of the world consider their central mission to be providing reliable, neutral research and analysis about the impact of public policies. Let the facts speak for themselves, whatever they might say about whether government interventions are working or not.

Much of that research over the years has identified shortcomings—including the sorts of unintended consequences that the neoconservatives of the 1960s warned against—along with the successes of liberal programs. But the presumption of the established think tanks, consistent with the principles of social science, was that learning from mistakes would help to point toward policy modifications that would produce better outcomes. The underlying belief system of those institutions continues to be scientific rather than political—much less militaristic. It wasn't until the creation of the Center for American Progress in 2003 when a think tank even approaching the combativeness of the Heritage Foundation came to pass on the left, and its policy proposals are just as moderate and scrupulously researched as those of older liberal counterparts were. The center just devotes far more energy to marketing its work, in recognition of the right's successes on that front.

The philosophies of the leading individuals who financed movement conservatism are far outside of the mainstream. (David H. Koch ran as a vice presidential candidate on the Libertarian Party ticket in 1980, receiving just over 1 percent of the vote—a typical showing for libertarians running for public office even today.) But the institutions receiving their largesse needed to concoct strategies for simultaneously keeping those funders happy while also building a broad political movement.

The real wonder of the conservative enterprise has been its ability to transform the rudimentary desire of a handful of wealthy families to gut the government into a set of public policy ideas that would help to accomplish that goal while sounding appetizing enough to attract large numbers of voters. Rather ingeniously, the simple, easy-to-understand ideas they developed are largely consistent with each other and elegantly link to a broader story line that the conservative movement has effectively sold with remarkable sophistication. That's how the right won the war of ideas. It's also the underlying reason why those ideas are failing.

In each of the chapters that follow, readers will come to recognize patterns in the evolution of each idea, the selling of it to the public, the causes of its failure once implemented, and the right's response as the bad outcomes became increasingly obvious. Part of the modus operandi invariably is to redefine each problem confronting the nation in a way that distracts the public from the real issue while pointing logically toward the remedy on the right's agenda—a remedy that always entails weakening government on domestic issues, exerting unilateral muscle in foreign policy and matters involving civil liberties. Overthrowing Saddam Hussein as a response to a terrorist attack executed by al-Qaeda is perhaps the most transparent of the bait and switches. Another example is the conservative claim explored in chapter 7 that public education is allegedly terrible simply because government bureaucracies and the teachers' unions prevent the kind of innovation and efficiency that arise in private markets for products and services. Never mind that the real systematic problems with public schools are confined to urban districts, which predominantly teach students from low-income families. And that studies show that students in non-unionized private and charter schools unencumbered by government bureaucracies perform no better than those in public schools, after taking into account differences in family income and social characteristics of students. In all the realms of policy explored throughout the book, there is a large gap between the conservative refrain about the nature of the problem and what the preponderance of evidence indicates to be the actual cause for concern.

Because the ultimate goal of movement conservatives is to roll back the government, the answer to domestic problems as they have defined them almost invariably entails the simple panacea of substituting the private sector for the public sector. Just turn everything over to markets, and let the collective wisdom of consumers, free enterprise, competitive pressures, and Adam Smith's "invisible hand" fix everything. Yet most existing government domestic programs came about in the first place because of what economists call "market failures." Experience over more than a century, consistent with economic theory, demonstrated that competitive firms acting to maximize profits in the absence of rules will impose harms on the broader public— harms that voters through the democratic process insisted be curtailed. So the government created laws, regulations, and enforcement systems to help ensure that the food supply would be untainted, that drugs and medical devices would be safe and effective, that price-gouging monopolies be broken up, that securities markets be fair, that transportation systems be safe, that the environment be protected, that racial discrimination be outlawed, that fraudulent sales practices be criminalized, that workplaces be safe, and so on. It also created economic protections such as Social Security, Medicare, Medicaid, unemployment insurance, and food stamps to cushion economic blows for citizens who fared poorly in the rough and tumble of the marketplace, and for older and disabled Americans out of the workforce.

While many on the right recognize in the abstract the need for some degree of government activity in such realms, movement conservatives fighting the "war of ideas" leave no doubt in the day-to-day combat over all those issues that the private sector wears white and the government black. Less government is always preferable, they argue, because unfettered markets, no matter what the realm, create incentives that lead to better outcomes. Costly and cumbersome regulations do more harm than good. Public insurance only discourages people from taking care of themselves. Rampant waste, fraud, and abuse can always be cut painlessly. And slashing taxes will cure whatever ails us.

On foreign policy, as chapter 3 will examine, the neoconservative perspective that came to hold sway over the movement is no less simplistic and no less divorced from historical experience. In a sense, though, its overarching mission internationally is the inverse of the crusade to cripple the government's domestic capabilities. Abroad, the goal is to aggressively exert America's might, unilaterally if need be, in order to build on the dominance we gained in the aftermath of the Soviet Union's collapse while deterring other countries from challenging our leadership. In and of itself, the right's diametrically opposed views about the government's inherent domestic ineptitude, alongside the prowess to effectively bend to our will the actions of the rest of the world, display an incongruity that further helps to explain the failures of conservatism both within and beyond our borders. But those crystal-clear positions also made it easy to develop politically powerful rhetoric that by design enabled Republicans to win elections over Democratic candidates who held more nuanced—in the right's parlance, "wishy-washy"—views.

As experience in the United States has demonstrated again and again, progress almost never comes about easily or through simplistic solutions. When the nation has successfully confronted complex and

daunting public policy challenges, both domestically and internationally, it has always involved energetic government led by committed
individuals who over time through the course of trial and error managed to help make conditions better for Americans. In the hands of liberals, moderates, and pragmatic conservatives—Democrats and
Republicans—the public sector's many successes over the years have,
without question, also come with significant failures. Movement conservatives harped on those unmet goals and disappointments to rise to
power. But now that they have held the reins of government for a good
while, both at the federal and the state levels, it's time to ask why *they*
don't have a single meaningful success to point to.

Forgotten Wisdom

The conservative ideas explored in this book have been tried—here
and in other countries—and failed. But the right nonetheless has
pressed forward with the same agenda, distorting that history along the
way, because of an obsession with fundamentally undercutting the
role of government in the United States. The traditionalist Russell
Kirk often referred to H. Stuart Hughes's aphorism that conservatism
is "the negation of ideology," and Benjamin Disraeli defined his own
brand of conservatism as "muddling through." The modern right's
neglect of that wisdom has much to do with the damage documented
throughout this book. Since moderates, for all intents and purposes,
have been marginalized from the Republican Party, it will be up to
Democrats, drawing in part on the demonstrated strengths of traditional conservatism—building on the successes of the past, avoiding
the repetition of failures, and aggressively fighting radicalism—to
begin the reconstruction.

PART I

Ideas for Making America Safer and Stronger

1

"A Heckuva Job"

Politicizing the Government

The American public witnessed the worst display of U.S. governmental failure in our lifetimes when Hurricane Katrina ravaged New Orleans and the surrounding region in late August and September 2005. The most comprehensive report documenting what went wrong, produced by the Senate Committee on Homeland Security and Governmental Affairs, weighs in at 732 pages and conveys a relentless succession of miscalculations, managerial negligence, turf battles, ignored warnings, dysfunctional communication, and sheer ineptitude at all levels of government.[1] Those screwups produced agonizing farce amid the tragedy: evacuation buses sitting in lots within a few hundred miles of the flooded region; Secretary of the Department of Homeland Security (DHS) Michael Chertoff learning from a radio reporter for the first time about thousands of people trapped without food and water in the Ernest Morial Convention Center; an aide to Federal Emergency Management Agency (FEMA) Director Michael Brown insisting that he be allowed to enjoy a leisurely restaurant dinner during the height of the crisis; President George W. Bush's non sequitur, "Brownie, you're doing a heckuva job"; police officers abandoning their duty; ice-delivery trucks roaming to Maryland, Idaho, and Maine rather than the Gulf Coast; thousands of mobile homes intended as temporary housing sitting empty in the middle of nowhere; and on and on.

The reasons for the failures are manifold and complex, not the least of which was a storm so overwhelming that human beings had no chance of completely defeating it. Still, the past governmental response to many other natural disasters, as well as to the Oklahoma City bombing, has been far more effective. Honing in on the particular strand of the Katrina tragedy related to the managerial history of FEMA—since 1979 the lead national office responsible for preparing for and responding to major calamities—reveals a great deal about why the conservative movement's arguments about public leadership, bureaucracies, and civil servants are fundamentally wrong. Everyone by now knows that FEMA director Brown, whose most significant prior job had been as a commissioner of the International Arabian Horse Association (a position he was forced to leave), had no emergency-management experience and conforms to all the conventional definitions of an old-fashioned political crony. But there's far more to the story than one unfortunate political appointment at an inopportune moment. The politicization that contributed to FEMA's failures occurred throughout the executive branch under Bush in accordance with conservative ideology, with comparably harmful, if less visible, consequences for the American public.

Bull's-Eye on the Bureaucrat

In the weeks immediately preceding and following George W. Bush's first inauguration, the Heritage Foundation issued a flurry of reports, briefs, and op-eds with titles like "Taking Charge of Federal Personnel," "Why the President Should Ignore Calls to Reduce the Number of Political Appointees," and "Keep 'em Coming: In Defense of Political Appointees." The thrust of the Heritage argument was that an ample supply of officials appointed by the president at the top levels of federal agencies is essential to ensure that his goals will be carried out in the face of resistance from the career civil service.

In a *Washington Times* op-ed on January 16, 2001, Heritage director of domestic policy studies Robert Moffit wrote:

> Having the right number of political appointees is crucial to every president's success. He can't fulfill his mandate alone or with only a handful of staffers in the West Wing. Nor can his Cabinet implement his policies without a cadre of like-minded, personally committed appointees within the agencies. This is especially true in today's political climate with a narrowly divided Congress provid-

ing a perfect excuse for those who merely want to perpetuate the status quo.

It goes without saying that Heritage engaged in no such advocacy upon the occasion of either of Bill Clinton's inaugurals. (Heritage remained opposed to proposals to limit presidential appointments during the Clinton administration, though, noting that when Republicans returned to the White House they would want the flexibility to hire their own people.) But the right's call for greater reliance on political appointees after Bush's election was consistent with an extensive body of public administration research and argumentation emanating for many years from conservative outposts, all in one way or another targeted at career government employees and the unions representing them. The intellectual foundation undergirding much of that work is the branch of economics dating back to the 1950s called "public-choice" (and its extremely close cousin "rational-choice") theory, which attempts to explain the motivations and behavior of government workers, politicians, voters, and lobbyists as analogous to consumers and producers in the marketplace who are driven, the theory goes, entirely—or at least predominantly—by self-interest.

Public-choice models invariably show government employees behaving in ways that are unconnected or opposed to the broader public interest. For example, one of the ways that current Cato Institute chairman William A. Niskanen first made a name for himself was by publishing a 1968 paper using public-choice theory to purportedly demonstrate that "bureaucrats" will always act to maximize their budgets.[2] (Niskanen neglected the possibility that motivations beyond self-interest might influence the behavior of government officials, including, as the economist Anthony Downs has emphasized, pride in performance, loyalty to a program, and a wish to best serve their fellow citizens.) The lowest rungs of the civil service ladder also fare poorly under the public-choice framework, due to the so-called principal-agent problem. Because managers cannot perfectly and costlessly monitor the activities of line staff who are layers below in the bureaucracy, the theory goes, civil servants will invariably goof off on the job, subvert the intentions of policymakers, and even steal.

For many years the right has drawn on public-choice arguments as the basis for claiming that systematic approaches need to be pursued to weaken or bypass civil servants. In addition to making career government workers more submissive to political appointees (preferably conservative ones), the right has devoted abundant energy at all levels of government to pushing for privatization and contracting out of government services, weakening civil service employment protections, and diminishing the capacity of public employees to impose and monitor regulations. Public choice's theoretical claims about the shortcomings of government workers, buttressed by elaborate economic equations beyond the comprehension of most journalists and average citizens, were used by the conservative movement as justifications for replacing the public sector in one way or another with private, competitive markets. The costs and risks associated with making those transitions usually receive short shrift, at best, in public-choice literature.

Historically, the two presidencies most closely associated with the politicization of government agencies were the administrations of Republicans Richard Nixon and Ronald Reagan.[3] Nixon was suspicious of civil servants, most of whom joined the government under Democrats John F. Kennedy and Lyndon B. Johnson as it expanded to take on tasks of little interest to him. Viewing government workers as disloyal bureaucrats tied to patrons in Congress, agency clienteles, and interest groups, Nixon pursued a variety of tactics to gain greater control of executive branch departments. After his initial attempts to strengthen the policy clout of the White House and reorganize agencies largely failed, in his second term he replaced existing appointees with loyalists while inserting more of his own people deep into departments and bureaus. In the process, he relied on what was called "Malek's Manual," named after Office of Management and Budget (OMB) official Fred Malek, which detailed a variety of elaborate techniques for sidestepping civil service laws and replacing unwanted careerists.

Similarly, Reagan believed that environmental and social welfare agencies were mainly populated with Democrats far more loyal to the programs they were managing than to the White House. Thus he, too, distributed more political allies throughout the government so that by 1986–1987, both appointees and civil servants were more Republican and conservative than in 1970.[4] The Princeton University political scientist David E. Lewis notes that the Reagan administration was especially effective in using reorganizations and reductions in force as ways of downgrading the pay and the responsibilities of career civil servants, increasing their rates of attrition.

Democrat Jimmy Carter, who gained the presidency after campaigning as a Washington outsider, was also suspicious of the civil service and was responsible for the greatest post-1960 increase in political appointments when he created the so-called Senior Executive Service. So party affiliation, in and of itself, has not strictly determined in the past whether any particular president has been more likely to increase the politicization of the executive branch.

The Real Problems with Bureaucracy

The growing consensus in recent years, outside of the large, well-funded enclaves of movement conservatism, is that *less* reliance on political appointees is better for government. (Carter's abysmal managerial record helped to clarify the issue for many Democrats.) So-called good-government reformers, including many of the dwindling number of nonideological Republicans, approach issues about public administration from the standpoint of making government more responsive, efficient, and effective without assuming that civil servants will inherently act to the detriment of those goals. Graduate and undergraduate schools of government and public policy, foundations, think tanks, advocacy groups, and public employee unions committed to the idea of good government take seriously the belief that public employees as a class have strengths as well as weaknesses. They focus on strategies for applying the knowledge and experience of the career workforce while chipping away at the rigidities that have indisputably arisen in the past. Movement conservatives, in contrast, perceive anything that undermines civil servants to be an accomplishment in its own right.

The public-management reforms pursued during the eight years of the Clinton administration were consistent with the good-government heritage. Ideas arising from Vice President Al Gore's National Performance Review, which focused on "reinventing government," were explicitly presented as ways to combat "creativity-stifling bureaucracy," rather than reining in "power-hungry bureaucrats." Paul C. Light, one of the nation's leading public administration scholars, wrote that Clinton's deliberate semantic shift "allowed the Clinton administration to simultaneously claim victory in the war on bureaucracy while liberating the bureaucrats from a host of needless rules."[5] Under Clinton, for example, the ten-thousand-page *Federal Personnel Manual* that had previously defined human resources rules throughout the federal government was literally thrown away, and agencies were given greater flexibility to design their own performance appraisal and rewards systems. Procurement practices were overhauled and streamlined so that the past emphasis on rules, hierarchy, and system design was reoriented toward accomplishing goals in ways that gave more discretion to career civil servants.[6] Gore also pushed for reforms, which weren't enacted by Congress, that would have tied the pay and the bonuses of government managers more closely to performance evaluations, including to the results of customer and employee satisfaction surveys.[7]

Most nonideological observers viewed Clinton and Gore's reinventing government reforms to be at least moderately successful steps in the right direction, though by no means a panacea. A subsequent bipartisan commission led by the former Federal Reserve chairman Paul A. Volcker, which included Republicans Kenneth M. Duberstein, Constance Horner, and Vin Weber, issued a report in early 2003 that focused on persisting problems including:

- *Organization.* A clear sense of policy direction and clarity of mission is too often lacking, undercutting efficiency and public confidence.
- *Leadership.* Too few of our most talented citizens are seeking careers in government or accepting political or judicial appointments.
- *Operations.* The difficulties federal workers encounter in just getting their jobs done have led to discouragement and low morale.[8]

The Volcker report, the latest major effort in the good-government tradition, proposed a number of recommendations, most of which would continue moving in the same basic direction as the Clinton administration. Particularly noteworthy is this one: "Congress and the President should work together to significantly reduce the number of executive branch political positions." Diametrically opposed to the Heritage viewpoint, the bipartisan commission argued:

When a new administration takes office or a new agency head is appointed, it often seems too politically difficult, or the time horizon too short, to reshape the top ranks or to improve accountability. So more leadership posts are created to help agency heads and presidents work around old leadership posts they cannot control or remove. Compounded over the decades, this pattern has yielded a federal management structure that is top-heavy, cumbersome, and contrary to the goals of effective leadership and meaningful accountability.[9]

Following the Heritage Plan

In a March 26, 2005, article in the *National Journal* titled "By the Horns," the reporter Paul Singer recounts calling Robert Moffit at Heritage to ask him about one of the papers he coauthored four years earlier urging President Bush to reassert managerial control of government through political appointees. "Reminded of this paper recently, [Moffit], who has moved on to other issues at Heritage, dusted off a copy and called a reporter back with a hint of rejoicing in his voice. 'They apparently are really doing this stuff,' he said."

Singer's article documented a variety of reorganizational efforts in different agencies that strengthened the leverage of politically appointed officials while weakening the discretion and influence of career civil servants, including changes at the Centers for Disease Control, the Environmental Protection Agency, NASA, and even the obscure National Resources Conservation Services—a division of the Agriculture Department. Other media reports raised concerns about politicization in the Food and Drug Administration,[10] the Civil Rights Division of the Justice Department,[11] and the Office of Special Counsel, which is supposed to protect career service whistle-blowers who disclose waste, fraud, and abuse.[12]

The numbers support the abundant anecdotes. Princeton's Lewis, reviewing data from the Office of Personnel Management, found that political appointments escalated during the first term of the Bush administration after declining substantially during Clinton's eight years. From 1992 to 2000, political appointees in the federal government dropped by nearly 17 percent—from 3,423 to 2,845. From 2000 to 2004, that figure climbed back up 12.5 percent to 3,202.[13] Similarly, the political scientist Paul C. Light found that after holding steady during most of the Clinton administration, the number of senior title holders increased by 9 percent, to 2,592, between 1998 and 2004—the vast majority of which occurred under Bush. Light also found that fourteen departments added new executive titles between 1998 and 2004. The Department of Veterans Affairs topped the list with six additional titles, followed by Defense, Education, Energy, and Justice with four, and Labor with three. Light wrote,

> The fastest spreading titles continue to be "alter-ego" deputies, including chiefs of staff to secretaries, deputy secretaries, under secretaries, deputy under secretaries, assistant secretaries, deputy assistant secretaries, associate deputy assistant secretaries, associate assistant secretaries, administrators, deputy administrators, associate administrators and assistant administrators.[14]

Who says conservatives hate bureaucracy?

Down on the Turkey Farm

Before FEMA was born, the main orientation of the assortment of scattered federal agencies involved in preparing for disasters was the threat of a nuclear attack from the Soviet Union. Hurricanes, tornadoes, and other acts of nature were generally considered to be state and local responsibilities. But in the 1970s, several high-profile calamities led state and local governments to put pressure on Congress to get the feds to play a more active role, resulting in the Federal Disaster Relief Act of 1974. That law allowed the Defense Department's Civil Defense Preparedness Agency (CDPA) to become "dual use" in extending its purview from potential nuclear attacks to natural disasters. Five years later, President Carter created FEMA in an elaborate reorganization that combined the CDPA with more than a hundred existing federal disaster-response programs, which collectively reported to twenty different congressional committees. The University of Virginia political scientist Patrick S. Roberts wrote about FEMA's creation:

> To appease interest groups and congressional committees, the reorganization plan transferred each program's political appointees

to FEMA, which created isolated divisions or "stovepipes" with their own connections to Congress and interest groups but little connection to each other. One participant in the reorganization recalled that "It was like trying to make a cake by mixing the milk still in the bottle, with the flour still in the sack, with the eggs still in the carton."[15]

President Reagan picked as his first FEMA director Louis O. Giuffrida, who had directed the California Specialized Training Institute, an outfit that had focused on subduing riots and student protests when Reagan was governor in the 1960s. Giuffrida, consistent with Reagan's focus on nuclear competition with the Soviets, strived to make FEMA a player in national security as the lead agency responsible for responding to terrorist attacks, and he created an Office of National Preparedness to that end. In the process, he developed a secret contingency plan in the event of a national crisis that called for a declaration of martial law and suspension of the Constitition, with FEMA in effect taking over the country. Attorney General William French Smith put the kibosh on that idea, and in 1985 Giuffrida resigned after being the subject of a federal investigation of alleged fraud and mismanagement.[16]

For the rest of the Reagan administration and the presidency of George H. W. Bush, FEMA remained an ineffective amalgamation of programs pulled in competing directions by its dual civil defense and natural disaster missions. So, on the one hand, FEMA dabbled in activities such as building a secret 112,544-square-foot bunker under the Greenbrier resort in West Virginia to house Congress during a nuclear war. On the other hand, when localized or medium-size storms hit, FEMA often equivocated about whether to intervene—a persistent cause of frustration for states and localities. After bigger natural disasters struck, the agency's response was usually slow and overly bureaucratic.[17] For example, after Hurricane Hugo in 1989 caused a record $4 billion in damage, mainly on the American Virgin Islands and in the Carolinas, stories circulated about FEMA requiring the submission of cost assessments before complying with state and local requests for generators and other desperately needed supplies. That prompted South Carolina senator Ernest Hollings to famously denounce FEMA's staff as "a bunch of bureaucratic jackasses."[18]

The lowest of FEMA's lows came after Hurricane Andrew struck Florida, Georgia, and Louisiana in 1992. The federal response was so disorganized that three days afterward, Dade County Director of Emergency Preparedness Kate Hall held a press conference saying, "Where the hell is the cavalry on this one? We need food. We need water. We need people. For God's sake, where are they?" President George H. W. Bush, recognizing the political damage FEMA was inflicting on him in the midst of his reelection campaign, in effect shunted the agency aside by sending nearly twenty thousand navy, air force, and coast guard troops to take over the efforts in Florida under the leadership of Transportation Secretary Andrew Card and a group of military brass.[19]

By this time, FEMA's reputation was in a shambles. One House committee underscored that the agency had become a dumping ground for political appointees, calling it "the federal turkey farm."[20] The agency was featured prominently in a November 1992 *Washingtonian* magazine article titled "Perfect Places for Those Hard-to-Place Contributors."[21] The *Washington Post* described FEMA as "the agency that everybody loves to hate."[22] Several independent assessments were commissioned to devise reforms. The National Academy of Public Administration (NAPA)—the ultimate embodiment of a "good-government" institution—produced the most influential report. It broached the possibility of a "death penalty" for FEMA but settled on the idea that "the time has come to shift the emphasis from national security to domestic emergency management using an all-hazards approach." An all-hazards approach meant preparing plans that would be effective regardless of the nature of a particular calamity, rather than specialized tactics that varied for floods, hurricanes, earthquakes, and so on. The report also criticized "the uneven quality of its political executives" and recommended a limit on the number of presidential appointees, while filling leadership positions with the most qualified FEMA employees.[23]

A Model Agency

Upon taking office, President Clinton appointed as FEMA director James Lee Witt, who had served under Clinton in Arkansas as director of the state's Office of Emergency Services. Witt, with Clinton's endorsement, proceeded to implement the lion's share of recommendations in the NAPA report. One of Witt's first actions was to eliminate ten presidentially appointed management posts—about one-third of the total number of appointees at the agency.[24]

Clinton also acceded to Witt's request to have an opportunity to interview the individuals whom the president was considering for the agency's remaining appointments. In contrast to prior practice, Clinton's selections almost uniformly had strong relevant experience, as opposed to just lending a hand in political campaigns. Examples included Deputy Director Robert M. Walker, who as undersecretary of the army had supervised the Defense Department's response to domestic disasters; Lacy E. Suiter, who for twelve years had been director of the Tennessee Emergency Management Agency; and Michael Armstrong, who had worked for more than ten years in Colorado state and local government specializing in conservation, land use, and personnel matters.[25]

Witt, further following NAPA's counsel, forcefully and relentlessly clarified FEMA's new central mission as providing support for "all-hazards, comprehensive emergency management." Previously, according to NAPA, FEMA was "a check-writing agency, an intelligence agency, a social service agency, and an insurance agency, with a fire administration thrown in."[26] Witt's "all-hazards" mantra transformed that pastiche into a straightforward mission focusing on activities that would be beneficial to the public, regardless of the precise nature of a particular crisis. So, for example, it would devote far more resources and energy than in the past toward "mitigation," which meant reducing the potential loss of life and property long before a disaster occurred by helping to move out people and protect structures in locations that were highly vulnerable. Rather than having multiple response plans and coordinators tailored to different types of emergencies, FEMA helped to develop a single strategy that would be universally applicable for police, fire, and emergency personnel, regardless of whether a hurricane, a tornado, or a flood hit a particular area. At the same time, the agency's past focus on civil defense dissipated after Witt convinced Congress that funds previously allocated for that purpose could now, in the aftermath of the Soviet Union's collapse, be more effectively devoted toward improving the government's response to natural disasters.[27]

As he greatly clarified FEMA's mission, Witt also undertook a major reorganization of the agency that reinforced support for the all-hazards approach while reinvigorating its career civil servants. Witt asked the most senior career employees to switch to different jobs, suggesting that the change would enable them to bring fresh perspective and new ideas to the restructured institution. That process reduced each manager's incentive to react defensively to subsequent reforms, since none had a personal stake in defending the way his or her part of the organization had done things in the past. Witt and his team also emphasized the importance of achieving concrete results, regardless of the means used to get there. A sign in Witt's office said, "When entering this room, don't say, 'We've never done it that way before.'" In 1996, President Clinton elevated Witt's post to cabinet level, providing the agency with a direct connection to the Oval Office.

In interviews with longtime FEMA staff, Jerry Ellig of George Mason University found that two consistent themes emerged under Witt's leadership:

> 1) Individuals are more willing to actually take responsibility for things that they were supposed to be responsible for all along. They make decisions and accept the resulting criticism or praise, whereas previously they were more prone to duck decisions or criticism. 2) Individuals have a much better understanding of how their specific responsibilities relate to FEMA's overall customer service mission. As a result, people focus on helping citizens prevent or solve problems, rather than simply complying with standard procedures.[28]

Morale escalated throughout Witt's eight years at the helm, and job applications for open positions soared—a stark contrast to the previous era, when half of all FEMA employees surveyed said they would take a job elsewhere if offered one.[29]

Witt's reforms produced improvements that were so concrete and dramatic that his tenure became a model for government managers. In 2000, two glowing studies of his accomplishments were published.[30] Testimonials flowed to the agency from members of Congress and others who previously had lambasted it. After Florida was wracked by tornadoes, floods, and forest fires in an unprecedented series of natural disasters in 1998, Senator Bob Graham (D-Fla.) said that FEMA's response represented "a 180-degree turnaround" from its efforts after Hurricane Andrew just six years earlier.[31] Florida's director of emergency services called FEMA "[m]uch more proactive, more sensitive to the consumer, in this case the disaster victim. They have just made a tremendous turnaround in improvement."[32] Senator Tim Hutchison (R-Ark.) said in 1998, "Prior to [Witt's] arrival, FEMA was rivaled probably only by the IRS as the most disliked federal agency." But after tornadoes hit Arkansas in 1997, he remarked, "FEMA's reaction was outstanding. People were receiving checks within days of the disaster. At times, it is difficult to identify owners of property because of hand-shake sales, yet, to my knowledge, there was little or no complaint in the filling of requests. This is an outstanding turnaround for a very important agency."[33]

Back to the Turkey Farm

Notwithstanding the logic of staying the successful course, newly elected president George W. Bush's choice for FEMA director in 2001 immediately signaled not only a change in direction for the agency but also a reversion to the past. Joseph M. Allbaugh, like most pre-Witt FEMA leaders, was far more experienced in political campaigns — having just managed Bush's as part of his "iron triangle," along with Karl Rove and Karen Hughes — than in emergency management. Leo Bosner, an emergency-management specialist who had worked at FEMA since its creation in 1979 and is now head of the agency's union, told *Rolling Stone*, "There are plenty of Republican emergency managers, fire chiefs, or police chiefs around. And they pull this guy who's a campaign manager?"[34]

In the months ahead, Allbaugh proceeded to reaffirm his desire to stamp a conservative imprint on the agency, just as Heritage pre-scribed, by choosing for presidential appointment slots other top officials who shared both his ideology and lack of emergency-management credentials. Among them was Michael Brown, who initially joined FEMA as general counsel in February 2001. With the exception of a single FEMA employee who served as acting director of operations, none of the other individuals in the agency's front office during All-baugh's tenure had any prior emergency-management experience.[35] Beyond reverting to FEMA's old turkey-farm hiring practices, All-baugh reestablished the Office of National Preparedness that Reagan's failed director Giuffrida had originally set up under the same name in 1981. That action restored the civil defense mission that had been near and dear to the heart of conservative icon Reagan, which Witt had largely dropped in order to sharpen the agency's focus. Allbaugh's decision to reinstate under the same name an office that had once embarrassed the government sent a signal that only conservative ideologues could interpret positively.[36]

Allbaugh's tenure further followed the conservative movement's playbook by emasculating much of his corner of the federal government—dropping programs (despite their success), shedding responsibilities to states and localities, and privatizing activities by contracting out a greater share of work that agency personnel had previously conducted. In testimony on May 16, 2001, before a Senate appropriations subcommittee, Allbaugh said, "Many are concerned that federal disaster assistance may have evolved into both an oversized entitlement program and a disincentive to effective state and local risk management. Expectations of when the federal government should be involved and the degree of involvement may have ballooned beyond an appropriate level."[37] That is pure conservative movement boilerplate, which conformed with what the heads of many Bush administration agencies were saying at the time. For example, budget director Mitch Daniels told a federal audience in April 2001, "The general idea that the business of government is not to provide services, but to make sure that they are provided, seems self-evident to me."[38]

What did Allbaugh's efforts mean in practice for an agency that by all accounts, from the perspective of many Republicans as well as Democrats, had experienced a remarkable turnaround in the previous eight years? One telling example was Allbaugh's decision to eliminate Project Impact, a Witt disaster-mitigation initiative that provided relatively small grants—between $500,000 and $1 million—to spur local and private support to pursue plans to better defend communities against potential disasters. The relatively inexpensive $25-million-a-year program was widely credited with such results as the construction—mostly funded with private and local money—of tornado-safe rooms in about ten thousand homes across Oklahoma, the installation of storm shutters and other hurricane-proofing devices on buildings in central and southern Florida, and the removal in the Seattle area of large water tanks from rooftops that could cave in during an earthquake.

Frank Reddish, the longtime Republican emergency-management coordinator of Miami-Dade County who credited Project Impact with raising the awareness of local officials about the need for disaster mitigation, said about Allbaugh's elimination of the program, "They politicized it. Just because it was invented by a Democrat doesn't mean it was bad."[39]

Allbaugh, an intimidating character at six feet, four inches, 280 pounds, with a flat-top crewcut, was less than diplomatic in communicating his devolution agenda to states and localities. Shortly after taking office, in late April 2001, Allbaugh went to Davenport, Iowa, which had experienced significant flooding after the Mississippi River reached near-record-high levels. He proceeded to chastise the city for refusing to build a floodwall that might have prevented the disaster. "How many times does the American taxpayer have to step in and take care of this flooding, which could have been prevented by building levees and dikes?" Allbaugh asked. The mayor of Davenport, incredulous at such a harsh statement in the midst of the crisis, called Allbaugh's attack "insensitive."[40] But his message was crystal clear that states and localities would be largely on their own in preparing for calamities, as they were before the Witt era.

Privatize, Devolve, and Cut

Contracting out a much larger share of FEMA's work—again in accordance with conservative dogma—was another Allbaugh priority. While virtually every federal agency relies to varying degrees on private providers to carry out public services through contracting, the doctrine of the right errs decisively on the side of farming out work—often to providers who have coughed up abundant campaign contributions. In the process, movement conservatives relative to good government supporters prefer less government oversight, fewer and looser performance requirements, and a greater use of no-bid contracts. The presumption on the right is that private-sector contractors can carry out activities at lower cost and more effectively because they have to compete in the marketplace with other private firms for profits and, in most cases, are not unionized and therefore can pay their workers less. Oversight by the dreaded government bureaucrats only gums up those virtuous market forces. But as anyone knows from reading the headlines in recent years about no-bid Defense Department contracts to Halliburton for Iraq rebuilding or FEMA's own post-Katrina no-bid contracts to politically connected companies like Bechtel and Fluor, overzealous contracting practices combined with lax government oversight squandered millions of taxpayer dollars.[41] As a small indication of how pervasive the privatization mind-set was from the get-go, in 2001 the White House, FEMA, and other agencies went so far as to begin contracting with the Bulletin News Network, run by Paul Roellig, a former policy analyst in George H. W. Bush's White House, to prepare daily morning summaries of customized news clippings. That activity had previously been performed mostly by volunteers, so it's not clear how the government became more efficient in the process.[42]

All of these ideologically driven changes—privatization, the elimination of successful programs, the resurrection of a failed Reagan-era enterprise, the devolving of responsibilities to states and localities, and the heightened reliance on political appointees with negligible qualifications beyond an abiding commitment to the conservative movement—predictably sent the morale of FEMA employees into a deep and rapid tailspin. Large numbers of the most experienced workers began to leave the agency, in many cases without being replaced. After the implementation of conservative ideology set in motion FEMA's downward spiral, its inclusion in the Department of Homeland Security following the September 11 terrorist attacks—a largely bipartisan but ill-fated decision that Witt presciently objected to—greatly exacerbated the agency's decline. Now Michael Brown, who succeeded Allbaugh upon the creation of DHS in 2003, didn't directly report to the president but was just one among twenty-two agency heads accountable upward through several chains of command to the secretary of DHS, including many additional layers of inexperienced conservative political appointees. Jane Bullock, who served as chief of staff for emergency management from 1995 to 2001, told *Rolling Stone*:

> The moment FEMA went into DHS, it was a death knell. When FEMA was independent, Witt could pick up the phone and call up the Secretary for Defense for assistance. He'd respond immediately, because he had seen Witt in Cabinet meetings. No one can tell me that if Mike Brown picked up the phone and called Don Rumsfeld, that Rumsfeld would even have known who Brown was.[43]

All of these forces accelerated the deterioration in staff morale that had begun under Allbaugh. By 2005, FEMA was operating with a 15 to 20 percent job vacancy rate, and many openings were not being filled because of funding shortfalls.[44] A June 21, 2004, letter written by sixteen-year FEMA veteran and then union head Pleasant Mann to several senators, and sent more than a year before the Katrina calamity, conveyed alarm:

> Over the past three years, FEMA has gone from being a model agency to one where funds are being misspent, employee morale has fallen, and our nation's emergency management capability is being eroded. . . . In a recent survey, 60 percent of FEMA head-quarters employees who responded said they would probably leave FEMA and take another job if one were offered, and nearly 75 percent said they would retire immediately if they could do so. . . . Over the past three-and-one-half years, professional emergency managers at FEMA have been supplanted on the job by politi-cally connected contractors and by novice employees with little background or knowledge of emergency management. At first this took place at the senior levels of FEMA, but it has now entered into the mid-level and working-level of the agency, and jobs are increasingly being filled by hiring inexperienced and unqualified persons.[45]

A survey of morale levels among all government agencies found that FEMA's ranked last, after having been among the leaders just a few years earlier.[46]

Conservative Leadership

At the time Katrina hit, five of FEMA's eight top officials had virtually no prior experience in emergency management. In addition to Brown, the other four novices with political connections were Chief of Staff Patrick J. Rhode, who had done advance work for Bush's presidential campaign; Deputy Chief of Staff Brooks D. Altshuler, another cam-paign aide; the acting director for risk reduction and federal insurance administrator David I. Maurstad, who was previously Nebraska's lieu-tenant governor until 2001; and Director of Recovery Daniel A. Craig, who came to the agency from the U.S. Chamber of Commerce after working previously as a lobbyist for the National Rural Electric Cooperative Association.[47] The Senate Homeland Security Committee staff reviewed the biographies of FEMA regional directors since 2001 and found that many of them had little or no emergency-management experience as well.[48]

The committee's investigation found that FEMA employees considered the root of the agency's problems to be its reliance on unqualified political appointees. Eric Tolbert, who was director of response at FEMA until February 2005, told the committee, "The impact of having political in the high ranks of FEMA . . . that's what killed us. In the senior ranks of FEMA there was nobody that even knew FEMA's history, much less understood the profession and the dynamics and the roles and responsibilities of the states and [of] local governments." The committee also released excerpts of an internal assessment by the nonprofit consulting firm MITRE in early 2005 (months before Katrina hit), exploring why FEMA was failing to deal quickly with disasters. Based on confidential interviews with eleven of FEMA's senior executives, the MITRE report emphasized both the high number and the poor qualifications of political appointees in the agency. Among the quotes cited: "The void is in leadership. There's none," and, "None of the senior leadership understand the dynamics of how response and recovery actually works. . . . This administration doesn't understand the value and importance of emergency management."[49]

The politicization of FEMA did, however, generate a certain sort of productivity when four successive hurricanes slammed the pivotal election state of Florida during the 2004 presidential campaign season. An investigation by the South Florida *Sun-Sentinel* found that concerns about the damage the storms could do to the president at the ballot box prompted FEMA to dole out disaster relief checks with unprecedented generosity. The paper reported that two weeks after a FEMA consultant raised alarms that the second of the hurricanes was creating a "huge mess" that could reflect poorly on Bush, a Florida official wrote that FEMA was handing out housing assistance "to everyone who needs it without asking for much information of any kind."[50] Subsequent investigations by the DHS's inspector general and the Senate Committee on Homeland Security and Governmental Affairs confirmed the *Sun-Sentinel* reports, finding that FEMA paid more than $31 million to thousands of Florida residents who were unaffected by the hurricanes. As Senator Susan Collins (R-Maine) described it at a contentious May 2005 hearing at which Brown parried heated questions, "FEMA approved massive payouts to replace thousands of televisions, air conditioners, beds and other furniture, as well as a number of cars, without receipts, or proof of ownership or damage, and based solely on verbal statements from the residents, sometimes made in fleeting encounters at fast-food restaurants."[51]

The wasteful spending in Florida prompted the Collins-Lieberman Committee to recommend numerous changes to improve fairness, accountability, and transparency in the administration of FEMA's disaster-assistance program. Other pre-Katrina, post–September 11 studies and reports examining the agency raised concerns and offered recommendations about the meager training of personnel, inadequate "surge capacity" to have temporary workers available to help during crises, its poor use of communications and information technology, the absence of standard operating procedures, a grossly understaffed procurement office, and excessive vacancies. But none of those warnings or ideas were heeded, and the consequences became horrifically obvious to everyone after Katrina hit.

In all of the postmortems about FEMA's failures, the explanations for what went wrong invariably boil down to a single word: leadership. It's a word that ultimately explains most government success stories as well, as Witt's turnaround of the 1990s demonstrates. The conservative movement produces leaders who are committed to Ronald Reagan's core belief that government is the problem, not the solution. The right also insists that after political victories, as many like-minded leaders as possible should be planted throughout the government to "exert control" over civil servants, who typically have much more experience and knowledge about public activities such as responding to emergencies. Allbaugh and Brown were exactly the kinds of leaders the conservative movement promised the public that it would bring to the executive branch: advocates of "limited" government; suspicious of career bureaucrats; believers in outsourcing, downsizing, and devolution; recruiters to the government hierarchy of more ideologues just like them. People who describe Allbaugh and Brown as simply incompetent or unqualified misunderstand why conservative government is failing. They did precisely what the right said its leaders would do.

The Defense Department's Ministry of Propaganda

Another emblematic demonstration of the Heritage approach to public sector management, and why it's deeply flawed, is the short, unhappy life of the Defense Department's Office of Special Plans (OSP). Chapter 3 will discuss the broader connections between movement conservatism and the invasion of Iraq, which has proved to be another debacle, but the creation of OSP also deserves dishonorable mention here because it was motivated entirely by the Bush administration's contempt for career civil servants standing in the way of an ideological mission.

OSP was molded in a policy office in the Pentagon that focused on the Near East and South Asia. At the direction of Defense Secretary Donald Rumsfeld, Deputy Secretary Paul Wolfowitz, and Undersecretary for Policy Douglas J. Feith, the unit began to evolve beginning in May 2002 into an enterprise primarily charged with providing administration talking points that could be used to justify an attack on Iraq. It conducted some scattershot intelligence of its own—reading Iraqi newspapers for reports that might incriminate Saddam Hussein in acts of terrorism, for example—but its main purpose was to develop arguments against his regime while questioning the reliability of CIA and other intelligence reports, including the Defense Department's own, that doubted his possession of weapons of mass destruction and connections to al-Qaeda.[52] The political appointees brought in to run OSP without exception were individuals who had long advocated Saddam Hussein's overthrow and adhered to Wolfowitz's neoconservative philosophy that forceful exertion of American hegemony should be the nation's overriding foreign policy priority. Among them was Deputy Undersecretary of Defense William Luti, who oversaw the Near East and South Asia section, a recently retired navy captain who had served as an aide to both Vice President Dick Cheney and Newt Gingrich.

The director of OSP was Abram Shulsky, who had been a housemate of Wolfowitz's during their college years and previously worked for the neoconservative Richard Perle. Shulsky, like Wolfowitz, a disciple of University of Chicago political scientist Leo Strauss, believed that tyrannical regimes are so dependent on deception that gathering valid intelligence about them can be an exercise in futility. Shulsky coauthored a 1999 essay that included this passage: "Strauss' view certainly alerts one to the possibility that political life may be closely linked to deception. Indeed, it suggests that deception is the norm in political life, and the hope, to say nothing of the expectation, of establishing a politics that can dispense with it as the exception." As George Packer wrote in *The Assassins' Gate: America in Iraq*, "It isn't such a long step from this insight to the creation of an office that conceals its work behind a deliberately obscure name like 'Special Plans.'"[53]

Veteran experts in the Near East and South Asia unit—including Joseph McMillan, James Russell, Larry Hanauer, and Marybeth McDevitt—were either transferred elsewhere or retired.[54] New recruits were hired from such ideologically driven think tanks as the Middle East Media Research Institute, the Washington Institute for Near East Policy, and the Jewish Institute for National Security Affairs.[55] Three of Luti and Shulsky's hires were men who had close ties to Ahmed Chalabi, the head of the Iraqi National Congress whom Perle had long touted as the logical replacement for Saddam Hussein after an overthrow, notwithstanding Chalabi's uncertain, at best, popular support in the country. Those three individuals were Colonel William Bruner, a former military aide to Gingrich; Michael Rubin, an Iran scholar at the American Enterprise Institute (AEI); and Harold Rhode, another AEI fellow. OSP served as a channel for passing along intelligence provided by Chalabi, almost all of which turned out to be false.[56]

Lieutenant Colonel Karen Kwiatkowski, a self-identified conservative with twenty years of military service, had been working as a staff officer in the Pentagon's policy office on sub-Saharan Africa when she was "volunteered" to work in the Near East, South Asia directorate. Her summation of what she witnessed inside OSP:

> I saw a narrow and deeply flawed policy favored by some executive appointees in the Pentagon used to manipulate and pressurize the traditional relationship between policymakers in the Pentagon and U.S. agencies. I witnessed neoconservative agenda bearers within OSP usurp measured and carefully considered assessments, and through suppression and distortion of intelligence analysis promulgate what were in fact falsehoods to both Congress and the executive office of the president.[57]

Paul R. Pillar, who served as national intelligence officer for the Near East and South Asia from 2000 to 2005 at the end of a long career in the CIA, wrote in *Foreign Affairs*:

> The administration used intelligence not to inform decision-making, but to justify a decision already made. . . . The Bush administration deviated from the professional standard not only in using policy to drive intelligence, but also in aggressively using intelligence to win public support for its decision to go to war. This meant selectively adducing data—"cherry-picking"—rather than using the intelligence community's own analytic judgments.[58]

It almost goes without saying now, but the United States would be stronger and safer today if the administration had recognized the value of career civil servants like Kwiatkowski and Pillar.

The Bush Scorecard

As compelling as the FEMA and OSP stories are in making the case against excessive politicization of government agencies, they are only two examples. But thanks to the Bush administration's own innovation in instituting a new management-grading system, it has become possible to more systematically evaluate whether political appointees or career civil servants are more effective managers—using the conservative Bush team's criteria for defining *effective*.

The grading system developed by the Office of Management and Budget, first implemented in 2002, is called the Program Assessment Rating Tool, or PART. Under PART, four categories of management receive grades—program purpose and design, strategic planning, program management, and program results—based on a series of twenty-five to thirty yes-or-no questions filled out jointly by agencies and OMB examiners. The raw scores are weighted and combined to produce a total numerical score, as well as a grade for each category, ranging from 0 to 100. Those tallies are translated into verbal assessments: ineffective, results not demonstrated, adequate, moderately effective, and effective. Disagreements between the OMB and the agencies are resolved by appeals up the OMB hierarchy—tantamount to giving the

White House the last word. To date, a total of 614 federal programs have been evaluated under PART.[59]

David E. Lewis set about to compare how the PART grades of programs managed by political appointees compared with those run by career administrators. He found that 245 different bureau chiefs administered the programs that were assessed (some managers were responsible for more than one). Of the 242 Lewis was able to ascertain background information about, he found that 62 percent were Senate-confirmed political appointees, 11 percent politically appointed members of the Senior Executive Service (SES), and 25 percent career SES managers.[60]

After comparing the scores through statistical regression analysis, Lewis found that "the programs administered by appointees get systematically lower grades than careerists—even when controlling for differences among programs, substantial variation in management environment, and the policy content of the programs themselves." In other words, the data show decisively that experienced civil servants are judged to be more effective managers than are political appointees—a result that is not dependent on differences in the kinds of programs that the two groups might be more likely to manage. If anything, those findings are apt to be skewed in favor of political appointees and against career managers. Because the administration uses the PART grades to help make judgments about budgets for particular programs, its ideological predilections favoring political appointees would be more likely to bias the results against activities managed by career staff. In addition, Lewis found that programs created by Democratic presidents received lower grades, which suggests that evaluations of policy content may be working their way into the administration's evaluations of management performance.[61] Again, that tendency would be more likely to benefit politically appointed managers.

Lewis's study also attempted to discern from the data *why* programs administered by appointees receive lower grades. Additional regressions showed that two characteristics that were more prevalent among career managers—previous experience within the bureau and relatively longer tenure in the job—appeared to matter in producing higher performance grades. He found that political appointees had higher levels of education and a broader range of experience, including in private sector management, on average. But those traits did not correlate with the PART performance grades.

Robert Shea, who oversees the PART program at the OMB, told the *Federal Times* that Lewis's findings don't prove anything: "It's safe to say that almost all of the programs that [he] compared are managed by a political appointee, not a career employee. All careerists eventually report to a political appointee. The career folks they've isolated as managers of programs are under the day-to-day management of a political appointee."

Lewis responded that he simply chose the managers for each program as listed on the OMB's worksheets. If every program is, in effect, ultimately under the control of a political appointee, then why would his calculations turn up systematically better outcomes for those directly managed by career officials?[62] One would think that an executive of the OMB, which is supposed to be concerned with improving government efficiency, would respond that maybe more research could be conducted to see whether Lewis might be on to something. But, no, the right's ideology is clear: political appointees, good; career civil servants, bad.

Circular Reasoning

Everyone recognizes that government can be painfully inefficient. On the other hand, it also has often accomplished impressive goals and demonstrated the capacity to reform itself to become more effective and avoid past mistakes. But the conservative movement's central mission of weakening the government's domestic capabilities while exerting muscularity abroad doesn't allow for nuance in thinking about public sector management. The right's diagnosis of the problem is simple: bureaucracies are always inherently inefficient because they are run by useless, stubborn, unmanageable civil servants. The solution that follows logically from that assessment is to put the government as much as possible in the control of conservatives who share the mindset that career bureaucrats are standing in the way of achieving the right's overarching goals. Unfortunately for the country, ideologically driven Bush appointees have not only created one mess after another, they also have left future administrations with a government workforce littered with unqualified believers just like them. This will

only make it that much harder to rebuild an effective public sector—
a result not unlike the argument of President Reagan's budget director David Stockman that high federal deficits would impede government long after Reagan left office. It's all part of the right's plan for
America.

Many conservatives pounced on the Katrina failure as a reaffirmation of their views about the inherent ineptitude of government. For
example, the *New York Times* columnist David Brooks wrote:

> The paradox at the heart of the Katrina disaster . . . is that we really
> need government in times like this, but government is extremely
> limited in what it can effectively do. Katrina was the most antici-
> pated natural disaster in American history, and still government
> managed to fail at every level. For the brutal fact is, government
> tends toward bureaucracy, which means elaborate paper flow but
> ineffective action. Government depends on planning, but plan-
> ners can never really anticipate the inevitable complexity of
> events. And American government is inevitably divided and power
> is inevitably devolved.[63]

David Boaz of the libertarian Cato Institute was even more forceful:

> You've got to hand it to the advocates of big government. They're
> never embarrassed by the failures of government. On the contrary,
> the state's every malfunction is declared a reason to give govern-
> ment more money and more power. Take Hurricane Katrina, a
> colossal failure of government at every level—federal, state, and
> local. . . . Let's look at the facts. Government failed to plan. Gov-
> ernment spent $50 billion a year on homeland security without,
> apparently, preparing itself to deal with a widely predicted natural
> disaster. Government was sluggish in responding to the disaster.
> Government kept individuals, businesses, and charities from re-
> sponding as quickly as they wanted. And at the deepest level, gov-
> ernment so destroyed wealth and self-reliance in the people of New
> Orleans that they were unable to fend for themselves in a crisis.[64]

But as we have seen, the quality of the government's performance
was far from identical after previous major disasters—that's why both
Democratic and Republican senators kept referring to FEMA's "turnaround" under Witt. For a theory like public choice to be robust, it

needs to be useful not only in explaining something that happened in the past but also in predicting what will happen in the future. The fundamental problem with public-choice theory is that its empirical applicability seems to make sense only in explaining past governmental failures such as the Katrina episode. But it doesn't have anything remotely useful to offer about Witt's accomplishments. It can't explain Lewis's findings that government programs run by career managers seem to be systematically more effective than those run by political appointees. And it can't predict whether FEMA, intelligence agencies, or any other government branch or department will improve or decline over time, because all it has to offer is that government will always fail to promote the public interest due to the intrinsic flaws of bureaucracies and civil servants.

Many in the conservative movement are convinced, and want the public to believe, that government can do no better than it did after Katrina. According to the right's worldview, the debacle we all witnessed was an inevitable consequence of forces beyond the capacity of leadership to overcome. But that philosophy is self-fulfilling. If you believe that government is predestined to fail, and you choose leaders who share that belief, your ideology will be borne out. No institution will succeed unless the people running it are committed to its success. Politicizing the government by putting civil servants under the thumb of individuals lacking that deeply held commitment—not to mention relevant experience, knowledge, and familiarity with policies that have historically proved to be effective—is a sure path to failure. Yet government, when managed by individuals who reject conservative ideology, has succeeded many times in the past. The lesson is pretty easy to follow.

2

The Nixon Doctrine
The Unitary Executive

T hree years after resigning from the presidency, Richard Nixon sat for a series of taped televised interviews with the journalist David Frost. At one point, Frost asked Nixon about the "Huston Plan"—an effort in which the CIA, the FBI, and other police and intelligence agencies would systematically use wiretappings, burglaries, mail openings, and infiltration of antiwar groups to comply with Nixon's demands for better intelligence about his opponents. Deputy White House Counsel Tom Huston, who convened the meetings that produced the plan, warned Nixon that some of the activities were clearly illegal. Nixon approved the enterprise anyway, though it was ultimately withdrawn after FBI Director J. Edgar Hoover opposed it. Here's an excerpt from the interview:

> Frost: So what, in a sense, you're saying is that there are certain situations, and the Huston Plan or that part of it was one of them, where the president can decide that it's in the best interests of the nation or something, and do something illegal.
>
> Nixon: Well, when the president does it, that means that it is not illegal.
>
> Frost: By definition.
>
> Nixon: Exactly. Exactly. If the president, for example, approves something because of the national security, or in this case because

of a threat to internal peace and order of significant magnitude, then the president's decision in that instance is one that enables those who carry it out, to carry it out without violating a law. Otherwise, they're in an impossible position. . . . Just so that one does not get the impression that a president can run amok in this country and get away with it, we have to have in mind that a president has to come up before the electorate. We also have to have in mind that a president has to get appropriations from the Congress. We have to have in mind, for example, that as far as the CIA's covert operations are concerned, as far as the FBI's covert operations are concerned, through the years, they have been disclosed on a very, very limited basis to trusted members of Congress. I don't know whether it can be done today or not.

Considering that the main upshot of Nixon's views about executive power was what his successor Gerald Ford termed "our long national nightmare," ending in Nixon's own resignation and disgrace, one might think that his philosophy of "when the president does it, that means that it is not illegal" would also be relegated to ignominy. But that would be wrong. Many of Nixon's fellow conservatives have continued to believe in the validity of his assertions about the authority of the president to act unencumbered by constraints—particularly in wartime—whether from existing laws and treaties, congressional oversight, or executive branch agencies pursuing agendas at odds with his priorities.[1] The same impulses that have driven conservatives to politicize the government, weaken career civil servants, and disembowel the regulatory process drew them to see the Constitution as empowering the president in ways not spelled out, as Nixon put it, "in every jot and in every tittle." To a large extent, those impulses derive from a desire to thwart Democrats in Congress and the civil service by any means necessary. But the right needed more persuasive justifications than Nixon's if they were to resurrect a constitutional interpretation that virtually equates the president with a sovereign. The evolution of that effort is yet another demonstration of how money, creativity, and groundless spin combined to produce ideas that, when acted upon by the administration of George W. Bush, proved to be at least as disastrous as Watergate.

The New "Federalists"

The single most determined individual to keep Nixon's flame alive is Dick Cheney. As chief of staff to President Ford, a Republican congressman from Wyoming during the Reagan years, secretary of defense under President George H. W. Bush, and now vice president under George W. Bush, Cheney repeatedly took umbrage at what he perceived to be inappropriate congressional encroachments on the executive branch. The assortment of post-Watergate laws that reined in the presidency, as well as the 1973 War Powers Resolution, directly fenced in Cheney when he worked for Ford. The congressional vote to cut off military funding to the South Vietnam government before Saigon fell in 1975 particularly rankled him. Kenneth Adelman, a high-ranking Pentagon official under Ford, told Jane Mayer for a *New Yorker* article that Saigon's fall was "very painful for Dick. He believed that Vietnam could have been saved—maybe—if Congress hadn't cut off funding. He was against that kind of interference."[2] In December 2005, Cheney told reporters, "I do have the view that over the years there had been an erosion of Presidential power and authority. . . . A lot of the things around Watergate and Vietnam both, in the seventies, served to erode the authority that I think the President needs."[3]

After the Iran-Contra scandal under Reagan, Cheney was the ranking Republican on a House select committee assigned with investigating the secret arms sales to Iran that produced funds diverted to support the Contras fighting the leftist Sandinista government in Nicaragua; both selling weapons to Iran and using government funds to finance the Contras clearly violated laws and the administration's publicly stated policies. Cheney's team produced a Minority Report in 1987 arguing that it was actually Congress, not the president, that had overstepped its authority. The report said that Reagan had been driven by "a legitimate frustration with abuses of power and irresolution by the legislative branch." It also defended the legality of ignoring congressional intelligence oversight, arguing that "the President has the Constitutional and statutory authority to withhold notifying Congress of covert actions under rare conditions."[4]

Cheney's frustrations with Congress, which not coincidentally happened to be under the control of Democrats throughout most of the 1970s and 1980s, were widely shared in conservative circles. But as Cheney's Minority Report demonstrates, conservatives hadn't moved much beyond Nixon's insistent assertions in explaining how their beliefs could possibly square with the plain language of the Constitution regarding checks on executive power and the president's responsibilities to faithfully execute the laws. Providing some semblance of intellectual footing for their monarchist interpretation—a "reading" based at root on annoyance with unwanted meddling from congressional Democrats rather than on a well-developed philosophy—came to be a job for the Federalist Society.

Established in 1982 by a group of conservative lawyers and law students at the University of Chicago, Yale, and Harvard, the Federalist Society was initially conceptualized as a networking organization on campuses opposed to what was perceived to be liberal orthodoxy taught at law schools. The idea was to identify and feed promising young conservative attorneys into clerkships and positions in the Reagan administration, while winning over and indoctrinating law students who would be exposed to the insights of leading conservative legal figures.[5] Early founders and supporters of the society included such icons of the right as Edwin Meese, Irving Kristol, William Rehnquist, Antonin Scalia, and Robert Bork. Over the years, money supporting the Federalist Society has flowed from the always generous Scaife, Olin, Bradley, and Earhart foundations. It has grown to include lawyers' chapters in about sixty cities and student chapters on almost all of the nation's accredited law school campuses.

The Federalist Society is not a think tank akin to the Heritage Foundation or the Cato Institute. It does not have a stable of full-time "scholars" issuing reports and commentary on the issues of the day or a big media operation to feed quotes to journalists. The Federalist Society's approach toward fostering and spreading ideas is more reliant on convening conferences, training sessions, and other gatherings, including "practice groups" in which members brainstorm about strategies that participating litigators working for conservative activist groups might pursue. It also runs a speaker's bureau and provides a conduit for members to share their written work with one another. Although the Federalist Society's leaders like to refer to it as merely a "debate club," it undeniably has played an important role in fertilizing conservative legal thought and strategy on a wide range of issues, while greasing the path for conservative law students to attain influential jobs.

One of the ideas massaged over the years in Federalist Society circles is the concept of the "unitary executive," a label whose meaning has mutated but which has ultimately come to embrace by some of its adherents, in essence, the Nixon doctrine of executive power. In its original incarnation in the 1980s, the concept applied mainly to legal claims of executive authority in managing the executive branch. That is, the unitary executive tenet held that the president had the right to take actions such as revising regulations developed in agencies or the right to fire civil servants because the Constitution endowed him, rather than Congress, with the authority to manage government departments. In a 2000 speech to the Federalist Society, Samuel Alito, now a Supreme Court justice, recalled that when he worked in the Office of Legal Counsel (OLC) at the Justice Department under Reagan, "We were strong proponents of the theory of the unitary executive, that all federal power is vested by the Constitution in the president." Steven Calabresi, who helped to found the Federalist Society as a Yale law student and went on to serve under Reagan attorney general Meese, told the *New Republic*'s Jeffrey Rosen, " 'Unitary executive' was a phrase that was commonplace around the Justice Department while I was working there, although I was the first to defend it in a law review article in 1992. The inspiration for the phrase was Alexander Hamilton's call for 'unity' in the executive."[6]

It is unarguably true that Hamilton was a forceful defender of the need for a vigorous presidency with a degree of independence from the other branches of government. In Federalist Paper 70, for example, he wrote, "Energy in the executive is a leading character in the definition of good government," and "unity is conducive to energy." He elaborated, "Decision, activity, secrecy, and despatch will generally characterize the proceedings of one man in a much more eminent degree than the proceedings of any greater number; and in proportion as the number is increased, these qualities will be diminished." And in Paper 71 he asked, "To what purpose separate the executive or the judiciary from the legislative if both the executive and the judiciary are so constituted as to be at the absolute devotion of the legislative?" He also supported a four-year term for presidencies, with an opportunity to run for additional terms, to give the executive the time to perform well and "secure to the government the advantage of permanency in a wise system of administration."

On the other hand, Hamilton also emphasized the importance of such congressional checks on presidential power as the requirement of Senate confirmation of ambassadors and Supreme Court justices, and for two-thirds of the Senate to vote for treaties for their ratification. The Hamilton biographer Ron Chernow wrote, "In his essays on the need for executive branch vigor, Hamilton continually invoked the king of England as an example of what should be *avoided*, especially the monarch's lack of accountability. . . . Hamilton was as quick to applaud checks on powers as those powers themselves, as he continued his lifelong effort to balance freedom and order."[7]

As developed in law review articles in the 1990s by such Federalist Society members as Calabresi, Saikrishna B. Prakash, and Kevin Rhodes, the initial incarnation of the unitary executive idea relies heavily on the "vesting clause" in Article II, Section 1 of the Constitution, which states, "[T]he executive Power shall be vested in a President of the United States of America." In combination with the "take care" clause—"[The President] shall take care that the laws be faithfully executed"—those two broad grants of power give the president, under the unitary executive theory, unfettered control of all government officials who implement the laws. One conclusion adherents have drawn is that the advent of independent agencies and special counsels created by legislation is unconstitutional because they violate that unity.

That argument is plenty radical, and one that has been effectively rebutted by scholars.[8] But the concept has since broadened greatly from that framework in the minds of many, though not all, Federalist Society members and Bush administration officials. Now it goes so far as to interpret the powers granted to the president as commander in chief of the armed forces as superceding any enacted laws or treaties ratified by Congress, especially during wartime. Hence the difficulty of discerning any distinction between the unitary executive idea and Nixon's belief that "when the president does it, that means that it is not illegal."

Yoo Who?

Two Bush administration officials were primarily responsible for pushing the boundaries of the unitary executive concept and using that legal rationale as the basis for carrying out a variety of unprecedented actions. One is David Addington, Cheney's chief of staff and former legal counsel whose longstanding connection to the vice president extends back to playing a lead role in producing the Minority Report on Iran-Contra. Widely regarded as a powerful infighter in the administration, Addington has been called "Cheney's Cheney" and "Cheney's hit man" and invariably takes the position that the administrative branch needs maximum "flexibility" if it is to beat terrorism.[9] The other is John C. Yoo, who served as a midlevel lawyer in the Office of Legal Counsel in the Justice Department during Bush's first term. A former clerk to Clarence Thomas, Yoo—while he was a young law professor at the University of California at Berkeley and a Federalist Society member in the 1990s—had written a number of articles arguing that the Constitution empowers the executive to a greater extent than does the consensus view.

Usually together but occasionally separately, and sometimes in combination with other officials, Yoo and Addington wrote memos using the principle of the unitary executive to defend warrantless electronic surveillance, indefinite detention, military tribunals, and disregard of the Geneva Conventions. And President Bush, in more than a hundred written statements issued when he signed legislation, referred to his authority to "supervise the unitary executive branch" as justification for disregarding bill provisions he considered to be objectionable.[10] For example, in December 2005, upon signing the antitorture legislation sponsored by Senator John McCain, Bush issued a statement saying in part that the executive branch "shall construe" a portion of the act relating to detainees "in a manner consistent with the constitutional authority of the President to supervise the unitary executive branch and as Commander in Chief and consistent with the constitutional limits of judicial power." According to research by Christopher Kelley of Miami University, Bush's predecessors rarely used the term *unitary executive* in signing statements or executive orders—Clinton never did, George H. W. Bush used it six times, and Reagan just once.[11]

The most fully developed defense of Bush's authority to carry out those actions is provided in a book Yoo published after leaving the Justice Department in 2003 titled *The Powers of War and Peace: The Constitution and Foreign Affairs after 9/11*, which draws in part from his writings in the 1990s.[12] Yoo's book primarily bases its case on what he contends the framers of the Constitution, its ratifiers, and the public understood as its meaning at the time it was drafted. That "originalist" approach, not incidentally, also happens to conform with widely held Federalist Society beliefs—shared by such members as Antonin Scalia, Clarence Thomas, and Robert Bork—about the most appropriate way to interpret the Constitution generally. In Yoo's view, the genesis of the Constitution demonstrates that the founders intended for the president to have unilateral authority to (1) initiate wars without congressional approval; (2) violate or terminate treaties at will; and (3) exercise unilateral authority unchecked by law in all matters related to foreign affairs in times of war. While Yoo acknowledges that the Constitution gives Congress the power to "declare war," he argues that a declaration merely "recognizes a state of affairs—clarifying the legal status of the nation's relationship with another country—rather than authorizing the creation of that state of affairs." If Congress opposes the president's war, Yoo argues, it can deny appropriations in support of it. But that's about the full extent of its role, as Richard Nixon suggested.

One line of Yoo's originalist argument focuses on legal thinkers of the time, particularly those from Britain such as William Blackstone, whose view of his country's constitution was that "the monarch has no need to declare war before beginning hostilities against another nation." In England, the king alone had the power to oversee the military and initiate war without any kind of formal declaration. Yoo argues that "[T]he Framers would have looked to recent British political theory as much as to intellectual thought on the separation of powers" in claiming that the Americans would have logically adopted the English system in devising their own.

Considering that rebellion against the British monarchy was the reason that the Constitutional Convention came about in the first place, Yoo's claims that the framers would naturally have looked to England as a model certainly deserve credit for bold counterintuitiveness. The deep suspicions that the founders harbored toward unchecked executive power as demonstrated by the throne across the ocean would seem to make his argument a nonstarter without even delving into the particulars. But delve we must. As the University of Chicago law professor Cass Sunstein noted in a careful dissection of Yoo's book for the New Republic:

There is specific evidence that the British model was rejected. Just three years after ratification, [Pennsylvania's James Wilson, a Constitution drafter and leading legal scholar of the time] wrote, with unambiguous disapproval, that, "in England, the king has the sole prerogative of making war." Wilson contrasted the United States, where the power "of making war and peace" is in the legislature. Early presidents spoke in similar terms. Facing attacks from Indian tribes along the Western frontier, George Washington, whose views on presidential power over war deserve respect, observed: "The Constitution vests the power of declaring war with Congress; therefore no offensive expedition of importance can be undertaken until after they have deliberated on the subject, and authorized such a measure." As president, both Thomas Jefferson and John Adams expressed similar views. In his influential *Commentaries*, written in 1826, James Kent wrote that "[W]ar cannot lawfully be commenced on the part of the United States, without an act of Congress."[13]

John Hart Ely, the former dean of Stanford Law School, has commented that while the original intention of the founders on many matters is often "obscure to the point of inscrutability," when it comes to war powers "it isn't."[14]

Yoo's arguments about the commander in chief's constitutional flexibility to ignore laws and unilaterally abrogate treaties are only marginally less shaky even from his own originalist standpoint. As Sunstein notes, *The Powers of War and Peace* reads like a lawyer's brief that puts forward only evidence in support of predetermined conclusions while ignoring or dismissing masses of information that contradict his views—a style of argumentation emblematic of the modern conservative movement. Perhaps even worse, Yoo's focus on the late 1700s gives short shrift to the nation's extensive history since then in wrestling with questions about wartime separation of powers. Yoo argues that such history lacks current relevance because everything is different since the September 11 attacks on U.S. soil by nonstate enemies. But dismissing on that basis accumulated precedents that have proved to serve the country well is a flimsy rationale for such a radical position. Over and over across the decades, the Supreme Court has consistently ruled that in time of war, the president must obtain explicit authorization from Congress for actions that threaten to abridge individual liberty.

Supreme Court Justice Anthony Kennedy, a Reagan appointee, took direct aim at Yoo's unitary executive construction precisely on that basis in his concurring opinion in the case of *Hamdan v. Rumsfeld*. That ruling relates to a Yemeni national named Salim Hamdan, who was taken prisoner in Afghanistan on a battlefield in 2001 and held in Guantanamo and who challenged the authority of the president to try him by a military commission that would be subject to unprecedented rules designed by the administration. Kennedy, joined by Justices Souter, Ginsburg, and Breyer, wrote in support of the 5–3 decision in Hamdan's favor:

> Military Commission Order No. 1, which governs the military commission established to try . . . Hamdan for war crimes, exceeds limits that certain statutes, duly enacted by Congress, have placed on the President's authority to convene military courts. This is not a case, then, where the Executive can assert some unilateral authority to fill a void left by Congressional inaction. It is a case where Congress, in the proper exercise of its power as an independent branch of government, and as part of a long tradition of legislative involvement in matters of military justice, has considered the subject of military tribunals and set limits on the President's authority. Where a statute provides the conditions for the exercise of governmental power, its requirements are the result of a deliberative and reflective process engaging both the political branches. Respect for laws derived from the customary operation of the Executive and Legislative Branches gives some assurance of stability in times of crisis. The Constitution is best preserved by reliance on standards tested over time and insulated from the pressures of the moment.

For anyone who remains skeptical about whether the Nixon analogy is fair, here's a brief exchange at a December 1, 2005, debate in Chicago between Yoo and the Notre Dame professor and international human rights scholar Doug Cassel:[15]

> Cassel: If the president deems that he's got to torture somebody, including by crushing the testicles of the person's child, there is no law that can stop him?

Yoo: No treaty.

Cassel: Also no law by Congress. That is what you wrote in the August 2002 memo.

Yoo: I think it depends on why the President thinks he needs to do that.

As history has demonstrated all too often, when immoral ideas catch on, immoral acts follow.

"*Animal House* on the Night Shift"

No one in the Bush administration even attempted to argue that the horrific photographs from Baghdad's Abu Ghraib prison depicting American soldiers abusing and humiliating Muslim detainees were anything other than a major blow in the "war on terror." It was immediately self-evident that the pictures, first publicly shown on the CBS *Evening News* on April 28, 2004, could do nothing but inflame greater hostility toward the United States in the Islamic world while infuriating allies who already had become alienated over America's Iraq invasion. More fundamentally, they diminished the hard-earned moral standing of the United States as the world's leader toward progress on human rights and the rule of law. The photos have been converted into posters available widely in locations with high concentrations of Muslims, from Marrakesh to Jakarta, and they appear prominently on Web sites run by militant groups.[16] The extent to which the photos have helped the recruitment efforts of al-Qaeda and other terrorist groups is unknown, but it is difficult to imagine a more generous gift the United States might have provided to them—with the exception of the Iraq War itself. Leaders of every nation, regardless of their political views, condemned the conduct in Abu Ghraib.

The Bush administration's response has consistently been to blame what happened on a handful of renegade guards and low-ranking officers. In a May 2004 speech, for example, Bush said, "A new Iraq will also need a humane, well-supervised prison system. Under the dictator, prisons like Abu Ghraib were symbols of death and torture. That same prison became a symbol of disgraceful conduct by a few American troops who dishonored our country and disregarded our values."[17] The "few bad apples" explanation was shared by the former defense secretary James R. Schlesinger, who chaired an independent investigation into Abu Ghraib. Schlesinger concluded that while the military's civilian leadership bore "indirect responsibility" for the abuses, the central cause was the sadism of a small number of guards whose actions he likened to "*Animal House* on the night shift."[18]

But in the months that followed, other investigations found that Abu Ghraib was anything but aberrant. Government documents reveal that torture and other degrading and inhumane treatment has been widespread, including multiple cases at Camp Cropper, Camp Bucca, and other detention centers in Mosul, Samarra, Baghdad, and Tikrit in Iraq, as well as Orgun-E in Afghanistan and the Guantanamo facility.[19] At least twenty-seven of the more than one hundred detainees who died in U.S. custody have had their deaths listed by the Army as confirmed or suspected homicides.[20] A 2006 report by Amnesty International stated:

> While it seems that some practices, such as "waterboarding," were reserved for high value detainees, others appear to have been routinely applied during detentions and investigations in Afghanistan, Guantanamo, and Iraq. The latter include hooding, stripping and shackling of detainees in painful positions as well as using military dogs to intimidate blindfolded detainees; prolonged isolation, deprivation of food and sleep and exposure to extremes of temperature also appear to have been common practice to punish detainees for failing to cooperate or to "soften them up" for interrogation. . . . Standard practices as well as interrogation techniques believed to have fallen within officially sanctioned parameters appear to have played a role in the ill-treatment.[21]

If bad apples are primarily responsible, it seems mystifying that there would be bushels full of them in every place the military ran a prison where interrogations occurred. Colonel Lawrence Wilkerson, who served as chief of staff to Secretary of State Colin Powell and served in the U.S. Army for thirty-one years, connects the dots:

> What else other than policy could have been responsible? A variety of people in a variety of units, in different locations at different times with different groups of detainees (a majority of whom, in every place, indisputably were innocent of being terrorists), handled by soldiers, Marines, CIA and contractors, . . . abused and even murdered detainees. Why did they do it? Can the behavior

of such disparate groups, across all areas and in all three services, be explained by any theory other than that they all thought they were doing what they were supposed to—and had a plausible reason for thinking so? . . . And the reason why we only have hundreds of cases and not thousands is the basic decency of the American fighting man and woman—and their leaders—most of whom refused to follow this policy?[22]

In a situation like this one in which policies set at the very highest levels of government make their way down through extended and complicated chains of command, assigning culpability with sufficient precision and evidence to stand up in court is enormously difficult. But there is no question that the top officials in the office of the vice president, the Justice Department, and the Defense Department actively and repeatedly took steps that at a bare minimum created ambiguity about appropriate procedures for the interrogation and treatment of prisoners. Fully recognizing that those new policies might be perceived as not complying with the Geneva Conventions or with U.S. statutes, David Addington and John Yoo were in the thick of the effort to legally justify why those laws did not apply to the handling of detainees captured in Afghanistan and in connection with the war on terrorism generally.

The Torture Memos

The door to Abu Ghraib opens with a memo John Yoo and special counsel Robert J. Delahunty sent on January 9, 2002, to Defense Department general counsel William J. Haynes II on the subject of "Application of Treaties and Laws to al Qaeda and Taliban Detainees."[23] Yoo and Delahunty argued that because al-Qaeda is not a nation-state, it can't be a party to a treaty like the Geneva Conventions, which requires that prisoners of war must at all times be humanely treated and protected against acts of violence or intimidation. Similarly, Taliban militia, the memo argued, were not entitled to POW status under the Geneva Conventions because the Taliban was not a government and because Afghanistan was not a functioning state. Later that month, then White House counsel Alberto Gonzales circulated a draft memo for President Bush endorsing Yoo and

Delahunty's analysis and recommended that Bush declare the Taliban and al-Qaeda to be outside the coverage of the Geneva Conventions and the War Crimes Act of 1996—a declaration that would protect U.S. officials from exposure to the act's severe penalties. Gonzales wrote that the war on terror, against nonstate actors who killed U.S. citizens on American soil, "renders obsolete" and "quaint" the "strict limitations on questioning of enemy prisoners" required by the Geneva Conventions.

Secretary of State Colin Powell almost immediately reacted to Gonzales's memo by pointing out that a sweeping pronouncement that the Geneva Conventions don't apply to Taliban or al-Qaeda prisoners would pose a multitude of "cons," with the only "pro" being the provision of "maximum flexibility." The cons Powell listed included undermining the protections of the laws of war for our troops, both in this specific conflict and in general; a high cost in terms of negative international reaction, with immediate adverse consequences for our conduct of foreign policy; undermining public support among critical allies, making military cooperation more difficult to sustain; legal problems raised in European and other countries with extradition or other forms of cooperation in bringing terrorists to justice; and making the government more vulnerable to domestic and international legal challenges while undermining an important legal basis for trying the detainees before military commissions. Gonzales prevailed, with President Bush in February 2002 issuing a directive noting that "[T]he war on terrorism ushers in a new paradigm" and that "the United States armed forces shall continue to treat detainees humanely and, to the extent appropriate and consistent with military necessity, in a manner consistent with the principles of Geneva." Bush did not elaborate on what he meant by "appropriate and consistent with military necessity," but it obviously signals a qualification to "the principles of Geneva."

In August 2002, the Office of Legal Counsel head Jay S. Bybee issued a memo to Gonzales that was drafted by Yoo with help from David Addington that set out to define in detail appropriate standards for overseas interrogations by the CIA. This is the memo that notoriously asserted:

> [F]or an act to constitute torture as defined in [Section 2340A of the U.S. Code, which derives from the Geneva Conventions] it must inflict pain that is difficult to endure. Physical pain amount-

ing to torture must be the equivalent in intensity to the pain accompanying serious physical injury, such as organ failure, impairment of bodily functions, or even death. For purely mental pain or suffering to amount to torture under Section 2340, it must result in significant psychological harm of significant duration, e.g., lasting for months or even years. . . .We conclude that the statute, taken as a whole, makes plain that it prohibits only extreme acts.

That definition obviously leaves plenty of room for "flexibility." Kicking kneeling prisoners in the stomach, sleep deprivation, the use of painful physical positions, and using dogs to intimidate detainees and nudity to humiliate them all fell explicitly or implicitly within the bounds of acceptability. All the more so since Bybee's memo reiterates the now familiar Yoo/Addington mantra:

> Even if an interrogation method arguably were to violate Section 2340A, the statute would be unconstitutional if it impermissibly encroached on the President's power to conduct a military campaign. As Commander-in-chief, the President has the constitutional authority to order interrogations of enemy combatants to gain intelligence information concerning the military plans of the enemy. The demands of the Commander-in-chief in power are especially pronounced in the middle of a war in which the nation has already suffered a direct attack. In such a case, the information gained from interrogations may prevent future attacks by foreign enemies. Any effort to apply Section 2340A in a manner that interferes with the President's direction of such core war matters as the detention and interrogation of enemy combatants thus would be unconstitutional.

A New Yorker article by Jane Mayer about the futile efforts of U.S. Navy general counsel Alberto J. Mora to stop what he came to recognize as an unlawful policy of cruelty toward terror suspects traces the origins of coercive interrogations at Guantanamo to October 2002— two months after the Bybee memo circulated. Major General Michael Dunlavey, the commander of the joint task force assigned with gathering information at the Cuban prison to help determine al-Qaeda's next move, requested that interrogations be made more aggressive. Shortly thereafter, Major General Geoffrey Miller assumed command of Guantanamo and pushed his superiors hard for more flexibility in interrogations. On December 2, Defense Secretary Donald Rumsfeld gave approval for the use of "hooding," "exploitation of phobias," "stress positions," "deprivation of light and auditory stimuli," and other tactics normally forbidden by the army field manual. Beside his approval signature, Rumsfeld wrote by hand, "However, I stand for 8–10 hours a day. Why is standing limited to 4 hours?" Powell's chief of staff Colonel Wilkerson told Mayer about Rumsfeld's scrawled aside, "It said, 'Carte blanche, guys.' That's what started them down the slope. You'll have My Lais then. Once you pull this thread, the whole fabric unravels."[24]

Six weeks later, after military lawyers rebelled, Rumsfeld suspended his authorization of the harsh interrogation techniques and created a working group of a few dozen lawyers from all branches of the armed services who would come up with recommendations after considering the constitutionality and effectiveness of various tactics. The group ended up approving a list of thirty-five possible methods, with large portions of its report drawn directly from the Bybee torture memo. Rumsfeld authorized twenty-four of them, generally leaving out the harshest, for use in Guantanamo.[25] The working group report also included the Yoo-Addington boilerplate: "In light of the President's complete authority over the conduct of the war, without a clear statement otherwise, criminal statutes are not read as infringing on the President's ultimate authority in these areas." Publicly, the administration was reassuring Congress that the Pentagon's policy was never to engage in torture or in cruel, inhumane, or degrading treatment. At the same time, secret documents like Yoo's memo and the working group report circulating at the highest levels of government were offering what amounts to legal protection to operations officials who undertook interrogation tactics that could be construed as torture.[26]

It is unclear the extent to which harsh tactics were actually implemented in Guantanamo. A New York Times report included accounts of prolonged sleep deprivation, shackling prisoners in uncomfortable positions for many hours, and subjecting prisoners to bright flashing lights in their eyes and loud music.[27] But it is indisputable that the kinds of tactics endorsed in the working group report became commonly used in Iraq and Afghanistan, even though the Defense Department never specifically authorized them beyond Cuba. One factor contributing to the migration to Iraq was the transfer of Guantanamo overseer Miller to supervise all U.S. prisons in Iraq in August 2003, when the insurgency there was beginning to take hold and the military was growing frustrated with the lack of good intelligence it was obtaining. Miller brought with him a group of interrogators from Guantanamo, called the Tiger Team. A Pentagon investigation led by Major General George Fay into Abu Ghraib found that legal advisers to the senior commander in Iraq, General Ricardo Sanchez, were using the working group report as a reference in determining the limits of their authority—even though it was supposed to apply only to Guantanamo and Rumsfeld had signed off on only a subset of the report's approved tactics.[28] Fay's investigation also concluded that "DoD's development of multiple policies on interrogation operations for use in different theatres of operations confused Army and civilian interrogators at Abu Ghraib."[29] Exacerbating the confusion about legal authorization for various interrogation tactics, according to several government investigations, was a lack of training among the guards and a low ratio of military police to inmates—at Abu Ghraib, there was only one guard for every seventy-five detainees in a prison that held as many as eight thousand.[30]

In belated recognition that it had created a monster, the administration furtively backpedaled from its swaggering legal arguments. In December 2003, the new head of the Office of Legal Counsel, Jack Goldsmith, informed the Defense Department that it could no longer rely on the previous legal analysis by Yoo, who had left the government by then, partly because its interpretation of the president's powers was overly broad. According to an investigative report by *Newsweek*,

> It is almost unheard-of for an administration to overturn its own OLC opinions. Addington was beside himself. Later, in frequent face-to-face confrontations, he attacked Goldsmith for changing the rules in the middle of the game and putting brave men at risk, according to three former government officials, who declined to speak on the record given the sensitivity of the subject.[31]

Likewise, in March 2005, the Pentagon declared that the working group report, which also had asserted sweeping presidential authority consistent with unitary executive theory, was a nonoperational "historical" document.[32]

Those concessions would seem tantamount to admissions that the torture policy had failed—that Powell had been right. But movement conservatives rarely acknowledge their failures. Witness Bush's continuing use of signing statements expressing his "unitary executive" authority. Yoo himself has been anything but contrite, bemoaning the Supreme Court's decision in the *Hamdan* case: "The court has just declared it is going to be very intrusive in the war on terror. . . . It could affect detention conditions, interrogation methods, the use of force. It could affect every aspect of the war on terror."[33] Indeed. If, instead of invoking the unitary executive theory, Yoo and the others in the top ranks of the administration had clearly stated their determination to strictly adhere to the Geneva Conventions and other laws, does anyone believe that Abu Ghraib and the widespread horrors described in Amnesty International's reports would have happened to the extent that they did?

When the Facts Are Deemed Not to Matter

As for the commentariat, two prominent conservative intellectuals vented withering revulsion not so much over torture but over the apparent retreat from coercive interrogations prompted by the reaction to Abu Ghraib. Heather MacDonald of the Manhattan Institute, New York City's oasis for right-wing thinkers funded by Olin, Bradley, et al., wrote, "Timidity among officers prevents the energetic application of those techniques that remain. Interrogation plans have to be triple-checked all the way up through the Pentagon by officers who have never conducted an interrogation in their lives."[34] MacDonald's piece heroically attempts to argue that the sundry torture memos and working group report didn't influence the actions down through the chain of command, although investigations by Fay and others that followed, as well as Jane Mayer's reporting, decisively undercut that thesis.[35] She blames what happened at Abu Ghraib on poor planning by the Defense Department, which was only part of the problem and doesn't explain the hundreds of abuses in all of the other prisons where interrogations occurred. Perhaps more important, MacDonald argues that coercive interrogation tactics (though she draws the line short of the "hair-raising" procedures endorsed in the Bybee memo) work in the sense of helping to provide useful information. That effective tool, she argues, should not be sacrificed just because of the preventable abuses that occurred in Abu Ghraib.

Going even further along the same track, the conservative columnist Charles Krauthammer wrote in the *Weekly Standard* that he would carve out two contingencies in which torture would be legal: (1) the proverbial ticking-time-bomb scenario (when the prisoner is believed to have information that could prevent an imminent attack) and (2) the slower-fuse high-level terrorist, such as Khalid Sheikh Mohammed, who was indeed reportedly "waterboarded" to the point where he confessed in between two and two and a half minutes[36] (a confession not likely to be of much use in any court worth its salt). Krauthammer argues that there is actually a moral imperative to conduct torture

> if you have even the slightest belief that hanging [a terrorist] by his thumbs will get you the information to save a million people. . . . Is one to believe that in the entire history of human warfare, no human has ever received useful information by the use of pressure, torture, or any other kind of human treatment? It may indeed be true that torture is not a reliable tool. But that is different from saying it is *never* useful.

MacDonald's defense of coercive interrogations and Krauthammer's of torture, which generally received enthusiastic responses in conservative circles, may not be crazy theoretically but unravel when the real world is brought into the debate. First, their arguments presume that the government knows that the individuals to be tortured or coercively interrogated are in fact terrorists. But the International Red Cross was told by military intelligence officers that "between 70 percent and 90 percent of the persons deprived of their liberty in Iraq had been arrested by mistake."[37] As for Guantanamo, which held a peak of nearly eight hundred prisoners, a former CIA operative who spent a year there told PBS's *Frontline*, "[O]nly like 10 percent of the people [there] are really dangerous, that should be there and the rest are people that don't have anything to do with it . . . don't even understand what they're doing there."[38] Brigadier General Jay Hood, who was the commander of the Camp Delta facility on Guantanamo, said that expectations about intelligence from the base may have been "too high" and "Sometimes we just didn't get the right folks."[39] The possibility of torturing innocent people demolishes basic principles of justice and human rights that the United States has come to stand for more than any other country. More pedantically, torturing innocents—as we have seen, accidents happen all the time, particularly under intense pressure—can't possibly provide useful information.

The Pulitzer prize–winning journalist Joseph Lelyveld, in a *New York Times Magazine* piece, interviewed numerous interrogators in the United States and Israel—which has considerable experience with torture—to try to discern the extent to which different tactics ranging from extreme force to "torture lite" (approaches such as subjecting detainees to loud music and temperature changes) to nonphysical threats and manipulative practices, have produced reliably useful information.[40] Lelyveld wrote: "If I pressed my question about violence in these and other conversations, the almost invariable answer, as if learned by rote in the same school, was that too much violence produced unreliable information because people will say anything, admit to anything, as a way of gaining surcease from unbearable pain. Torture, in other words, is a useful tool in gaining confessions when the facts are deemed not to matter."

Only a handful of specific cases, including Khalid Sheikh Mohammed's, are commonly cited as demonstrations that torture or lesser forms of coercion have prevented future attacks. But almost without exception, the evidence supporting those claims ranges from negligible to meager. The only example that Lelyveld considered to be credible was the case of Nasim Za'atari, who had scouted out potential targets for Hamas and helped suicide bombers prepare attacks in Israel. Information he provided under questioning—which Lelyveld was told did not "fall within the definition of torture in international law" but which presumably entailed force—led to the assassination of a Hamas recruiter and the seizing of bomb belts that attackers would have worn. Lelyveld concluded, "[O]n the basis of the scant amount of information available to those of us who will never be shown interrogation logs, I still think the case for actual torture remains shaky even by the most amoral and pragmatic standard."

It is worth noting that after the Bush administration released a transcript of Khalid Sheikh Mohammed's confession to masterminding the September 11 attacks—as well as the beheading of journalist

Daniel Pearl and the planning of roughly two dozen other operations—the international response ranged from skepticism to indifference. The conservative *Washington Post* columnist Anne Applebaum
observed:

> The *Daily Telegraph*, normally the most pro-American newspaper
> in Britain, wrote that it hardly mattered whether he was guilty,
> since whatever the conclusion of the military tribunal that will try
> him, 'the world will condemn the procedures by which the ver-
> dicts were reached.' Germany's *Frankfurter Allgemeine Zeitung*
> concluded that the 'Bush administration has nobody but itself to
> blame for the fact that the actions and motives of the perpetra-
> tor are now playing second fiddle to the practices used by the
> Americans in fighting terrorism.' . . . This is concrete proof, as if
> more were needed, that it is not merely immoral to operate out-
> side the rule of law, it is also profoundly counterproductive. Who
> would have imagined, in September 2001, that one of the master-
> minds of the attacks on the World Trade Center and the Penta-
> gon would make his confession and the world would hear it with
> indifference?[41]

At a press briefing in September 2006 to announce revisions to the
army field manual for human intelligence collector operations, Lieu-
tenant General John Kimmons, the army's deputy chief of staff for
intelligence, said:

> No good intelligence is going to come from abusive practices. I
> think history tells us that. I think the empirical evidence of the
> past five years—hard years—tells us that. . . . Any piece of intelli-
> gence that is obtained under duress through the use of abusive
> techniques would be of questionable credibility. . . . It would do
> more harm than good when it inevitably became known that abu-
> sive practices were used. We can't afford to go there.[42]

The Geneva Conventions have arguably been the single most
important and effective source of progress on international human
rights in the last century. Unilaterally carving out even the narrowest
of exceptions to its ban on torture invites other countries to make their
own exceptions while opening the door to our adding more contingencies later. Sometimes slippery slope arguments can be hyperbolic,

but the slope from John Yoo's January 2002 memo about the inapplicability of the Geneva Conventions descending to Abu Ghraib and the widespread torture in other prisons proved to be undeniably slick and fast. As Michael Kinsley has written:

> The strength of an absolute ban on torture—or an absolute rule of any sort—is its relative immunity from salami slicing, both in theory and in practice. It is hard to say why you would torture a teenager abducted into a terrorist gang if this would save a dozen lives, but would not torture a military officer in order to save a thousand. It is not hard to explain why you would not torture anybody at all. The argument may be wrong, but at least it is clear. The policy—just don't do it—is hard to misunderstand, making it easier to teach and enforce. And the principle can be abandoned, but it can't easily erode.[43]

Another such absolute principle to be preserved is that the president is not above the law. Yoo, in the *New York Times* article recording his reaction to the *Hamdan* case, said, "What the court is doing is attempting to suppress creative thinking."[44] Given the immense damage caused by Yoo's kind of creative thinking, which is characteristic of the simple-mindedness disconnected from historical lessons that is pervasive in the right's idea factories, the country would be much better off if such thoughts forevermore remain imprisoned in the salons of the Federalist Society.

3

"We Will, in Fact, Be Greeted as Liberators"
Benevolent Hegemony

In March 1992—two and a half years after the fall of the Berlin Wall and a year after the Gulf War victory—a front-page *New York Times* scoop reported on a forty-six-page draft document circulating at the highest levels of Defense Secretary Dick Cheney's Pentagon. Written under the supervision of Under Secretary for Policy Paul D. Wolfowitz, the statement proposed a bold new vision for U.S. foreign policy, asserting that America's political and military mission in the post–Cold War era will be to ensure that no rival superpower is allowed to emerge in Western Europe, Asia, or the territories of the former Soviet Union. Emphasizing the dangers posed by the use of nuclear, chemical, or biological weapons, even in conflicts that do not directly engage U.S. interests, the document stated that "The U.S. may be faced with the question of whether to take military steps to prevent the development or use of weapons of mass destruction." The draft document, called the Defense Planning Guidance, made clear that the American government should be prepared to take such preemptive action when it deems fit under those circumstances, even in the absence of international support. "The United States should be postured to act independently when collective action cannot be orchestrated," the statement said.

Intended in part as a justification for sustaining a 1.6 million-member military over five years at a cost of $1.2 trillion, the Defense Planning Guidance's endorsement of aggressively building on America's post–Cold War hegemony dovetailed with assertions that other countries would come to recognize that their own interests benefited from a supremely powerful United States. The document stated that part of America's mission will be "convincing potential competitors that they need not aspire to a greater role or pursue a more aggressive posture to protect their legitimate interests." And that the United States "must sufficiently account for the interests of the advanced industrial nations to discourage them from challenging our leadership or seeking to overturn the established political and economic order." In sum, "While the U.S. cannot become the world's 'policeman' . . . we will retain the pre-eminent responsibility for addressing selectively those wrongs which threaten not only our interests, but those of our allies and friends, or which could seriously unsettle international relations." The *Times* reporter Patrick E. Tyler wrote, "With its focus on this concept of benevolent domination by one power, the Pentagon document articulates the clearest rejection to date of collective internationalism, the strategy that emerged from World War II when the five victorious powers sought to form a United Nations that could mediate disputes and police outbreaks of violence."[1]

The article unleashed a torrent of criticism from Democrats outraged at the Defense Planning Guidance's implicit dismissal of the United Nations and transparent attempt to continue lavishing the military-industrial complex with funding, despite the Soviet Union's collapse. But attacks came from the right as well. The isolationist Patrick J. Buchanan, running as a Republican presidential candidate at the time, said, "It's virtually a blank check given to all of America's friends and allies that we'll go to war to defend their interests."[2] Ultimately, the final version of the plan that Cheney released was written in a considerably less hubristic tone and included more acknowledgments of the value of cooperation. It said, for example, "Our preference for a collective response to preclude threats or, if necessary, to deal with them is a key feature of our regional defense strategy." But the general thrust remained that the United States should strive to build on its hegemonic role in the world and stand ready to militarily act on its own, if necessary, to preempt perceived threats.

During the 1996 presidential campaign, as it was becoming clear that Republican Bob Dole had little hope of defeating President Clinton, William Kristol coauthored with Robert Kagan a widely discussed article in *Foreign Affairs* titled "Toward a Neo-Reaganite Foreign Policy."[3] Both conservatives are recognized across the political spectrum as keen intellects and strategists—when they write something together, people pay attention. In their *Foreign Affairs* article, they noted with alarm that "Dole was reduced to asserting . . . that there are no real differences between him and the president"—a position lacking political potency. They went on:

> Conservatives will not be able to govern America over the long term if they fail to offer a more elevated vision of America's role. What should that role be? Benevolent global hegemony. Having defeated the "evil empire," the United States enjoys strategic and ideological predominance. The first objective of U.S. policy should be to preserve and enhance that predominance by strengthening America's security, supporting its friends, advancing its interests, and standing up for its principles around the world. The aspiration to benevolent hegemony might strike some as either hubristic or morally suspect. But a hegemon is nothing more or less than a leader with preponderant influence and authority over all others in its domain. That is America's position in the world today. The leaders of Russia and China understand this. At their April summit meeting, Boris Yeltsin and Jiang Zemin joined in denouncing "hegemonism" in the post–Cold War world. They meant this as a complaint about the United States. It should be taken as a compliment and a guide to action.

Within months after Dole's defeat, Kristol and Kagan created a think tank, chaired by Kristol, called the Project for the New American Century (PNAC). Launched with core financial support from the Bradley Foundation, along with contributions from Scaife, Olin, and other conservative foundations, PNAC's founding statement of principles echoed the themes of the *Foreign Affairs* article:

> The history of the 20th Century should have taught us that it is important to shape circumstances before crises emerge, and to meet threats before they become dire. . . . Such a Reaganite policy of military strength and moral clarity may not be fashionable

today. But it is necessary if the United States is to build on the successes of this past century and to ensure our security and our greatness in the next.

The twenty-five signatories to that document included Cheney, Wolfowitz, Donald Rumsfeld, Wolfowitz, and I. Lewis (Scooter) Libby, the future chief of staff to Vice President Cheney, as well as the conservative movement notables Gary Bauer, Frank Gaffney, and Steve Forbes.

In January 1998, during a period when Kristol and his colleagues were casting about for enemies for the United States to fight to create a more favorable political environment for Republicans, according to lapsed neoconservative Francis Fukuyama,[4] PNAC sent a letter to President Clinton arguing for an overthrow of Saddam Hussein.[5] It said the only "acceptable strategy" toward Iraq was "one that eliminates the possibility that Iraq will be able to use or threaten to use weapons of mass destruction. In the near term, this means a willingness to undertake military action as diplomacy is clearly failing. In the long-term it means removing Saddam Hussein and his regime from power. That now needs to be the aim of American foreign policy." In addition to Rumsfeld and Wolfowitz, signatories who would later serve in high-ranking Bush administration posts included John Bolton, Douglas Feith, Richard Armitage, Zalmay Khalilzad, Elliott Abrams, and Robert B. Zoellick.

Although neither Bush nor his top advisers said much that sounded like neoconservative rhetoric during the first nine months of his administration, to the growing consternation of Kristol and other neocons, that changed within days of the September 11 attacks. At a meeting led by Rumsfeld that afternoon, aides took notes that said, "best info fast. Judge whether good enough hit S.H. [Saddam Hussein] at same time. Not only UBL [Usama bin Laden]. Go massive. Sweep it all up. Things related and not." According to Richard Clarke, who was the top antiterrorism official in the government at the time, the next day Bush ordered, "See if Saddam did this. See if he's linked in any way."

Clarke replied, "But Mr. President, al Qaeda did this." To which Bush responded, "I know, I know, but . . . see if Saddam was involved. Just look. I want to know any shred." In the flurry of meetings that followed, Wolfowitz repeatedly argued that Iraq should be the target of the initial U.S. response. Although Bush decided to attack Afghanistan first, he concurred with Wolfowitz's assessment of Iraq's culpability. Six days after 9/11, Bush told his team, without any evidence, "I believe Iraq was involved."[6]

In George Packer's superb book *The Assassins' Gate: America in Iraq*, both Kagan and neoconservative Richard Perle argue that Bush had independently fixated on Iraq rather than falling under Wolfowitz's neoconservative spell. Kagan told Packer:

> Paul may have brought it up, but Bush from the beginning was thinking about Iraq. I think that Bush had Iraq on the brain. Paul, who is a deputy secretary of defense who does not get along with his secretary of defense and whose time alone with the president is probably minimal, fighting giants like [Secretary of State Colin] Powell, who was much stronger than he was? I think it had to be the president. This is what the president wanted to do.

Concurs Perle, "Nine-eleven had a profound effect on the president's thinking. It wasn't the arguments or the positions held by me, or Paul, or anyone else before that. The world began on 9/11. There's no intellectual history."

But Packer goes on to underline how important neoconservatism proved to be in leading to the invasion of Iraq:

> [T]here was already in place across the top levels of the national-security bureaucracy a group of people with a definite intellectual history, who could give the president's new impulses a strategy, a doctrine, a worldview. . . . What mattered was who held positions of power. "The people are important, and the ideas are important in connection with the people," Perle told me. . . . "But the ideas themselves—let's put it this way: If Bush had staffed his administration with a group of people selected by Brent Scowcroft and Jim Baker, which might well have happened, then it could have been different, because they would not have carried into it the ideas that the people who wound up in important positions brought to it. The ideas are important only as they reside in the minds of the people who were directly in the decision process."[7]

The shift in focus from al-Qaeda to Saddam, and the administration's energetic efforts to convince the public of the validity of that shift, is emblematic of how ideologically driven leaders substitute their own philosophical fixations for much more complex realities. The genuine problem that everyone but the neocons recognized as the foremost post–September 11 priority was destroying al-Qaeda and developing an effective strategy for defusing future terrorist threats. That challenge, as the administration itself acknowledged, amounted to a mostly off-the-radar-screen "war without end" — one that we could never be certain we were winning. Taking down Saddam Hussein, in contrast, held out the political payoff of delivering a clearcut "mission accomplished," as well as the opportunity to exert our military muscle in a highly visible way that neoconservatives believed would yield all kinds of salutary residual benefits — intimidating Iraq's neighbors, impressing the "Arab street," creating a new beachhead for democracy, providing new strategically advantageous military bases, and so on. A full-bore effort to prevent terrorism, which to be effective would have to include nonmilitary efforts, was far less satisfying to the neoconservative mind-set than starting an old-fashioned war. Making the sale to the public wouldn't be easy, but if there's one thing movement conservatives can do well, it's sell.

During the buildup to the Iraq War, neoconservatives mocked the United Nations Security Council for expressing reservations about the planned invasion based on weapons inspections that had turned up nothing. Mohamed ElBaradei, the head of the UN nuclear agency, told the Security Council on March 7, 2003, after his team had conducted 247 inspections at 147 sites in Iraq, that it had found "no evidence of resumed nuclear activities . . . nor any indication of nuclear-related prohibited activities at any related sites." Hans Blix, who led a team of UN inspectors who carried out 731 inspections between November 2002 and March 2003, found no evidence of stockpiles of chemical and biological weapons or any active program to build such weapons.[8] But Kagan and Kristol scoffed at their findings in the *Weekly Standard*: "What are the chances that Mr. Blix will want to blow the whistle on Saddam — knowing that he may thereby signal the start of a war that he and his backers at the Security Council want to avoid?"[9] The administration was no more respectful of the UN inspections or the Security Council's objections to the invasion. The war was on, and neoconservatives were jubilant. To be sure, many others who dissent from neoconservatism endorsed the war as well — leading Democrats among them — based largely on a belief that the administration's claims about Iraq's weapons of mass destruction were accurate. Unbeknownst to the public at the time, neoconservatives within the administration were actively manipulating intelligence, as chapter 1 discussed, and developing misleading talking points to bolster what turned out to be erroneous claims.

The Problem with Their Solution

Toppling Saddam Hussein, a brutal tyrant who himself invaded the neighboring countries of Iran in 1980 and Kuwait in 1990, in and of itself was a significant military accomplishment. And the ratification in October 2005 of a constitution and the National Assembly elections of December 2005 seemed at the time to be concrete steps in the direction of creating democracy in Iraq—the new mission the administration was forced to adopt after it became clear that there were no weapons of mass destruction to seize. But by the spring of 2006, U.S. generals were acknowledging that conditions had deteriorated into a "low-grade" civil war between Shiite and Sunni factions, with a robust insurgency continuing to carry out highly deadly attacks in Baghdad and other key cities and regions with little sign of receding. Barring a miraculous turnaround that would defuse the civil war, quash the insurgency, and leave in place an Iraqi police force capable of sustaining security, the benefit of deposing Saddam Hussein increasingly pales in comparison to the ever-mounting costs:

Diminished U.S. government credibility. The Bush administration, along with the British government, launched the invasion based on what turned out to be utterly false pretenses. The rationale President Bush gave for attacking Iraq in the months leading up to the war was that Iraq was actively developing nuclear, chemical, and biological weapons to use against other countries, possibly including the United States by way of Iraq's purportedly close ties with al-Qaeda and other terrorist organizations. Vice President Cheney unequivocally proclaimed in August 2002, "Simply stated, there is no doubt that Saddam Hussein now has weapons of mass destruction."[10]

Here's what Bush said in his 2003 State of the Union address, two months before the March invasion:

> With nuclear arms or a full arsenal of chemical and biological weapons, Saddam Hussein could resume his ambitions of conquest

in the Middle East and create deadly havoc in that region. And this Congress and the American people must recognize another threat. Evidence from intelligence sources, secret communications, and statements by people now in custody reveal that Saddam Hussein aids and protects terrorists, including members of al Qaeda. Secretly, and without fingerprints, he could provide one of his hidden weapons to terrorists, or help them develop their own. Before September the 11th, many in the world believed that Saddam Hussein could be contained. But chemical agents, lethal viruses and shadowy terrorist networks are not easily contained. Imagine those 19 hijackers with other weapons and other plans—this time armed by Saddam Hussein. It would take one vial, one canister, one crate slipped into this country to bring a day of horror like none we have ever known. We will do everything in our power to make sure that that day never comes.

But after the invasion, no evidence was ever found that Hussein's regime had been actively pursuing a nuclear program or stockpiling chemical and biological weapons. Nor was any credible evidence ever provided demonstrating a relationship between the Baathist government and al-Qaeda, which isn't surprising since the secularist Saddam Hussein was known to detest religious militant groups like Osama bin Laden's. A declassified October 2005 CIA assessment released by the Senate Intelligence Committee found no evidence that Saddam Hussein had a prewar connection with al-Qaeda's leader in Iraq, Abu Musab al-Zarqawi, or his operatives. The report said that prior to the war, Saddam's government "did not have a relationship, harbor, or turn a blind eye toward Zarqawi and his associates." The committee also released documents showing that even before the war, the CIA had been raising questions about whether any ties existed. In a previously classified January 2003 report, for instance, the CIA concluded that Hussein "viewed Islamic extremists operating inside Iraq as a threat."[11]

While faulty intelligence was partly to blame for the cavernous gap between what we now know to be the truth and what the public was told in advance of the war, the long-term damage to U.S. credibility was greatly compounded by the administration's manipulation and cherry-picking of prewar government assessments. For example, the public was never made aware of opposing prewar analysis by the State

Department's Bureau of Intelligence and Research, known as INR. Knight Ridder found important differences between the public version and the then top-secret version of the October 2002 National Intelligence Estimate, the crucial document synthesizing what the U.S. government knew about Iraq's capabilities and activities. While the public version declared that "most analysts assess Iraq is reconstituting its nuclear weapons program" and that "if left unchecked, it probably will have a nuclear weapon within this decade," the INR's dissenting view was omitted. The secret version of the same document included INR's conclusion that

> The activities we have detected do not, however, add up to a compelling case that Iraq is currently pursuing what INR would consider to be an integrated and comprehensive approach to acquire nuclear weapons. Iraq may be doing so, but INR considers the available evidence inadequate to support such a judgment. . . . INR is unwilling to . . . project a timeline for the completion of activities it does not now see happening.[12]

In addition to selectively revealing the government's analysis of intelligence to the public, the vice president's office and the Defense Department internally applied extensive pressure for the answers they wanted to hear about WMD in Iraq and connections to al-Qaeda. For example, as discussed in chapter 1, the Defense Department in September 2002 created an Office of Special Plans specifically to build the case for war against Saddam Hussein. The *New Yorker*'s Seymour Hersh first reported that according to an unnamed Pentagon adviser:

> [OSP] was created in order to find evidence of what [Deputy Defense Secretary Paul] Wolfowitz and his boss, Defense Secretary Donald Rumsfeld, believed to be true—that Saddam Hussein had close ties to al Qaeda and that Iraq had an enormous arsenal of chemical, biological, and possibly even nuclear weapons that threatened the region and, potentially, the United States.

The goal of Special Plans, Hersh's source said, was "to put the data under a microscope to reveal what the intelligence community couldn't see."[13] As Paul R. Pillar, who oversaw Iraq intelligence for the CIA from 2000 to 2005, wrote, "[A]nalysts . . . felt a strong wind consistently blowing in one direction. The desire to bend with such a wind is natural and strong."[14]

A document that has come to be called the Downing Street Memo provides perhaps the most conclusive evidence that the Bush administration had made up its mind to invade Iraq by the summer of 2002 regardless of what any additional intelligence showed or any actions Saddam Hussein or the UN might take. The minutes to a July 23, 2002, meeting of the highest officials of the British government, including Tony Blair, the prime minister of England, and Foreign Secretary Jack Straw, the Downing Street Memo describes a presentation by Richard Dearlove, the head of MI6 (the British equivalent of the CIA): "[Dearlove] reported on his recent talks in Washington. There was a perceptible shift in attitude. Military action was now seen as inevitable. Bush wanted to remove Saddam, through military action, justified by the conjunction of terrorism and WMD. But the intelligence and facts were being fixed around the policy."[15]

America's credibility and moral standing have historically been at least as important as its military power in persuading other nations to follow its leadership, whether in pursuit of military actions such as the first Gulf War and the Kosovo intervention or nonmilitary undertakings like the Marshall Plan and the Camp David accords. Dearlove told the journalist James Fallows that by the end of the Cold War, there was no dispute worldwide about which side held the moral high ground—and that made his work as a spymaster far easier. "Potential recruits would come to us because they believed in the cause."[16] The long-term impact of losing much of that hard-earned credibility in the selling of the Iraq War remains to be seen, but no one disputes the seriousness of the damage. In light of the ultimate absence of either WMD or an Iraq–al-Qaeda connection, the Bush administration's prewar fixed preconceptions, unwillingness to publicly reveal competing evidence, and manipulation of information demonstrate yet again how a rigid mind-set impervious to facts can lead directly to failure—a familiar lesson that the conservative movement refuses to learn. Cheney's prewar promise that "we will, in fact, be greeted as liberators," neatly encapsulates how the premises undergirding benevolent hegemony are utterly divorced from reality. The credibility shortfall has only worsened with the administration's relentless spinning and attacking of war critics as conditions in Iraq deteriorated—Cheney and Rumsfeld repeatedly chastised "self-defeating pessimists" and drew ludicrous analogies to Neville Chamberlain's attempts to appease Hitler.

Casualties. As of mid-March 2007, the Pentagon reported that just fewer than 3,200 American soldiers had been killed in Iraq and at least 23,400 wounded in action. By way of perspective, the September 11 terrorist attacks claimed 2,973 lives. Another 258 coalition soldiers, mostly from the United Kingdom, also died. In both 2004 and 2005, slightly fewer than 850 U.S. soldiers were killed, with the trend remaining roughly steady with 821 fatalities in 2006.[17] But among Iraqi civilians, the death rate has been accelerating. In the last four months of 2006, according to the chief of the UN Assistance Mission for Iraq, 13,423 Iraqi civilians were killed—an average of about 110 a day—with the death rate generally escalating throughout the year. The estimated toll for all of 2006: 34,452.[18] The estimated total of Iraqi civilians killed during the entire war through March 2007, according to the Web site Iraq Body Count, which attempts to track the numbers based on information from morgues, the UN, and news accounts, was between 58,637 and 64,444. No reliable numbers are available for wounded civilians, but it's safe to say that figure exceeds 100,000.[19] Other estimates are much higher.[20]

Readers can reach their own judgments about whether the ousting of Saddam Hussein and the increasingly remote possibility of a democratic Iraq justify the loss of those lives and the physical and emotional damage inflicted on so many more. But honing in on the question of whether the Iraq War has made Americans less vulnerable to future terrorist attacks, which was the ostensible purpose of the enterprise, it should be mentioned that the Al Jazeera Arabic-language television station has regularly broadcast graphic images of the extensive civilian casualties to its estimated audience of more than 40 million viewers. It doesn't take a lot of imagination to recognize that the video and the photographs of carnage, far from deterring future attacks against the United States, would motivate otherwise nonpolitical Muslims to become militant. Time will tell.

Squandered resources. In September 2002, White House economic adviser Lawrence Lindsey was publicly reprimanded by the administration when he estimated that the cost of invading Iraq would be between $100 billion and $200 billion—a forecast that Budget Director Mitch Daniels proclaimed to be "very, very high." Deputy Defense Secretary Paul Wolfowitz shared Daniels's optimism, testifying to Congress that Iraq's oil reserves would finance postwar reconstruction at virtually no cost to the United States. As it turned out, however, Lindsey's projection was very, very low. An April 2006 Congressional Research Service report concluded that $261 billion had already been spent and that by the end of the conflict the cost would exceed the more than $549 billion spent (taking inflation into account) on the Vietnam War. But even that estimate, which accounts only for war-fighting appropriations, significantly understates the true economic costs of the war.[21]

The economists Joseph E. Stiglitz and Linda Bilmes calculated that the total budgetary cost to the federal government would be in the range of $750 billion to $1.2 trillion, conservatively assuming that the United States would have begun to withdraw troops in 2006 while maintaining a diminishing presence in Iraq over the next five years. By way of comparison, in 2005 the federal government devoted roughly $400 billion to all domestic and homeland security spending subject to Congress's annual discretion. Included in Stiglitz and Bilmes's estimate are such government obligations as additional Veterans Administration medical care costs for returning veterans, disability pay, increased future defense spending to replace worn-out equipment and increasingly difficult-to-recruit troops and officers, and interest payments on the added federal debt attributable to such Iraq-related costs.[22] The overall economic costs to the United States beyond those to the government, taking into account the lost productivity of killed and wounded soldiers, opportunity costs of resources that otherwise would have been used for other purposes, effects on oil prices, and so on, are significantly higher but also much more difficult to quantify. In any case, the purely financial cost of the Iraq War will be greater by orders of magnitude than anyone in the administration acknowledged before the invasion.

One crucial component has been the billions of dollars squandered by private corporations under government contract, usually without competitive bidding, to carry out rebuilding and provide other services in Iraq. The Los Angeles Times reporter T. Christian Miller's Blood Money: Wasted Billions, Lost Lives, and Corporate Greed in Iraq documented a multitude of examples of waste on the part of a small number of favored American multinational firms like Bechtel, Fluor, Parsons, and the Halliburton subsidiary KBR, formerly Kellogg Brown & Root. Miller estimated that KBR alone has billed more than $1 billion in questionable costs, including $200 million for meals that it never served, and twice as much for imported fuel as a Defense Department agency performing the same function. Miller described the $30 billion that Congress appropriated to rebuilding Iraq this way: "What appeared to be a remarkably generous foreign aid package was in fact a remarkable program of domestic handouts and corporate welfare." Adhering to the conservative movement's dictates to rely as much as possible on corporate contractors with minimal governmental interference, those outcomes were a predictable outgrowth of the right's ideology. Wrote Miller, "Action was more important than accountability."[23]

An overextended military. Primarily because of the Iraq War, the army's level of preparedness has eroded to its lowest point since the end of the Vietnam War and its immediate aftermath.[24] In 2006, two-thirds of the U.S. Army's active forces were officially classified as "not ready for combat."[25] Not a single nondeployed Army Brigade Combat team in the United States was ready to be sent into action.[26] Every available combat brigade from the active duty army had already been to Afghanistan or Iraq at least once for a twelve-month tour, with many of them in their second and third tours of duty. Moreover, about 95 percent of the Army's National Guard combat battalions and special operations units have been mobilized since September 11. All active Marine Corps units have been used on a "tight" rotation schedule—seven months deployed, less than a year back at home, then another seven months in action—and all of its reserve units have been mobilized.[27]

Not surprisingly, signs were beginning to emerge of recruiting shortfalls and a decline in retention rates. As of the end of fiscal 2005, the active army fell 6,627 recruits below its annual goal of 80,000, with a higher than normal percentage labeled with the lowest aptitude level of "category IV." The Army Reserve was 16 percent below its annual recruiting target, and the National Guard was 20 percent short of its goal. While the army met its overall retention goal, both the Army National Guard and Army Reserve fell short of their targets among those deciding whether to renew their commitment for the first time.[28] In January 2006, the army raised the maximum age for enlistment from thirty-five to forty—only to find it necessary to raise it to forty-two in June. Basic training, which for decades was an important tool for testing the mettle of recruits, has increasingly become a rubber-stamp ritual. Through the first six months of 2006, only 7.6 percent of new recruits failed basic training, down from 18.1 percent in May 2005.[29] Those adjustments, along with bonuses of up to $40,000 per recruit, helped to enable recruitment targets to be met for 2006.[30]

Throughout the Iraq War, the army and the Army National Guard have experienced periods of critical equipment shortfalls, with the problems becoming increasingly severe. Army chief of staff General Peter J. Schoomaker testified to Congress that while in 2004 the cost of repairing or replacing war equipment was $4 billion, by 2006 the amount needed had climbed to between $12 billion and $13 billion. Schoomaker anticipated that those figures would continue to increase the longer the war lasted, noting that the army is using up equipment at four times the originally anticipated rate. He traced the problem to entering into the war in 2003 with a $56 billion shortfall in equipment, which required the army to keep the same gear in Iraq as fresh units were rotated in. That equipment wore out faster than investments were made to produce replacement gear.[31]

Diminished international respect for the United States. In the immediate aftermath of the 9/11 terrorist attacks, the citizens of virtually all other countries had a higher opinion of the United States than at any other time since such surveys had been taken. But that sympathy, which presented an opportunity for the U.S. government to work closely with other countries in fighting jihadists and addressing other international challenges, transformed into widespread anti-Americanism, particularly in the aftermath of the 2003 Iraq invasion. The Pew Global Attitudes Project reported in June 2006 that "The war in Iraq is a continuing drag on opinions of the United States, not only in predominantly Muslim countries but Europe and Asia as well. And despite growing concern over Iran's nuclear ambitions, the U.S. presence in Iraq is cited at least as often as Iran—and in many countries much more often—as a danger to world peace." Even in Great Britain, America's most important ally in Iraq, 60 percent of the people say the war has made the world more dangerous, while just 30 percent feel it has made the world safer—the ostensible rationale for the invasion.[32]

International public opinion matters because it affects the ability of the U.S. government to persuade the leadership of other countries to do what it asks. If cooperating with the United States is likely to hurt support for the heads of other governments in their own countries— whether they are democracies or not—they will be less likely to share intelligence, sign trade agreements, or otherwise help to advance U.S. interests. The power of internal political forces can be far greater than U.S. military might in determining whether other nations will follow us. Most of the Bush administration's other foreign policy failures—for example, the lack of progress on the Israeli-Palestinian conflict, the inept response to North Korea's advancing nuclear program, squandered diplomatic openings from Iran, the negligent indifference to global warming—have more to do with ideological arrogance and obstinacy than with the unwillingness of other countries to cooperate with the U.S. due to the Iraq War. But in each case, anti-Americanism made a bad situation worse. Conversely, if the United States had acted in ways that sustained something close to its post–September 11 international popularity levels, it is easier to imagine how better results might have transpired—if one can imagine, that is, what might have happened in an administration contemptuous of neoconservatism.

For the ideas behind benevolent hegemony to make any sense at all, other countries would have to perceive that America's actions are entirely born of goodwill and serve the interests of those other countries as well. But, as former neocon Francis Fukuyama has come to recognize, that presumes an almost absurd degree of naïveté on the part of other nations. Fukuyama wrote, "The idea that the United States behaves disinterestedly on the world stage is not widely believed because it is for the most part not true and, indeed, could not be true if American leaders fulfill their responsibilities to the American people."[33] In the eyes of other countries, our actions in Iraq are just belligerent—not benevolent.

A thriving terrorist movement. While it is true that as this is written, no major terrorist attacks have occurred on U.S. soil since 9/11, it is also a fact that terrorism worldwide has accelerated since the Iraq invasion— largely but not entirely because of an increase in terrorist attacks within Iraq itself. The new National Counterterrorism Center began to issue annual reports tallying terrorist attacks beginning in 2004. Because it changed its methodology for computing those incidents, it is somewhat difficult to compare its 2004 and 2005 numbers. In its report for 2005, however, the NCC found:

- About 11,000 terrorist attacks occurred in 2005 and resulted in more than 14,500 deaths.
- Iraq accounted for almost 30 percent of the worldwide attacks (approximately 3,500) and 55 percent of the fatalities (about 8,300). The next highest country was India with 1,357 deaths, followed by Colombia (810), Afghanistan (682), and Thailand (500).
- Attacks on noncombatants increased significantly in Iraq in 2005; outside of Iraq, the total number of high-fatality incidents (those with 10 or more deaths) remained approximately the same in 2005 as in 2004—about 70 each year.
- Suicide attacks rose in a number of countries in 2005; about 360 suicide bombers accounted for about 20 percent of all deaths (about 3,000).[34]

The Memorial Institute for the Prevention of Terrorism, which maintains its own extensive database about worldwide terrorist attacks, reported that the number of terrorism incidents, according to its own consistent definition, increased from 1,905 in 2003, to 2,676 in 2004, to 5,023 in 2005.[35] Fatalities attributable to those attacks climbed in each year from 2,376 to 5,211 to 8,364. As with the U.S. government's statistics, the increase was largely attributable to more attacks in Iraq. But terrorist attacks that the institute concluded to have been carried out by al-Qaeda outside of Iraq also increased substantially from 2003 onward. In a study for *Mother Jones* magazine drawing from the same database, which examined the period from September 11 to the start of the Iraq War versus the comparable postinvasion time frame, the scholars Peter Bergen and Paul Cruickshank concluded that "the Iraq War has generated a stunning sevenfold increase in the yearly rate of fatal jihadist attacks, amounting to literally hundreds of additional terrorist attacks and thousands of civilian lives lost; even when terrorism in Iraq and Afghanistan is excluded, fatal attacks in the rest of the world have increased by more than one-third."[36]

It appears that U.S.-led military and intelligence operations in Afghanistan and Pakistan, as well as efforts to stifle the ability of al-Qaeda members to communicate, travel, and gain access to financial resources, have largely succeeded in dismantling the hierarchical organizational structure that Osama bin Laden formerly relied on. Now terrorists said to be affiliated with al-Qaeda are much more independent, fragmented, and dispersed, lacking the capability to coordinate effectively enough to plan and execute a major, complicated attack like the one on September 11, 2001. After interviewing some sixty experts for an article in the *Atlantic* assessing the state of the U.S. struggle against terrorism, James Fallows concluded that "al Qaeda's ability to inflict direct damage in America or on Americans has been sharply reduced."[37]

But that genuine progress, most analysts agree, has been offset to a significant extent by the Iraq War. Fallows quoted David Kilcullen, a senior adviser on counterterrorism at the State Department, as saying, "You only have to look at the Iraq War to see how much damage you can do to yourself by your response [to terrorism]." Based on his interviews, Fallows wrote:

> So far the Iraq War has advanced the jihadist cause because it generates a steady supply of Islamic victims, or martyrs; because it seems to prove Osama bin Laden's contention that America lusts to occupy Islam's sacred sites, abuse Muslim people, and steal Muslim resources; and because it raises the tantalizing possibility that humble Muslim insurgents, with cheap, primitive weapons, can once more hobble and ultimately destroy a superpower, as they believe they did to the Soviet Union in Afghanistan twenty years ago.[38]

In no small part because of the Iraq War, the number of individuals considered to belong to al-Qaeda has increased from 20,000 in 2001 to 50,000 now, according to the Memorial Institute. From January 1, 2003, to September 1, 2006, 22 attacks outside of Iraq were attributed to al-Qaeda, leading to 1,251 injuries and 206 fatalities. Those occurred in such countries as Saudi Arabia, Turkey, Bangladesh, Indonesia, and Kenya, where the targets in a number of cases were civilians from the United Kingdom and Australia—America's two principal allies in the Iraq invasion and occupation. (Spain withdrew from the coalition after the Madrid attacks in March 2004.) In its entire existence before September 11, 2001, al-Qaeda had carried out only 4 attacks, leading to 248 deaths. And in the post–September 11, pre–Iraq War period, al-Qaeda carried out only 3 attacks, leading to 100 fatalities.

Robert A. Pape, a University of Chicago political scientist who has written extensively about suicide terrorism, has determined that 95 percent of suicide terrorist attacks occur as part of coherent campaigns to compel modern democracies to withdraw military forces from territory viewed as the terrorists' homeland.[39] He noted that al-Qaeda recruiting videos more than anything else emphasize the casualties inflicted on Iraqis by American troops, as well as the occupation itself, rather than religious or economic messages.[40] "The operation in Iraq has stimulated suicide terrorism and given suicide terrorism a new lease on life," Pape said.[41]

In February 2005, CIA director Porter Goss told Congress that "Islamic extremists are exploiting the Iraqi conflict to recruit new anti-U.S. jihadists." He added, "Those who survive will leave Iraq experienced and focused on acts of urban terrorism. They represent a potential pool of contacts to build transnational terrorist cells, groups, and networks."[42] Some proponents of the Iraq War have argued that by luring foreign terrorists into the country, the invasion has enabled the U.S. military to efficiently kill them on the battlefield rather than trying to root them out in the caves of Afghanistan and Pakistan. But that so-called flypaper theory, to the extent one can discern any logic to it at all, presumes that there are a finite number of terrorists to be killed off. By motivating larger numbers of individuals to join or support radical Islamic jihadist movements, the Iraq War has actually served as a catalyst for worldwide terrorism. It also, obviously, has prompted hundreds of terrorist attacks leading to the deaths of thousands of Iraqi civilians. Pape told the *American Conservative* magazine, "People who make the argument that it is a good thing to have them attacking us over there are missing that suicide terrorism is not a supply-limited phenomenon where there are just a few hundred around the world willing to do it because they are religious fanatics. It is a demand-driven phenomenon. That is, it is driven by the presence of foreign forces on the territory that the terrorists view as their homeland."[43]

Iraq has also served as a training ground for militants to improve their tactical capabilities through trial and error. Anthony M. Cordesman, the well-known military strategist at the Center for Strategic and International Studies, detailed a multitude of "major adaptations" in the tactics and methods of attack used by insurgents in Iraq to increase their effectiveness. The new strategies that were learned from experience there include following one bomb with another after some delay in order to maximize casualties to police and rescue workers, carrying out complicated mixes of sequential ambushes, developing increasingly complicated and powerful "improvised explosive devices," and striking at key infrastructure points such as Iraq's northern export oil pipeline to inflict damage on political, economic, and social fronts in one fell swoop. After summarizing more than thirty such adaptations, Cordesman concluded:

> The problems such changes in insurgent tactics and technology created for U.S. forces often allowed them to fight below the threshold where U.S., British, and other coalition forces could exploit their conventional superiority. They kept casualties high enough to be serious and forced coalition forces to spend at least an order of magnitude more on countermeasures than the insurgents had to spend on new weapons and tactics.[44]

Iraq isn't flypaper; it's a place that is breeding increasingly lethal swarms of killers whose adaptations can now be used to inflict damage elsewhere—including Afghanistan.

The deterioration of conditions in Afghanistan, which the United States originally attacked with widespread domestic and international support in order to destroy al-Qaeda's training camps and the ruthless Taliban government that provided it with sanctuary, has also been an outgrowth of the Bush administration's preoccupation with Iraq. In March 2002, President Bush reportedly withdrew most of the special operations troops and their CIA counterparts in the paramilitary division who had been hunting for bin Laden in Afghanistan to prepare for war in Iraq. Flynt Leverett, who was serving in the National Security Council at the time, told the *Washington Post*: "I don't know of anyone who thought it was a good idea. It's very likely that bin Laden would be dead or in American custody if we hadn't done that."[45]

The U.S. role in Afghanistan after the Taliban's fall in late 2001 has been extremely limited, confined to less than twenty thousand troops (not even a fifth of the number deployed in Iraq at any time since that war) who mainly have been hunting for remnants of al-Qaeda in the country, as well as providing a limited peacekeeping role within the capital of Kabul. The absence of U.S. and international security forces beyond Kabul and negligible outside investment and assistance in building economic, social, and governmental institutions have enabled the Taliban to regroup while the economy has come to rely almost entirely on trafficking in opium poppies, which are the source of heroin. Roadside bomb attacks are up 30 percent, and both the number of suicide attacks and American casualty rates have doubled. In 2006, more than a hundred Americans were killed in Afghanistan, which as a share of forces deployed statistically means that it is now nearly as dangerous to be an American soldier in Afghanistan as it is in Iraq.[46] The general state of anarchy throughout the countryside, coupled with a militarily revitalized Taliban, threaten to re-create the conditions that enabled al-Qaeda to find safe haven in Afghanistan before September 11.[47] Few outside the administration would argue that the Iraq War has nothing to do with our negligence of Afghanistan and the consequent deterioration of conditions there.

The Iraq War has demonstrated not only the limitations of military power, but also how the arrogant application of our might can weaken us. That's the central blind spot of neoconservatism, in much the way that the right's advocacy of tax cuts and denigration of civil servants know no bounds, regardless of the consequences. Kristol's advocacy of military action against Iran,[48] as if the lesson of Iraq is that we need to be even more belligerent, is akin to the movement's support for even more tax cuts for the rich in the face of large and growing deficits. Their belief system trumps reality every time. The original challenges confronting the United States when the conservatives took power remain. But because of their ideologically driven solutions to the alternative problems they sold to the American public, we now have even greater difficulties—much greater—to deal with.

Autopsy of a Failed Idea

Because benevolent hegemony's Iraq failure is so stark and widely recognized across the ideological spectrum among all except neocon diehards, it provides the clearest illustration of why the multitude of ideas emanating from the right that share its traits has in practice produced results ranging from calamitous to counterproductive. One of the most consistent reasons that movement conservatives have succeeded in dominating one public policy debate after another has been their success in defining the problem to be resolved on their own terms. Stoking public fear has been central to that strategy, effectively precluding serious consideration of ideas tailored to addressing what concrete evidence shows to be the actual problem. So Social Security is like the *Titanic* headed for an iceberg. Any tax increase will invariably send the economy into a tailspin. Universal health insurance equates with a government takeover of the entire medical industry. And even voicing doubts about the conduct of the war in Iraq, and the decision to invade in the first place, amounts to appeasement of terrorists. In that context, the root causes of what movement conservatives identify as the problem include specific groups of individuals who are relentlessly caricatured for a panoply of intrinsic flaws. These are the plodding government bureaucrats, the "tax-and-spend liberals," the innovation-killing teachers' unions, the ambulance-chasing malpractice lawyers, and the antidemocratic United Nations thumb-twiddlers.

The right's habitual reliance on the modus operandi of promoting fear and attacking scapegoats, however effective politically, partly explains why its ideas have been failing in practice. The reality is that the country has nothing to fear from its real problems, which are at least as manageable as challenges the United States has successfully met in the past. And the groups castigated for causing nothing but trouble are here to stay for any number of good reasons and therefore have to be recognized as potentially effective participants in any initiatives with a hope of demonstrating actual progress. The nation's history shows again and again that successfully addressing both foreign and domestic problems—poverty among the elderly, air pollution, racial discrimination, the Soviet threat, Saddam Hussein's invasion of Kuwait, and on and on—requires leadership in educating the public honestly about the challenge, welcoming open and informed debate, uniting rather than dividing the country, reaching out to allies, recognizing both government's strengths and its limitations, and, perhaps most important of all, learning legitimate lessons from past experience.

One of the great ironies of the modern conservative movement is the extent to which it has inverted its traditional insistence on venerating history into a pathological compulsion to contort the past in ways intended to sell an agenda with no grounding whatsoever in what actually happened before. The selling of neoconservatism in the 1990s and the Iraq War after the September 11 attacks could not have been more ahistorical. The seminal Kagan and Kristol 1996 piece making the case for a "neo-Reaganite foreign policy" neglects all kinds of fundamental differences between their philosophy and Reagan's, and between the circumstances of the 1990s and 1980s—differences that the Heritage Foundation's very own Kim R. Holmes and John Hillen spelled out in a *Foreign Affairs* rebuttal later that year. Reagan and his top advisers were firmly committed to the realist worldview that American actions internationally should be closely tailored to U.S. national interests. Defense Secretary Caspar Weinberger, for example, adhered to a rigid and short list of conditions to be imposed on military interventions. Reagan pursued a moral crusade against Soviet communism not only because it was antidemocratic, as Kristol and Kagan emphasize, but also because he saw it as a mortal danger to American security. Holmes and Hillen also make the important distinction between a world with a central, indisputable enemy in the Soviet Union versus one in which "there are plenty of threats to U.S. interests, but they are scattered and come in many different stripes, from Cold War holdover regimes like North Korea to radical Islamic states like Iran. Because the threats they pose are philosophically, geographically, politically, and even militarily diverse, they are not amenable to the kind of single-minded crusade for democracy that Kristol and Kagan propose."[49]

During the period leading up to the invasion of Iraq, Kristol and other neoconservatives invoked a variety of historical analogies intended to defuse what turned out to be prescient concerns about the march to war. For example, against the objection that democracy cannot be imposed by military force, Kristol and the *New Republic* senior editor Lawrence F. Kaplan cited the cases of Japan, Germany, Austria, Italy, Grenada, the Dominican Republic, and Panama.[50] But none of those countries had experienced the long history of internal religiously based sectarian conflicts characteristic of the land now circumscribed by Iraq's borders. As for the nations conquered in World War II, their destruction and defeat at the hands of the allies was total, involving massive civilian casualties and a consequence of a vastly more ambitious military undertaking than anything ever contemplated for Iraq.

Perhaps the most commonly invoked historical analogy, both before the invasion and throughout the duration of the Iraq War, was Neville Chamberlain's "appeasement" of Adolf Hitler at Munich in 1938, when Germany was allowed to gain control over Czechoslovakia's Sudetenland. The same reference point was also used more generally in support of the neoconservative tenet endorsing preemptive, unilateral war in the face of even nonimminent threats. But the problem is that no one can accurately predict what other countries will do in the future. And no intelligence about the capabilities and intentions of a rival nation is ever complete, as the Iraq experience demonstrated with tragic consequences. As Ken Jowitt of the conservative Hoover Institution and the University of California at Berkeley explained with foresight in an article published just two months after the Iraq invasion:

> [T]he logic behind an anticipatory strategy is powerful. However, its strategic application demands the combined wisdom of Pericles and Solomon. To begin with, the premise for an anticipatory attack posits a hostile leader and regime platonically impervious to any environmental changes whether domestic or international. This is not always a mistaken premise—Hitler and Pol Pot are cases in point—but it is *almost* always mistaken. Over time, most regimes do change substantially if not essentially. One has only to look at the Soviet Union after 1956 and China after 1978.
>
> An anticipatory strategy also relies on American presidential administrations with an unerring ability to identify which leaders and regimes are impervious to environmental changes. Any mistake in identification would result not in preemption or anticipation, but in a war that could have been avoided.[51]

No author has been more effective at deconstructing why neoconservatism ideology has failed the United States in Iraq than the conservative columnist George F. Will, whose own historical references seem far more appropriate to current circumstances. Responding in the summer of 2006 to the *Weekly Standard*'s call to carry out another attack, this time of Iran, Will wrote:

> The administration, justly criticized for its Iraq premises and their execution, is suddenly receiving some criticism so untethered

from reality as to defy caricature. The national, ethnic and religious dynamics of the Middle East are so opaque to most people, but to the *Weekly Standard*—voice of a spectacularly misnamed radicalism, "neoconservatism"—*everything* is crystal clear. Iran is the key to everything. "No Islamic Republic of Iran, no Hezbollah. No Islamic Republic of Iran, no one to prop up the Assad regime in Syria. No Iranian support for Syria . . ." You get the drift. So, the *Weekly Standard* says:

"We might consider countering this act of Iranian military aggression with a military strike against Iranian nuclear facilities. Why wait? Does anyone think a nuclear Iran can be contained? That the current regime will negotiate in good faith? It would be easier to act sooner rather than later. Yes, there would be repercussions—and they would be healthy ones, showing a strong America that has rejected further appeasement."

"Why wait?" Perhaps because the U.S. military has enough on its plate with the deteriorating wars in Afghanistan and Iraq, which both border Iran. And perhaps because containment, although of uncertain success, did work against Stalin and his successors, and might be preferable to a war against a nation much larger and more formidable than Iraq. And if Bashar Assad's regime does not fall after the *Weekly Standard*'s hoped-for third war, with Iran, does the magazine hope for a fourth?[52]

Since movement conservatives remain determined to try to fool the American public about the lessons of history, much depends on the public's coming to grips with the lessons of the right's policy debacles. The failures won't end until voters recognize that the movement's belief system and ideas—not just some of its people—are responsible for the worsening damage to our country.

PART II

Ideas for Making Government Smaller and More Efficient

4

Lucky Duckies
Tax Cuts for the Rich

In August 1993, Congress passed President Bill Clinton's deficit reduction legislation by the narrowest possible margin. In the House of Representatives, the vote was 218 to 216—every single Republican voted against it, along with 41 Democrats. In the Senate, a 50–50 tie was broken by Vice President Al Gore, with all 44 Republicans joined by 6 Democrats on the losing end of an intensely fought tug-of-war. The bill's provisions included a tax rate increase on individuals with taxable incomes above $115,000 ($140,000 for married couples), a 1 percentage point increase in the corporate income tax rate, a 4.3 cent per gallon increase in the gasoline tax, a cut in military outlays (the so-called peace dividend following the Soviet Union's breakup), new constraints on Medicare and other entitlement spending, and a freeze on the overall cost of programs subject to annual appropriations.

The debate boiled down to a single question: should taxes be increased, mainly on the highest earners, to reduce large and growing federal budget deficits that virtually everyone agreed posed a serious threat to the nation's economic health? To the very last Republican, the answer was an unequivocal "no." Drawing on Heritage Foundation and other conservative think-tank talking points, the congressional opponents of Clinton's plan often sounded as confident as fortune tellers in describing the future damage that the tax hikes would inflict:

- Representative Dick Armey, (R-Tex.): "Clearly, this is a job-killer in the short-run. . . . The impact on job creation is going to be devastating."[1]

91

- Representative Newt Gingrich (R-Ga.): "I believe this will lead to a recession next year. This will be the Democrat machine's recession, and each one of them will be held personally accountable."[2]
- Senator Robert Packwood (R-Ore.): "I will make you this bet. I am willing to risk the mortgage on it. One year from now we will be back and . . . the deficit will be up, unemployment will be up; in my judgment, inflation will be up."[3]
- Senator Phil Gramm, (R-Tex.): "The deficit four years from today will be higher than it is today, not lower. . . . I believe this program is going to make the economy weak. I believe hundreds of thousands of people are going to lose their jobs. I believe Bill Clinton will be one of those people."[4]
- Senator Thad Cochran (R-Miss.): "Higher taxes will slow economic growth, cost us jobs, reduce our competitiveness in the international marketplace, and make it harder for working people to make ends meet. . . . A vote for this bill is a vote for a bigger federal government and a smaller economy."[5]
- Senator Bob Smith (R-N.H.): "I want my Democratic colleagues to know, with all respect, I wish them best of luck; I hope their predictions are right, I hope this package slashes the deficit, not only for their sake, but for America's sake. More importantly, I hope it creates jobs and reduces interest rates. If it does, the American people will see the wisdom of what you have done and reward you at the polls by millions of votes. If you are right, I will be the first Senator to stand up and put President Clinton's bust on Mount Rushmore. But I do not think Lincoln, Jefferson, Teddy Roosevelt, and Washington have to worry. I think the stone cutter will relax because it is not going to happen."[6]

Of those forecasts, the only one that came true was the failure of Clinton's bust to appear on Mount Rushmore—though former Senator Smith still owes him. As it turned out, the 1993 budget bill was the catalyst setting in motion a virtuous sequence of economic changes that produced an extended period of strong, broadly shared prosperity for the first time in more than two decades. Because Americans across the income spectrum earned higher incomes than anyone had predicted, more tax revenue flowed to the government—substantially reducing budget deficits. By the end of the 1990s, the federal budget was running large and growing surpluses that enabled the government to pay down some of the national debt that had built up over the preceding decades.

The unemployment rate, which reached a decade high of 7.8 percent in June 1992, fell steadily to 4.1 percent by the end of the 1990s—the lowest level since the late 1960s. The inflation rate defied economic theory and declined in tandem with unemployment, dropping from a peak of 6.3 percent in October and November 1990 to 2.7 percent by December 1999.[7] Over the second half of the decade, the annual productivity growth rate—which had languished near 1.4 percent for more than twenty years—averaged about 2.5 percent. In the five booming years from 1995 to 2000, the U.S. economy grew faster (more than 4 percent annually), maintained a lower unemployment rate, and generated less inflation than in the whole of the 1970s or the 1980s.[8] Even workers at the low end of the income ladder received wage increases above the inflation rate for the first time in decades, though rising inequality continued because the highest earners (the ones who bore the brunt of the Clinton tax increase) did even better.[9] A federal budget deficit of 4.7 percent of gross domestic product (GDP) in 1992, projected at the time to rise to 5.5 percent of GDP by 2000, transformed into an actual surplus of 2.4 percent of GDP by the end of the decade—an unprecedented swing of 7.9 percentage points.[10]

Pragmatism Works

Because conservative ideology does not countenance the possibility that tax increases can lead to anything good, it's instructive to briefly walk through how the 1993 budget bill played an important role in jump-starting such unexpectedly outstanding economic results. By way of context, remember that Clinton won the previous year's presidential election largely because of public unhappiness over the lingering effects of the 1990–1991 economic recession, coupled with H. Ross Perot's effective attacks against President George H. W. Bush's stewardship over a budget that was running large deficits. Bush's own tax increases in 1990 had disillusioned many in his party and proved to be insufficient to stanch the budget bleeding caused by the recession and the huge costs of mopping up after the savings and loan debacle—which averaged $60 billion a year in fiscal 1990 and 1991.[11]

Upon taking office, Clinton faced a bipartisan rebellion against his initial plans for a short-term economic "stimulus" package and quickly shifted his efforts behind a $473 billion deficit-reduction package proposed in February 1993. The underlying idea behind the plan—what became known as "Rubinomics," after Clinton's top economic adviser and former Goldman Sachs senior partner Robert E. Rubin—was that a credible set of proposals to significantly cut the deficit would restore the confidence of the bond market, leading to lower interest rates. Rubinomics worked. From the time Treasury Secretary Lloyd Bentsen first divulged details about the budget proposal in late January until October, the bond market surged and the yield on ten-year Treasury securities fell from about 6.5 percent to below 5.5 percent.[12] While a variety of factors can affect investment markets over any given period, the consensus at the time among journalists and economists was that bond market traders had perceived Clinton's deficit-reduction package to be serious enough to produce the rally. A month before the legislation was enacted, the unalterably circumspect Federal Reserve chairman Alan Greenspan acknowledged as much when he said, "I don't know how much of the long-term interest rate reduction is attributable to the expectation that there will be a credible reduction in the deficit out there. I suspect most of it is, rightly or wrongly."[13]

In the aftermath of the enactment of the budget agreement, the Federal Reserve pursued what has been widely acknowledged to be "extremely loose" monetary policy, keeping interest rates relatively low even as the economy heated up. The deficit-reduction bill helped to give the Fed greater flexibility to pursue that course, mainly because inflationary pressures are allayed when taxes are higher and government spending is lower. Subdued interest rates promoted by the combination of tight government budgets and loose monetary policy coincided with a boom in private investment spending, particularly on computers, software, and communication equipment in the second half of the 1990s, contributing to significantly improved productivity growth. Sorting out causes and effects is enormously complicated. Declining computer prices, for example, played an important role in the increased investment.[14] But it's also the case that one of the main goals of the deficit-reduction bill was to help boost investment by lowering interest rates, and that is exactly what happened—defying the conventional conservative wisdom that higher taxes inevitably discourage investment.

Some credit should also be given to the first President Bush's 1990 Budget Enforcement Act, which replaced the ineffective Gramm-Rudman-Hollings deficit targets of the 1980s with so-called pay-as-you-go (PAYGO) rules. Under PAYGO, any member of Congress who proposed a tax cut or an increase in spending on entitlements (programs like Social Security and Medicare in which government payments are owed to beneficiaries based on established eligibility criteria and benefit rules, rather than on annual appropriations) became obligated to propose offsetting revenue increases or cuts in entitlements to pay for the added cost. In addition, caps were set on annual appropriations for so-called discretionary (nonentitlement) programs. The 1993 budget act extended those rules, which were slated to expire in 1995, through 1998. PAYGO worked, playing pivotal roles in keeping government spending in check during several budget battles in the 1990s.[15]

A number of other forces, some of them serendipitous and not necessarily directly related to fiscal or monetary policy, further fueled the red hot economy of the second half of the 1990s: the acceleration in long dormant productivity as advances in information and communications technology diffused throughout workplaces, a temporary decline in health-care inflation during the early stages of managed care, a soaring dollar (caused in part by the deficit-reduction bill's bolstering of the federal balance sheet) that made imports cheaper, falling oil prices in 1997–1998, and a surging stock market (ultimately, a hyperinflated one by the end of the decade) that helped to encourage consumption by making investors feel wealthier.[16]

As the former Federal Reserve board members Alan S. Blinder and Janet Yellen point out in a meticulous analysis of what they call "the Fabulous Decade," economists have been preaching for decades that tight government budgets combined with relatively easy monetary policy can create a proinvestment macroeconomic climate by holding down interest rates.[17] That's basically what happened in the 1990s, though other factors obviously mattered as well. No one can say what would have occurred had a single vote in Congress switched from yea to nay over Clinton's deficit-reduction bill. But we can say with absolute certainty that not one of the long list of calamities that conservative opponents predicted as the inevitable outcome of tax increases actually transpired. To the contrary, the results were beyond the wildest dreams of even the plan's biggest boosters. What lessons did conservatives learn from the experience?

The "Everything-but-the-Kitchen-Sink" Theory

After George W. Bush decided to run for the presidency in 1999, he told the *Wall Street Journal* that his father's biggest political mistake had been to break his famous pledge: "Read my lips, no new taxes."[18] So it was no surprise that during the campaign, the Texas governor assembled some of the conservative movement's leading economic lights to assemble a package of tax cuts that would constitute the heart of his economic platform. Led by Larry Lindsey, a senior fellow at the American Enterprise Institute, the team included Reagan's former economic adviser Martin Feldstein and four economists based at the Hoover Institution: Martin Anderson, Michael Boskin, John Cogan, and John Taylor.[19] The centerpiece of the plan they developed was a reduction in marginal tax rates, including a cut in the top bracket from 39.6 percent (where Clinton had raised it from 31 percent in 1993) to 33 percent. The bottom rate would be reduced from 15 percent to 10 percent.[20]

That basic approach of slashing tax rates was consistent with the conservative "supply-side" vision propagated during the Reagan era and used to justify his huge 1981 tax cut, which held that reducing the share of taxes collected from every extra dollar a worker earns creates virtuous incentives. Among Bush's economic advisers, Lindsey, Feldstein, Anderson, and Boskin were especially committed supply-siders and in one way or another had been connected to the Reagan administration. Their belief is that tax cuts give individuals a stronger reason to work harder and longer, save more, and put their money in productive investments, all boosting the "supply" of resources that would enhance the production of goods and services. Arthur Laffer, the famous supply-sider, used to say, "Tax something, and you get less of it. Tax something less, and you get more of it." The most ardent supply-siders (not necessarily all the members of Bush's brain trust) go so far as to claim that tax reductions create so much additional economic growth that government revenues will become even higher than they otherwise would be, as Laffer's famous curve purported to show. Because the income tax system is progressive—it collects a much higher share from upper-income than from lower-income workers—across-the-board marginal rate reductions also happen to be far more beneficial to individuals at the top rungs of the economic ladder than to those at the middle and the bottom. So there's an elegant synergy between the conservative supply-side theory in support of tax rate reductions and the self-interest of the upper-crust political contributors to the Republican Party.

For the vast majority of mainstream economists, who were skeptical of supply-side-ism in the first place, the huge deficits and anemic levels of saving and investment during the Reagan era fully discredited the theory. The conservative economist N. Gregory Mankiw, who became an economic adviser to George W. Bush in the middle of his first term, wrote in the third edition of his textbook *Macroeconomics*:

> An example of fad economics occurred in 1980, when a small group of economists advised Presidential candidate Ronald Reagan that an across-the-board cut in income tax rates would raise tax revenue. They argued that if people could keep a higher fraction of their income, people would work harder to earn more income. Even though tax rates would be lower, income would rise by so much, they claimed, that tax revenues would rise. Almost all professional economists, including most of those who supported Reagan's proposal to cut taxes, viewed this outcome as far too optimistic. Lower tax rates might encourage people to work harder and this extra effort would offset the direct effects of lower tax rates to some extent, but there was no credible evidence that work effort would rise by enough to cause tax revenues to rise in the face of lower tax rates. . . . Nonetheless, the argument was appealing to Reagan, and it shaped the 1980 Presidential campaign and the economic policies of the 1980s. . . .
>
> People on fad diets put their health at risk but rarely achieve the permanent weight loss they desire. Similarly, when politicians rely on the advice of charlatans and cranks, they rarely get the

desirable results they anticipate. After Reagan's election, Congress passed the cut in tax rates that Reagan advocated, but the tax cut did not cause tax revenues to rise.[21]

Yet many movement conservatives like those who formed Bush's economic team during his campaign refused to let go of the supply-side idea that tax cuts significantly boost savings, investment, and work effort, and thereby productivity and economic growth. Its attractiveness as a political ruse was simply too appealing. One of the intellectual powerhouses of the conservative movement, Irving Kristol, was an early proponent of supply-side economics who later conceded that the concept's political virtues trumped its dubiousness as a theory. Writing in 1995, Kristol said of the supply-side doctrine, "I was not certain of its economic merits but quickly saw its political possibilities. . . . The task, as I saw it, was to create a new majority, which evidently would mean a conservative majority, which came to mean, in turn, a Republican majority—so political effectiveness was the priority, not the accounting deficiencies of government."[22] Much as Irving's son Bill embraced benevolent hegemony partly because he thought Republicans fare better when advocating for military confrontations with international foes, the senior Kristol cared more about the political appeal of a fraudulent rationale for tax cuts than the impact it might have in the real world.

Ronald Reagan himself deeply believed in the supply-side idea because he remembered when he made big money as a movie star during World War II and marginal tax rates were as high as 90 percent: "You could only make four pictures and then you were in the top bracket, so we all quit working after four pictures and went off to the country."[23] As Reagan adviser Richard Darman explained to the biographer Lou Cannon, "The president absolutely loathes and despises taxes."[24] To this day, the conservative movement shares its foremost icon's contempt, which has served it well politically.

At the time of the 2000 presidential campaign, the economy and the stock market were booming while budget surpluses were accruing. Although Bush and his advisers periodically alluded to supply-side shibboleths in pitching the tax rate cuts to the public, they mainly emphasized that the intent was merely to return to taxpayers about a quarter of the expected surplus. In his first debate with Al Gore, who proposed a tax cut of his own focused mainly on middle-class workers, Bush said:

> People need to know that, over the next 10 years, there's going to be $25 trillion of revenue that comes into our Treasury, and we anticipate spending $21 trillion. And my plan says, "Why don't we pass $1.3 trillion of that back to the people who pay the bills?" Surely we can afford 5 percent of the $25 trillion that are coming into the Treasury to the hard-working people who pay the bills. . . . I want to share some of that money with you, so you've got more money to build and save and dream for your families.[25]

But the rationale for tax cuts began to transform in December 2000, even before the Supreme Court delivered the presidency to Bush with its final decision on the Florida recount. Dick Cheney, then the vice president in waiting, asserted that a recession was looming and the tax cuts would be needed to stimulate the economy.[26] Although Cheney turned out to be right that a recession was at hand, the nature of Bush's proposed tax cuts was ill-suited to quickly goosing the economy. The bulk of the reductions was aimed at a relatively small segment of the population with high incomes, and they were to be phased in over a number of years. Countercyclical Keynesian tax cuts, which first took hold as a strategy to jump-start the economy during the Kennedy administration, are supposed to work by giving people more money to spend. But to the extent the Keynesian approach retains any theoretical credibility based on its checkered history—more often than not ending up in the hands of taxpayers well after the downturn had already ended—it needs to be implemented during a period of prolonged stagnation after it has become clear that lower interest rates and subdued inflation haven't self-corrected the economy. Still, Bush left his tax-cut proposal essentially intact while insisting that it would lead to a quick economic turnaround. The *Washington Post* columnist Sebastian Mallaby, a moderate, wrote in February, "This weird revival of Keynesianism says a lot about the rickety intellectual basis for a large tax cut."[27]

As evidence mounted that a recession was in fact under way, with surplus projections rapidly eroding with each passing month, politicians of both parties felt the need to take some kind of action. So they agreed to send out tax rebates ranging from $300 to $600 per taxpayer, which were distributed from July through September 2001. The checks were pitched as a down payment on the reduction in the lowest tax bracket from 15 percent to 10 percent that would be enacted later in the year as part of Bush's original package. The rebates were a mere drop in the entire Bush administration's tax cut bucket, and the Keynesian argument that Cheney and many Republicans marshaled in their defense is by no means a conservative plank, but it's worth mentioning that the rebates didn't work. Studies by Matthew D. Shapiro and Joel Slemrod found that the rebates appeared to be ineffective in jump-starting the economy because taxpayers parked most of the money in bank accounts rather than spending it.[28]

Even as the rebate checks were flowing through the mail in August 2001, President Bush interpreted the near-complete evaporation of the $4 trillion to $5 trillion in previously projected surpluses during his eight short months in office as "incredibly positive news." Why? Because it would put Congress in a "fiscal straitjacket."[29] With that remark, the president endorsed what has become the dominant conservative rationale for tax cuts in the wake of the failures of supply-side economics to live up to its theoretical promise during the Reagan administration. The argument is known as "starving the beast," a phrase widely attributed to the former Reagan budget director David Stockman. As Grover Norquist, a modern-day kingpin of the conservative movement, explained it to *U.S. News and World Report*: "The goal is reducing the size and scope of government by draining its lifeblood."[30]

As the Bush administration proceeded to barnstorm from one set of tax cuts to the next throughout the course of his first term, the rationales provided along the way coalesced into what might be called the "everything-but-the-kitchen-sink" theory: any particular tax cut was good because it offered virtuous long-term supply-side incentives *and* a short-term Keynesian boost to the economy *and* another calorie withdrawal for the federal government, *plus* tax relief to whatever overburdened group would benefit from a particular cut, *plus* fairness in eradicating sundry contrived injustices that the existing tax code imposed.

Of course, there are genuine, widely acknowledged problems with the income tax code. It is enormously complex for anyone who itemizes deductions, and particularly for the increasing number of middle-class families at risk of the so-called alternative minimum tax. It is unfair from a variety of standpoints, one of which is that taxpayers with similar incomes can owe wildly different tax bills depending on the tax breaks available to them. And it is tremendously inefficient, with some industries benefiting far more than others from various tax favors, and abundant resources devoted to tax-related paperwork and scheming to minimize tax burdens. Those inefficiencies impede the economy by diverting resources to relatively unproductive activities. The 1986 tax reform act, which received wide bipartisan support in Congress and was signed into law by President Reagan, significantly alleviated all of those problems while retaining the same revenue to the government. In stark contrast to that accomplishment, each of President Bush's tax changes—supported energetically by the conservative movement— without exception made the tax code much more complex, inequitable, and inefficient while depleting the Treasury. Again, the conservatives in power diverted the country's attention to imaginary problems while neglecting and then exacerbating the real ones.

Jackpot!

The scope, variety, magnitude, and complexity of the tax cuts that accrued from one year of the Bush administration to the next, combined with elaborate phase-in, phase-out, and expiration dates, was so mind-boggling that seasoned policy wonks, journalists, and even supportive legislators had great difficulty comprehending the changes— much less the rationales for them.[31]

As scattershot as the tax cuts and the justifications for them were, they did share a single unifying trait, but it was one that the administration and its conservative supporters did everything they could to obfuscate: singularly and collectively, the tax cuts were enormously generous only to the small fraction of Americans with very high incomes while providing modest-to-no benefit to the rest of the population. The widely respected economists William G. Gale and Peter R. Orszag calculated the effects of making the 2001 and 2003 tax cuts permanent and found that 73.1 percent of the benefits would go to taxpayers at the top fifth of the income ladder. The middle fifth would receive only 7.5 percent of the tax cuts, and the majority of the population in the lowest three quintiles would receive only 11.9 percent of the tax benefits. The very top 1 percent would get 30 percent of the entire tax cut with an average reduction in their tax bill of $56,051. In contrast, citizens in the middle fifth would receive an average tax cut of $699. Only 15.8 percent of those in the bottom fifth would get any tax cut at all.[32]

There are a number of reasons that the benefits of the tax cuts skew so much toward the highest earners. One, again, is that upper-income workers pay a higher share of all income taxes collected because the system is progressive, which means that they benefit more from across-the-board changes like reductions in tax rates. But in addition, many of the cuts are particularly targeted to the wealthy. Exhibit A is the reduction in the tax rate on capital gains and dividends, which most compensates individuals with sizable investment holdings outside of tax-deferred savings accounts (investment income in such accounts isn't affected because it isn't taxed as it accrues). In 2005, the proportion of taxpayers with incomes under $100,000 with *any* taxable capital gains was just 6.6 percent and, with dividends, 12.5 percent. Moreover, among households that collect investment income outside of tax-deferred accounts, the amounts involved are vastly larger for those with the highest earnings. Over half of all capital gains and dividend income flows to the 0.2 percent of households with annual incomes over $1 million. More than three-quarters—78 percent—of investment income goes to the roughly 3 percent of households with incomes over $200,000.[33]

Similarly, raising the limit on contributions to retirement savings accounts almost exclusively benefits the highest-income taxpayers because they're virtually the only ones who contribute the maximums, which are already very high. The estate tax is owed only by the very wealthiest families, who would be the exclusive beneficiaries of phasing it out. Eliminating the restrictions on write-offs for top-bracket taxpayers benefits only top-bracket taxpayers. The tax cuts for small business owners, who are disproportionately upper-income individuals, likewise skew toward the high end. By comparison, the new tax breaks for middle- and low-income households such as the marriage penalty adjustments and the write-offs for educational and child-care expenses help only a subset of taxpayers and even then only in modest amounts in most cases.

Despite the indisputable evidence that the Bush administration's tax cuts would predominantly reward the very small proportion of the population who prospered during an era of rising inequality, the right marshaled enormous creativity to present an alternative depiction of that reality. As the Princeton University economist and *New York Times* columnist Paul Krugman described in a 2003 article for his paper's magazine called "The Tax-Cut Con," Bush administration spokesmen repeatedly recited the phrase "92 million Americans will receive an average tax cut of $1,083" to sell that year's proposal. But that calculation left out the 50 million taxpayers who would receive no cut at all and used a mean average (computed by dividing the total tax cut by the number of taxpaying households), rather than median (which conveys the level at which half received more and half less), to create the impression that most people would get cuts of around $1,000. In fact, half of families received a tax cut of less than $100 and the great majority a reduction below $500. The mean average exceeds $1,000 because the small fraction of the population with very high incomes got far larger tax cuts.[34]

Even more artfully, the *Wall Street Journal* published periodic editorials developing the theme that low- and middle-income households are actually the ones who should be called "lucky duckies." Because their income tax liability is modest, the *Journal* argued, it's entirely appropriate to focus tax reductions on those who pay the most. To do otherwise, the paper unabashedly wrote, ran the risk that too many people would no longer have reason to be hostile to taxes and the government itself:

> [A]s fewer and fewer people are responsible for paying more and more of all taxes, the constituency for tax cutting, much less tax reform, is eroding. Workers who pay little or no taxes can hardly be expected to care about tax relief for everybody else. They are also that much detached from recognizing the costs of government. All of which suggests that the last thing the White House should do now is come up with more exemptions, deductions, and credits that will shrink the tax-paying population even further.[35]

The editorials mention only in passing that those lucky duckies also owe a payroll tax for Social Security and Medicare, which for almost all middle-class and low-income workers consumes a larger share of their earnings than income taxes do. Most households—71 percent—pay more in payroll taxes than in income taxes.[36] Unlike the progressive income tax, the payroll tax is regressive in that individuals with high incomes owe a smaller portion of their earnings than do those with lower salaries. For example, the average effective payroll tax rate in 2000 for someone in the middle fifth of the income scale was 9.6 percent, versus 6.3 percent in the top fifth.[37] People with the very highest incomes pay a much lower share. The main reason for that regressivity is that there's a ceiling on wages subject to the Social Security tax—$94,200 in 2006. (It also doesn't affect investment income at all, which predominantly is collected by the wealthy.) So the *Journal* really shouldn't be too concerned about average citizens not owing taxes—they pay their share. A question the paper might have at least tried to answer is why conservatives talk only about the merits of income tax cuts without ever raising the possibility that some sort of payroll tax relief might be a more equitable approach. Indeed, the *Journal* explicitly opposes the refundable earned-income tax credit, which in effect eases the burden of payroll taxes on low-income workers. Considering that the only genuine lucky duckies to enjoy rising real incomes as well as tax cuts are those with very high earnings, why leave payroll taxes off the table?

We Can Always Starve the Beast Later

As gung-ho as the *Journal*, right-wing think tanks, and the entire conservative movement were about the Bush tax cuts, the seeds for later dissent were planted when the Republican Congress first bypassed and then dropped entirely the PAYGO rules that had proved to be so effective at restoring balance to the federal budget during the 1990s. To enact the 2001 tax cut, the conservatives running the government agreed to suspend PAYGO—which would have required spending cuts to offset the lost revenue. (Those rules were also set aside in 1999 and 2000 to accommodate measures that decreased the surplus by much smaller amounts.) In 2002, Congress allowed PAYGO to expire entirely rather than renewing or strengthening it. Few on the right made much of a stink, both because they were fawning over their conservative president in his post-9/11 and pre–Iraq invasion glory days and because dropping the spending constraints greased the skids for more tax cuts. But dumping PAYGO, notwithstanding the starve-the-beast theoretical imaginings, virtually guaranteed that deficits would soar while little effort would be devoted to cutting the popular government programs decried by the conservatives attending Heritage luncheons who don't need votes to be reelected.

When President Bush came out of the gate in February 2003 with an "economic growth package" projected to cost twice as much as either supporters or opponents had expected—despite a ten-year deficit forecast that had ballooned to $1.3 trillion—some dissent started breaking out within the ranks of tax-cut enthusiasts.[38] That month, after Bush nominated N. Gregory Mankiw, the economist who had referred to supply-siders as "charlatans and cranks," Martin Anderson, one of the supply-siders who had advised Bush during the campaign, huffed to the *New York Times* about Mankiw's assertion: "It's stupid; it's simply not what a good economist writes. Anybody who puts that in a textbook for tens of thousands of students to read has a lot of explaining to do."[39]

Still, the fissures on the right over taxes during Bush's first term were relatively mild and inconsequential. Even as the budget picture continued to deteriorate before the eyes of the self-described "fiscal conservatives" running the Republican Congress, Bush's proposed tax cuts became law with mere tweaking at the margins. Whatever disagreements arose about the particulars, conservatives ultimately demonstrated yet again that their single most unifying trait is their embrace of tax cuts. While many on the right still firmly believe despite all evidence to the contrary that supply-side economics or starve-the-beast works, far and away the most significant reason that the movement is so deeply committed to tax cuts has to do not with economic theory but with *politics*. Support of tax cuts—and even more, opposition to tax increases—is extremely helpful in winning elections. Like Ronald Reagan, many voters dislike taxes at a visceral level. The right owes a large share of its success to bonding as Reagan did with a significant portion of the public over that hostility—without much regard for the consequences to the nation of pandering to that emotion.

The Oxymoron of "Fiscal Conservatism"

The United States has now experienced two grand experiments with major income tax cuts in the Reagan and Bush administrations that provide all kinds of useful evidence about whether those reductions accomplished what conservatives vowed they would. Before evaluating what we have learned, it's important to keep in mind that many factors affect how economies perform over periods of time, and it is impossible to say with great precision the extent to which a particular policy such as income tax cuts affects particular outcomes. It's also important to recognize that external events largely beyond the control of government—such as the devastation wreaked by the September 11 terrorist attacks and Hurricane Katrina—in their own right have important economic ripple effects. Still, while no one can claim with certainty what would have happened from 2001 onward in the absence of any or all of the tax cuts, economists have developed complex computer models that attempt to make such estimates based on historical experience.

Conservatives made many promises about the virtuous effects that the tax cuts would have. So as a starting point in assessing the degree to which those promises did or did not come true, let's look at some basic indicators of economic performance over the course of the Bush administration. By way of comparison, the Bush tax cuts amounted to about the same size as Ronald Reagan's—about 2 percent of GDP when measured against comparable baselines. (Reagan's 1981 cuts were larger but partially offset by his subsequent tax increases in 1982 and 1984.)[40]

In January 2007, the Center on Budget and Policy Priorities compared the performance of the U.S. economy since the recovery began in November 2001, as well as since the last business cycle peak in March 2001, with comparable periods post–World War II. The center looked at seven key indicators: GDP, personal consumption expenditures, private domestic fixed nonresidential investment, net worth, income from wages and salaries, employment, and corporate profits. For six of those seven indicators, the growth rates in the current period were below the average for the comparable postwar periods. Overall growth in GDP and fixed nonresidential investment, both of which supply-siders vowed would be boosted through the tax cuts, were among the below-average performers. Both employment and wage/salary growth have been much lower by historical standards in the current recovery, with job increases below *every* other comparable postwar period. The only aspect in which this decade's economy outperformed the average, and by a wide margin, was corporate profits.[41]

Even still, a study by the Federal Reserve economists Gene Amromin, Paul Harrison, and Steve Sharpe found that the 2003 dividend tax cuts did not raise U.S. stock values. Because stock prices in other countries without tax cuts closely tracked the levels in the United States, the authors inferred that other factors influenced the subsequent gains that occurred.[42] As the *Wall Street Journal* concluded in a story about the Fed report, "[T]he tax cut . . . was a dud when it came to boosting the stock market."[43]

From the standpoint of most Americans, the gauge that most closely captures whether they are prospering is median income in constant, inflation-adjusted dollars (the median level conveys the point at which half of all households earn more and half less). In 2005, the median household income increased for the first time over the previous year since the 1998 to 1999 period. At $46,326, it was still lower than the $47,671 level of six years earlier (in 2005 dollars).[44] Notwithstanding the economic recovery, the poverty rate increased from a low of 11.3 percent (31.6 million people) in 2000 to 12.6 percent (37 million Americans) in 2005.[45] In March 2006, Treasury Secretary John Snow tried to persuade reporters that everyone was sharing in economic prosperity, pointing to an 8.2 percent increase in the real after-tax income per person from January 2001 to January 2006. But he resorted to the administration's tried-and-true-but-misleading tactic of using a mean average, which gives added weight to the large income gains of the highest earners relative to the more revealing median.[46]

It's not surprising in light of such historically poor economic performance that the Bush team relied so heavily on misleading spin. For example, the administration argued that the unemployment rate in April 2006 of 4.7 percent was "below the average rate of the 1960s, 1970s, 1980s, and 1990s."[47] But comparing a reading for one month with entire decades is like comparing a batter's average for one unusually good game with the entire careers of better players. It also omits the inconvenient fact that unemployment was significantly lower when Bush took office and had declined throughout the preceding administration, in contrast to his own. Similarly, when Bush told Congress in his 2006 State of the Union address that "the tax relief you passed has left $880 billion in the hands of American workers, investors, small businesses, and families," he neglected to mention that the resulting budget deficits accruing as a result amount to future tax liabilities for Americans.

As in the 1980s, the condition of the federal budget deteriorated dramatically in the wake of the tax cuts. A surplus of 1.8 percent of GDP in 2001 transformed into a deficit of about 2 percent of GDP in 2006.[48] That huge 3.8 percentage point swing in the wrong direction stands in stark contrast to the restoration of fiscal health in the Clinton era. While many factors are responsible for the budget's deterioration, including the anemic levels of economic growth, the Congressional Budget Office (CBO) found that the tax cuts were far more to blame than was the pork barrel spending that preoccupies conservatives. CBO looked at the cost in 2005 of legislation enacted since January 2001, and concluded that 48 percent of the $539 billion in increased budgetary costs was due to the tax cuts, compared to 37 percent for spending on defense, homeland security, and international outlays, and 15 percent for domestic entitlement and discretionary programs.[49] How about discretionary domestic spending other than homeland security, which encompasses the pork that so rankles the Bush-bashers on the right? A meager 3 percent. The conservatives who are justifiably unhappy about rising deficits really ought to be pointing their fingers at their prized tax cuts rather than at nondefense spending.

To the average citizen, large federal deficits may seem like an unimportant abstraction. A January 2006 Pew poll found that only 2 percent of respondents said the budget deficit was the most important problem facing the nation, compared to 17 percent early in Clinton's first term in April 1993—when it ranked a close third behind unemployment and the economy generally, in large part because H. Ross Perot's famous graphs were still fresh in their minds.[50] It is true that the size of the gross federal debt is roughly the same now as a share of the economy, about 66 percent, as it was at the outset of Clinton's administration. But Clinton's actions moved the trend line downward while Bush's policies, especially the tax cuts, have contributed mightily toward forecasts of significant increases in the future. There are a number of reasons that the reversal in the budget picture alarms finance experts far more than it does the public generally:

- The big increase in federal budget deficits has coincided with a continuing decline in the household savings rate and widening trade deficits. Together, those interacting forces have left the United States increasingly dependent on huge inflows of money from abroad to finance our governmental and other deficits. As of 2004, the net amount of U.S. liabilities, including Treasury securities, held by foreigners amounted to 29 percent of America's GDP.[51] That figure continues to grow as our current account deficit—the combined balances on trade in goods and services, income, and net unilateral current transfers—has climbed to the highest sustained levels ever for a large industrial country.[52] The risk, which many economists consider to be large and growing, is that foreign investors will lose their enthusiasm for U.S. debt and will sell large quantities of it abruptly. That would send the dollar's value into a tailspin, cause interest rates to soar, and damage the U.S. economy. The best prevention against such a crisis would be an improved federal budget picture, which is unlikely if additional tax cuts are forthcoming.

- The aging of the baby boomers means that the rolls of Social Security, Medicare, and Medicaid (which covers nursing home care for many older Americans) will begin to swell around 2010 and continue to grow more rapidly than the working population for about two decades. Because health-care costs are sure to continue to escalate far faster than overall inflation, absent fundamental reform, outlays for Medicare and Medicaid are projected to increase especially rapidly (Social Security's growth is far more manageable, as explained in chapter 9). In anticipation of that demographic challenge, piling up large amounts of federal debt now is mindlessly shortsighted and will only compound the difficulty of providing adequate supports for tomorrow's elderly. The administration's tax cuts squandered budget surpluses that could have been used to help finance reforms in entitlement programs while minimizing future debt obligations.

- Even under the Bush administration's misleading budget projections—which don't fully account for the costs of the Iraq war, reforms to the "alternative minimum tax" that everyone agrees are essential to avoid unfair middle-class tax increases, and the long-term costs of the Bush tax cuts if they are extended beyond 2010—the budget item expected to grow fastest of all is interest on the federal debt. It is projected to increase by 75 percent between 2006 and 2011, consuming a growing share of each tax dollar.[53] In the process, the added borrowing will put upward pressure on interest rates attributable to the heightened government competition with private borrowers for capital. Higher interest rates, in turn, dampen economic growth.

In December 2005, the CBO released a report that evaluated the budgetary and economic effects of a 10 percent cut in income tax rates, using different economic models derived from observations of past experience. Those models took into account the "supply-side" effects that conservatives often complain are commonly omitted when economists make forecasts. The CBO concluded that supply-side factors, depending on the model, would offset only between 1 and 22 percent of the $466 billion in lost government revenues during the first five years after the tax cut; during the second five years, supply-side forces would offset no more than 32 percent of the additional $775 billion in lost government revenues over that period. The basic conclusion, after extensive study of supply-side effects as they have occurred in the real world, is that they are dwarfed by the direct loss in revenue attributable to tax reductions. Tax cuts do not pay for themselves, or anything close to it.[54]

Just as supply-side theories have been twice disproved in the wake of both the Reagan and the Bush tax cuts, it's also more than evident that the beast isn't starving this time around, either. The metaphor Reagan and Milton Friedman loved to tell about cutting off a child's allowance to prevent irresponsible spending has a pretty obvious shortcoming: it doesn't work if the kid can play with a full deck of credit cards. Over the first five years of Bush's administration, federal revenues as a share of GDP declined from 19.8 percent to 17.5 percent because of his tax cuts, while outlays increased from 18.5 percent to 20.1 percent. Contrary to widespread belief even among his conservative idolizers, Reagan didn't reduce federal spending much at all—it was 22.2 percent of GDP in 1981 and 21.2 percent in 1989 (he did, though, significantly cut expenditures on discretionary domestic programs while replacing those costs with his defense buildup). The big deficits arose during the Reagan era because revenues declined from 19.6 percent of GDP to below 18 percent for much of the 1980s, ending up at 18.4 percent by the end of his administration.[55] Alas, neither then nor now have tax cuts produced the conservative nirvana of a federal government, in Grover Norquist's charming phrase, drowning in a bathtub. Even Cato chief William Niskanen felt compelled by 2004 to concede the failure of the starve-the-beast tenet, presenting his own research to confirm the obvious.[56]

To convey how the modern conservative movement is responsible for corrupting the concept of "fiscal conservatism" to the point that it has become an oxymoron, a little history is useful. In the three decades preceding the Reagan administration, revenues as a share of national income were roughly stationary while expenditures rose only modestly. Each president, from Truman to Eisenhower to Kennedy to Johnson to Nixon to Ford to Carter, handed a lighter or comparable debt as a share of the economy to his successor. But during every single year of the presidencies of Reagan, George H. W. Bush, and George W. Bush, the national debt rose relative to the size of the economy. Combined, the debt-to-GDP ratio climbed by nearly 40 percentage points on their watch, while it fell by 6 points during the Clinton administration.[57] It's a record of irresponsibility and failure that speaks for itself.

The Legacy of Borrow-and-Squander Conservatism

To movement conservatives, anything that ever ails the economy can always be blamed on the same problem: income taxes are too high. The politically irresistible, uncannily simple solution is always the same: cut them. The Heritage Foundation, the Hoover Institution, and sundry other conservative think tanks and ideologically committed academics stand prepared to provide the media with talking points and elaborate research to defend any tax cut at any time—setting off smoke bombs that leave Americans who are highly inclined to like the sound of "tax relief" groping in a fog about the merits of the issue. Wealthy Republican contributors, about the only Americans who would benefit, keep sending big checks to the party. Meanwhile, problems that disappeared during the last half of the Clinton administration, such as stagnating incomes and federal deficits, return with a vengeance, in no small measure *because of* the conservative movement's solution.

The right is having great difficulty coming to grips with the profligacy of its political leaders and the further laying to waste of the two ideological pillars undergirding its adoration for tax cuts. In contrast to the post-Reagan era, when conservatives by and large stuck together in their comfort zone of hagiographic hyperspin, George W. Bush's economic policies have generated abundant finger-pointing and dissent in the movement. Typical of conservative efforts to rehabilitate Reagan's record, despite the prima facie evidence of the dubiousness of both supply-side economics and starve-the-beast, was a 1992 book by the late longtime proprietor of the *Wall Street Journal*'s editorial page, Robert L. Bartley, titled *The Seven Fat Years: And How to Do It Again*. To Bartley, "nay-sayers" and "elitists" had duped the public into believing that the Reagan era's "belle époque" was anything but. "Wallowing neurotically in arcane and ill-understood statistics, a gaggle of declinists denies a reality evident to everyone else in the world."[58] While it's true that the U.S. economy grew at a relatively strong average annual rate of 3.8 percent from the nadir of the recession in 1982 to 1988, that figure alone presents a misleadingly bright picture about the overall economic performance during that period—as well as about the impact of the 1981 tax cuts.

For example, a reader looking for more than a mention of median incomes throughout those fat years will search in vain through Bartley's three-hundred-plus pages. In 1981, when Reagan took office, the median household income in constant 2005 dollars was $39,125; by 1988, it was $43,168—that increase of about 1.5 percent a year may seem large by the standards of the current Bush administration, but it was modest relative to past periods of economic growth and was partly attributable to increasing numbers of two-income families. Bartley quickly dismissed the meager productivity increases over the period as something to be expected due to the increasing size of the workforce. Most audaciously, Bartley pooh-poohed the significant tapering off in both household savings and net investment rates—two of the most important factors that contribute to economic growth—with a few brusque non sequiturs related to what he perceived to be shortcomings in how those statistics are measured: "The savings rate, the object of much concern in the 1980s, has to be taken with a grain of salt. So, too, investment."[59] Actually, the economy deeply relies on that salt for fuel, and the whole basis of supply-side economics was that the tax cuts would produce more, not less, of both savings and investment.

As for the Reagan deficits, Bartley (himself an elite in his aerie at the *Journal*, it might be noted) offered all kinds of explanations and rationalizations attempting to minimize the extent to which his hero's huge increase in federal debt was problematic. But he also blamed Congress, suggesting that the budget would have been balanced if Reagan had his druthers. The common conservative refrain, after all, is not that office holders took wrongheaded theories too far, but that they didn't take them far enough. However, as the economist Benjamin M. Friedman pointed out in the *New York Review of Books*, "[Bartley] ignores the fact that even if Congress had adopted all eight of Mr. Reagan's budgets exactly as he submitted them, the deficit would still have averaged $159 billion per year during this period, not much below the $177 billion we actually had."[60]

Movement paladins have been far less kind to Bush, despite his unwavering devotion to tax cuts and an economic record that's not all that much worse than Reagan's. Approval ratings lurching below 40 percent have a way of converting political friends into backstabbers. The ostensible reason for all the hostility is that Bush and the Republican Congress have failed to sufficiently reduce federal spending. Heritage, Cato, the *Wall Street Journal*, and many of their disciples all have published rankings showing that the younger President Bush increased domestic discretionary spending at a higher rate than any other president since 1964. (They did not emphasize, though, that Democrats Carter and Clinton ranked at or near the bottom of the list, along with Reagan, depending on how the calculations were done.) Without question, the Bush administration and the Republican Congress have indeed squandered tax dollars to an unprecedented degree on wasteful activities with scant justification from a policy standpoint. All of the Heritage and Cato reports listing the explosion in so-called earmarks—the wonky term for pork barrel spending—are accurate to the extent that they document a level of wastefulness far beyond anything experienced when so-called tax-and-spend liberals were in power. Still, as noted earlier, the tax cuts that most of the same conservatives have applauded are far more responsible for the damage to the federal budget than domestic discretionary spending was.

All of the wailing on the right about Bush's purportedly vast expansion of the federal government should be recognized as nothing more than crocodile tears for political effect. If even the most ideologically committed presidents can't seem to deliver the right's nirvana of an emaciated beast, this time in collaboration with a conservative Congress, maybe it's time to recognize that the vision of right-wing ideologues is incompatible with both American democracy and the facts of economic life.

5

Rocky Mountain Lows
State Tax-and-Spending Limits

To Grover Norquist and his lobbying organization Americans for Tax Reform, the holy grail is a state constitutional amendment approved by the voters of Colorado in 1992. Dubbed TABOR—for Taxpayer's Bill of Rights—the amendment, among other things, restricts state revenues to the level of the previous year, plus the rate of population growth and inflation. Any excess tax collections over that threshold during times of prosperity must be refunded back to taxpayers. When times are bad and tax payments fall short of that year's limit, legislators have no option but to cut the budget unless they receive approval from voters for a tax increase. That reduced revenue level during a recession in turn constitutes the new, lower baseline for the following year—creating a further tightening of the budget called the "ratchet effect." The purported benefits of the TABOR law, in the eyes of Norquist and his followers, is that it will produce stability, tax relief, and economic growth without unduly reducing essential state services.

It's the holy grail because even among simplistic conservative ideas, this one is the most simple. If you want small, efficient government, just pass an amendment that says it has to be small and efficient.

Across the country, Norquist's extensive network of conservative allies, funded by Scaife, Koch, Olin, Bradley, and their wealthy brethren, have pushed other states to follow in Colorado's footsteps. None have as yet, although Alaska, Nevada, and Utah had previously enacted considerably weaker statutory population plus inflation limitations on their budgets. In 2006, sixteen state legislatures introduced tax and expenditure limits akin to TABOR, including Arizona, Kansas, Maine, Maryland, Michigan, Minnesota, Missouri, Montana, Nebraska, Nevada, Ohio, Oklahoma, Oregon, Pennsylvania, South Carolina, and Wisconsin. Ohio's legislature ended up adopting a less restrictive statutory measure, and the efforts in all but Maryland, Minnesota, and South Carolina were seriously considered before ultimately failing.[1] The voters of Maine, Nebraska, and Oregon rejected TABOR referenda.

Largely because TABOR is the antitax movement's holy grail, Colorado is its paradise, and the former Republican governor Bill Owens its messiah-in-waiting—at least he was until 2005. Owens, who consistently supported TABOR, extending back to its original passage when he was a state legislator from Aurora, emerged as a darling of the conservative movement not long after he became the first Republican to be elected Colorado governor in twenty-eight years when he won his first term in 1998.[2] For example, the *National Review* published a piece in 2002 titled "America's Best Governor: For Republicans, a Rocky Mountain High—Bill Owens," which said, "His instinctive conservatism on everything from taxes and education to guns and abortion has served him well during his first term, and also has set him apart from an older wave of Republican governors whose reformist impulses have waned."[3] The Cato Institute's report card for governors that same year put Owens at the top with an A grade. And a year later, George F. Will's column applauding Owens's support for fiscal austerity and school vouchers was headlined "Riding High in Colorado."[4]

But that adulation abruptly transformed into disdain among many conservatives in 2005. An August 2005 *New Yorker* profile of Norquist quoted the right-wing strongman saying of Owens, "He was a guy we trusted. The bad news is he's getting a lot of corporate pukes to support him. . . . Bill Owens, who I considered a presidential contender, he will never be president. He slit his own throat."[5] Owens's transgression? In the midst of a painful budget crisis, and just a few months after Democrats regained control of the state legislature largely because of that crisis, Owens agreed to support a referendum that would temporarily bypass TABOR's constraints.

Because TABOR is so central to what the modern conservative movement wants to accomplish at the state level, and because Colorado has operated under it for well over a decade, this chapter is devoted to understanding the experience there. Remember, the promise is that TABOR will provide states with stability, tax relief, and economic growth without unduly reducing essential state services. Decide for yourself how it has worked in practice.

Genesis

The TABOR idea did not emerge from a right-wing think tank, from one of the libertarian oracles of the academy, or from a task force of business executives. Rather, its author is one Douglas Bruce, a bombastic real estate investor and former lawyer who became Colorado's counterpart to Howard Jarvis. Bruce, whose business cards famously identified him as "Terrorist," worked as a Los Angeles County deputy district attorney in the 1970s before making an unsuccessful run in the Democratic primary for the California State Assembly in 1980. After losing a tax dispute that elevated his hostility toward the government, Bruce became a Republican, bought five properties in Colorado Springs in 1986, and transplanted himself there.[6]

Within months of his arrival, Bruce became the El Paso County spokesman for Amendment 4, an initiative on the 1986 ballot stipulating that state and local officials could not impose new taxes or increase existing ones without approval of the majority of the voters. Bruce was familiar with, but hadn't actively campaigned for, the California tax initiatives pushed by Jarvis and Paul Gann, including the Proposition 13 property tax rollback that passed in 1978. Amendment 4 ended up getting trounced by a margin of 24 percentage points, but Bruce had become a man with a mission to "end the tyranny of unlimited taxation."[7]

According to research by the political scientist Daniel A. Smith, a group of Amendment 4's supporters got together after its defeat to assess what went wrong. Bruce then drafted his own version of a new and improved tax limitation initiative, which ended up dividing the group into two factions. Those opposed to his alternative wanted something along the lines of Proposition 13, except that it would include commercial along with residential real estate in a property tax cut. Bruce stuck with his more expansive, and in his eyes more reasonable, approach, which supplemented Amendment 4's provisions with a 10 percent cut in state income taxes and a cap on residential property taxes of 1 percent of market value. He set up a political committee called the Taxpayer's Bill of Rights with the acronym TABOR and succeeded in gathering enough petition signatures to get his measure onto the 1988 ballot as Amendment 6, although he had to overcome a court challenge questioning the validity of some names.

During that year's campaign, Bruce described his measure as a "moderate, comprehensive, responsible tax-and-spend limitation policy" and "not a radical major cut." Bruce wasn't subtle in characterizing opponents of his amendment. "People will lie in order to get our money, and the government wants our money." When asked what would happen if Amendment 6 met the same fate in 1988 that befell Amendment 4 in 1986, the always colorful Bruce said, "If they buy this election, we will be back next time . . . with a two-by-four to hit them on the back of the head. . . . And like Dorothy, they will wake up in Kansas." After an independent poll a month before the election showed his amendment with a substantial lead, opponents quickly mobilized and ended up decisively defeating it by 62 percent to 38 percent.

Bruce went back to the drawing board and rewrote his plan, which became Amendment 1 on the 1990 ballot. This milder incarnation would restrict property taxes while requiring voter approval of any new or increased taxes or fees that exceeded an index based on the rate of inflation and population growth, but it also allowed for emergency tax increases. At 1,857 words, it was close to incomprehensible. *Forbes* magazine wrote, "For sheer complexity, [Amendment 1] deserves a prize." Still, Bruce's decision to reduce the rigidity of his proposal helped him to win endorsements from some key Republicans and more substantial financial contributions. This time, in a harbinger of what would soon come, Bruce's amendment fell short by only a 51 percent to 49 percent margin. Nonetheless, an embittered Bruce expressed resentment toward the political establishment, "who outspent and outscared us," and the voters themselves, who "did not fight back, but they timidly and gullibly surrendered to this blackmail."

The next time around, Bruce's proposed amendment was even more convoluted and replaced some of the constraints in his earlier versions with new ones. His revision included limitations not just on the taxes that state and local governments could impose, but also on their ability to spend resources. This version of what also was labeled

Amendment 1 required a popular vote to approve any new taxes, tax increases, or government debt; imposed a limitation on annual state spending equal to the rate of inflation plus (or minus) population changes; restricted local government spending to the rate of inflation plus changes in the property tax rate; and limited increases in school district spending to inflation plus changes in student enrollment. Bruce dropped the ceiling on property taxes and the requirement of voter approval for fee increases that were in his 1990 amendment. In the process, Bruce managed to shave off about 150 words while introducing even greater complexity. The *Denver Post* quoted John Lay, the chairman of the No On #1 Committee, as saying that even though proponents of the amendment "don't necessarily know what it's going to do, they know good and well it's not going to be positive. They just want to be disruptive."

In 1992, some degree of serendipity, combined with a higher degree of political competence on the part of Bruce and his corps, finally put TABOR over the top. For one thing, Amendment 1 shared the ballot with an even more controversial initiative restricting the rights of homosexuals. The Democratic governor Roy Romer, who had focused much of his energy on defeating Bruce's propositions during past campaigns, devoted more attention to the antigay measure as well as to his own referendum on education. In addition, as the political scientist Daniel Smith noted, Bruce helped his own cause by softening his tone and distancing himself from the initiative. "I'm no anarchist," Bruce told the *Post*. "I'm a short-haired, middle-aged bachelor with a paunch living in the suburbs with a puppy. I'm not a threat. I just don't like government paternalism." Amendment 1 may also have benefited from H. Ross Perot's complementary message in the presidential campaign of that year, which decried federal budget deficits and government wastefulness. Perot ended up with 23 percent of the vote in Colorado—one of his better states.

Amendment 1 won handily, by 54 percent to 46 percent. Bruce was triumphant, pronouncing, "We have sent a message to the politicians; thou shalt not steal. . . . It is a new day for Colorado. We shall be the freest state in America. We have proven beyond a doubt who is in charge in Colorado—we the people."

The state's eventual receptivity to Bruce's rhetoric and his body-slamming constitutional amendment apparently arose more from

Coloradans' long-standing skepticism toward government and cultural predilection for stubborn independence rather than anything out of the ordinary related to the state's tax-and-spending policies. In 1990, compared with other states, Colorado's 3 percent state sales tax was one of the lowest, its corporate income tax rates were among the lowest, and personal income taxes were in the middle of the pack. Local property taxes in 1992 were only slightly above the national average.[8] But polls showed that a majority of Coloradans believed that their state government was wasteful and inefficient, and that special interests had undue influence. Pollsters at the time concluded that "On balance, Coloradans are skeptical, if not hostile, to state government."[9] That finding was consistent with a heritage that the journalist John Gunther captured in 1947 when he wrote that "Colorado is conservative politically, economically, financially. . . . I do not mean reactionary. Just conservative, with the kind of conservativeness that does not budge an inch for anybody or anything unless pinched or pushed."[10]

What's most remarkable about what happened with TABOR in Colorado is that a single individual, pretty much winging it as he went along, concocted an almost indecipherable collection of tax-and-spending restrictions that landed as he drafted them directly into the state's constitution, dominating governance in the state for more than a decade. There was no underlying theory justifying any aspect of TABOR beyond the belief that state government required a tight, virtually unbreakable rein. The closest comparable counterpart to it was California's much-imitated Proposition 13 property tax limit, followed by other referenda there that further constrained both taxes and government spending. Peter Schrag's superb book *Paradise Lost: California's Experience, America's Future* documented the chaos and decline in state, county, and local government services that California's initiatives wreaked—chaos and decline that was well under way by the time TABOR was passed.[11] But no one, including Douglas Bruce, had the slightest idea how TABOR would change life in Colorado.

A Hole in the Boat

The most significant element of the TABOR amendment is the provision to restrict state revenues to the rate of growth in the population plus inflation. That idea certainly sounds reasonable and unlikely to cause pain. Many of the Colorado voters who supported it no doubt presumed as much. But state governments spend a large share of their budgets on health care and education, both of which consistently and over a long period of time experience cost increases far in excess of overall inflation. That's true for the private sector as well as for government. Within the consumer price index, medical and schooling costs have risen at about twice the rate of the overall average. Exacerbating that noose-tightening effect is faster population growth among citizens who impose high costs on the government. The Center on Budget and Policy Priorities calculated that while the total U.S. population grew by 15.4 percent from 1990 to 2002, the state prison population increased by 83 percent, disabled children in schools grew by 35 percent, and the number of elderly and disabled persons on Medicaid grew by 70 percent. As a result, the seemingly innocuous population-plus-inflation limit is actually a highly constraining double whammy.[12]

In Colorado, TABOR's impact on state programs took hold quickly even though conditions couldn't have been much more favorable. During the 1990s, the state's population was among the fastest growing in the nation, and rapidly climbing housing prices in the Denver area elevated its inflation rate. Those forces caused TABOR's population-plus-inflation threshold to rise significantly. At the same time, the economy was strong—as it had been in the years preceding TABOR—producing sizable revenue growth enabling state spending to rise. Several accounting maneuvers also allowed the state's general fund to spend more in most years than the population-plus-growth formula. Pressure was further eased because health-care costs rose at a relatively low rate, and the state was able to devote money from the tobacco settlement to medical outlays. It wasn't until 1997 when the first TABOR-mandated tax rebates were paid, amounting to a total of $3.25 billion then and in the years that followed.[13]

Nonetheless, the state's national rankings in providing Medicaid health insurance coverage, as well as both K-12 and higher education, declined precipitously in the 1990s. When the state's economy finally began to turn sour in 2001, TABOR really came home to roost with a vengeance. The decline in tax revenues without recourse to tax increases or access to an adequate "rainy day" fund available in many other states—but which TABOR denies—combined with the year-to-year "ratchet effect" to force draconian budget cuts even as taxpayers received TABOR-mandated refunds. By 2004, exasperated state legislators of both parties acknowledged that Bruce's amendment had inflicted serious damage on the state. Brad Young, the Republican chairman of the legislature's joint budget committee, said in 2004, "There is a hole in the bottom of the boat—that is the TABOR spending limit. It works for a little while, but you go out in the future and you sink the boat." Democratic representative Tom Plant concurred, "We are broke. We are more than broke. According to the Constitution we have no money. We don't have money next year. We don't have money the year after that."[14] Few in the state of either party dissented from those views, which amounted to mainstream opinion.

The post-TABOR declines in public services that preceded the recession worsened greatly in this decade. Colorado, despite its status as one of the nation's wealthiest states with the tenth highest median household income, now ranks near the bottom in the share of low-income citizens covered by Medicaid—the federal-state health insurance program. From 1992 to 2005, the portion of low-income children lacking health insurance doubled in Colorado even as it fell in the nation as a whole. Colorado ranks dead last among the fifty states in covering low-income children. The percentage of low-income adults under sixty-five without health insurance dropped the state's overall ranking by that measure from twentieth to forty-eighth.[15]

One connection between that austerity and public health in Colorado has been the impact on pregnant women. Largely because of reductions in Medicaid coverage and relatively meager support for health clinics, Colorado's national ranking in access to prenatal care declined from twenty-third in 1990 to forty-eighth in 2004.[16] Only 67 percent of Colorado's pregnant women received adequate care, compared to the national average of 76 percent.[17] Nationally, Colorado ranked sixth worst in deliveries of low-birthweight babies—with the rate of such births increasing over the course of the 1990s.[18] Although TABOR was not the only factor contributing to the increase, it clearly prevented the state from acting effectively to reverse the negative trends. For example, the state initially responded in 1996 by creating the Prenatal Plus Program, but inadequate state funding forced a number of its clinics to drop the program.[19]

In 2004, the state imposed a rule change—ostensibly aimed at preventing illegal immigrants from receiving Medicaid coverage but also intended to save the state money—that ended the practice of initially presuming eligibility for pregnant women when they sought prenatal care. Instead of health-care providers being assured of state reimbursements regardless of whether a patient is ultimately verified to be eligible, typically after a period of up to three months, they became responsible for bearing the financial risk for treating patients determined to be ineligible for Medicaid. The policy led some health-care providers to stop treating uninsured women altogether and discouraged some women from seeking care. Testifying before a state congressional committee, Dr. Steve Volin of the Women's Health Group said, "We are seeing patients much, much later in the course of their prenatal care. They're not coming in until their Medicaid is approved, because they know they'll be financially responsible if they're not approved."[20] In one publicized case, a pregnant Colorado woman who was eligible for Medicaid but never received prenatal care because she wasn't sure whether she would qualify for coverage, lost her baby at thirty-seven weeks of gestation.[21] The state legislature eventually restored the policy of presumptive eligibility, but the experience dramatically highlighted the strong connections between government-subsidized health insurance coverage, TABOR-imposed cost pressures, and medical outcomes.

Similarly, Colorado ranked last among all states in vaccinations for two-year-olds in 2002 and 2003, with coverage rates of just 63 percent in 2002 and 68 percent in 2003;[22] its ranking increased to forty-fourth in 2004.[23] Medicaid coverage and state funding for health are not the only factors determining immunization rates, and Colorado tracked just below the national average until 2002. But TABOR was clearly responsible for the state's decision to suspend its requirement that students be fully vaccinated against diphtheria, tetanus, and pertussis (whooping cough) between April 2001 and October 2002. During that period, a national shortage of the vaccine led most states to purchase higher-priced vaccines with state funds. The Colorado legislature, though, decided it couldn't afford to take the same steps.[24]

The incidence in Colorado of whooping cough, which is life threatening in children under six months, began to soar well ahead of the national average in 2002 and has continued to increase. In 2005, more cases of whooping cough were reported in Colorado than in any other state.[25] A report by the Colorado Institute of Health indicated that there is likely a connection between the state's relatively low vac-cination rate against whooping cough and its vulnerability to out-breaks of the disease.[26]

The impact of the health-care budget squeezing extends to all Coloradans, not just to the poor. That's because the costs of providing health care to the uninsured are passed along to people with coverage in the form of higher premiums, which have induced an unusually high share of Colorado employers to drop their coverage for workers. In 1998, the rate of Colorado employer-based health-care coverage was ahead of the national average by 69.5 percent to 62 percent; by 2003, the respective rates were less than a point apart—61.2 percent and 60.4 percent. During that period, the percentage of Coloradans with employer-based health insurance coverage fell by 14 percent.[27] Employees who retained coverage at work found themselves con-fronting much higher deductibles and copayments. Referring to the state's Medicaid cuts, Jay Picerno, the chief financial officer of Cen-tura Health, Colorado's largest hospital system, said, "They are going to have a substantial impact on the cost of health care for everyone. Any savings the state accumulates is an indirect tax."[28]

We Don't Need No Education

Even under the enormously favorable conditions during the 1990s, TABOR's constraints were largely responsible for a steep decline in spending on K-12 education as legislators struggled to remain under the inflation-plus-population-growth limit. As a consequence, class-room sizes escalated so that student-teacher ratios in Colorado—one of the most prosperous states in the country—were worse than in all but eight states.[29]

Concerns about the TABOR-induced problems in the public schools prompted the emergence of a successful initiative on the state ballot in 2000 called Amendment 23, which mandated the state to match the cost of inflation, plus an additional 1 percent per year for K-12 for the following ten years. While Amendment 23 gave some protection to public schools against a continuation of deep cuts, it also put even more of a squeeze on the rest of the budget in the context of the overarching TABOR limitations. More money for schools meant less resources for other purposes.

Even for the schools, Amendment 23 was little more than a Band-Aid. In 2004, Superintendent Emily Romero of the Centennial R-1 School District in Southern Colorado asked for $11.5 million for a new school to replace one that had fallen into complete disrepair. Sewage spilled into the hallways. Because some classrooms had no ventilation, temperatures could run 80 to 90 degrees in the winter. But the state didn't provide a cent for capital improvements to the district, where more than 70 percent of the students qualify for free or reduced-price lunches. "I'm disappointed that they're willing to put us on the back burner," Romero said. "Kids in affluent communities wouldn't ever go to school here. No parent would allow their kids to attend school with sewage in the hallway." The explanation from Nancy Spence, the Republican state legislator from Centennial: "The fact is, the state doesn't have any money."[30]

Paul Teske, the director of the Center of Education Policy Analysis at the University of Colorado-Denver, assessed Colorado's public school finances in a 2005 report for the Donnell-Kay Foundation. He concluded that largely because of TABOR, "The picture is not a pretty one. For a state with the resources that come from a population that ranks tenth among states in per capita income and second in the percentage of adults with college degrees, some might be surprised to see that our spending rankings look more like those of a poor Southern state."[31]

Teacher shortages have become acute, in both Colorado's cities and its rural areas. The ratio of teacher salaries to average private-sector earnings is lower in Colorado than in any other state.[32] In 2005, for example, Denver's school system was so desperate for substitute teachers that it began asking parents with bachelor's degrees to consider applying for the vacancies. After daily pay for substitutes was reduced from $120 to $81 in order to provide a raise to full-time teachers, about 9 percent of the system's requests for substitutes went unfilled, compared to just 1 percent in the previous school year. The Denver Public Schools spokesman Mark Stevens, referring to the letter urging parents to sign up for classroom duty, told the *Denver Post*, "If you have a college degree, you may never have stopped to realize this may be a good opportunity to pick up some money to work in your child's school." But the substitute teacher Anne Kaye's reaction seemed hard to dispute: "To me, it's a sign of desperation. If I were a parent, I'd be horrified to get a letter like this."[33]

Colorado's public higher educational system likewise has deteriorated severely, due mainly to TABOR. From 1991 to 2005, total state support to colleges and universities in Colorado grew at the second-slowest rate in the nation—averaging 1 percent annually, far below the rates of inflation and growth in college-age population. Now Colorado ranks forty-eighth in the U.S. for state higher education funding as a share of personal income. The state's contribution toward higher ed per $1,000 in income plummeted from $7.40 in 1992 to $3.67 in 2004.[34] State spending per public college student is about $2,400 in Colorado, compared to a national average of about $10,000.[35]

As the state reduced its contribution to state colleges and universities by 21 percent from fiscal 2001 to fiscal 2005, it also raised four-year tuitions and fees by between 16 and 51 percent, depending on the school. Overall, the decline in resources available to public colleges and universities amounted to 21 percent from 2001 to 2005.[36]

The upshots of those cuts were obvious to anyone paying attention. Listen to Colorado University regent Michael Carrigan: "There's deteriorating facilities, skyrocketing tuition, and fleeing faculty." Dennis Jones, the president of the National Center for Higher Education Management Systems, a Boulder-based consulting group, said, "Colorado is systematically de-investing. It's showing up in class size, maintaining and recruiting faculty, and keeping up with technology. There's an awful lot of institutions out there just waiting to hire Colorado faculty." David Longanecker, the executive director of the Western Interstate Commission on Higher Education, which provides data and analysis for governors and legislators, said, "I'm often quick to say the sky is not falling. Now, I can't find the data that suggests Colorado is not in trouble. I was in Arizona recently before a state higher-education board, and they were saying, 'Life could be worse—we could be in Colorado.' "[37]

After the share of the flagship University of Colorado's funding from the state dropped to 8.7 percent—compared to 25 percent just a decade earlier—it reclassified itself as a "publicly assisted enterprise university."[38] Dropping below the 10 percent threshold legally shed the school from TABOR's revenue restrictions, but it also reflected the reality that the state had been emphatically moving in the direction of abandoning public higher education entirely. In 2004, the Republican state senator Ron Teck proposed a referendum that would do precisely that. While his idea didn't get far, some supporters of the state higher educational system thought it might serve as a useful wake-up call. Western State College president Jay Helman, who had to cut his faculty by 20 percent over two years, said, "If we are going to dismantle public higher education in Colorado, that should be a policy decision and not the unintended consequences of a constitutional logjam that's tying the hands of our legislators and our leadership in the state. Did the voters intend to strangle higher ed? If we did, let's say it and get it over with."[39]

Many debates over the future of education in the state refer to the "Colorado Paradox": the fact that more than 80 percent of high school freshmen never receive a college degree in the state with one of the highest concentrations of college-educated residents. But the explanation for that seeming contradiction is obvious. Those highly educated voters, an unusually large percentage of whom came to the state from elsewhere (including Douglas Bruce), approved an amendment in 1992 that has been directly responsible for a severe top-to-bottom deterioration in the state's entire public educational system—as well as in health care and other public services. In 2005, largely in recognition of the damage TABOR had caused, the state's voters passed Referendum C, which allows the state to spend all the revenues it collects at current tax rates for five years, even if they exceed TABOR limits. It remains to be seen whether that vote signals the beginning of the end for the conservative movement's treasured hogtie on state government. But at the very least, it demonstrates that a majority of Coloradans are willing to forgo tax refunds to stop the public sector's bleeding.

Does TABOR really protect taxpayers against any excessive levies that they can't resist for themselves at the ballot box when their governor and legislators run for reelection? Nationwide, the state and local tax burden has risen relatively modestly as a share of GDP—from 14.5 percent in 1987 to 16.1 percent in 2002, according to the Census Bureau. On a per capita basis, in 2002 dollars, that amounts to an increase of $1,371, from $4,479 to $5,850—less than $100 a year.[40] Keeping in mind that most costs that states confront have risen much faster than inflation, it seems reasonable to conclude that governors and legislators have been far from overzealous in taxing their residents. At the same time, most states have managed to sustain their services without experiencing the virtual meltdown in health, education, and other public needs that Colorado encountered. The power of the vote for representation, in and of itself, appears to be an effective check on excesses or inadequacies in either governmental spending or taxation.

Spin Zone

The conservative movement's devotion to implanting TABOR amendments in state constitutions across the land necessitates that its machine contrive an alternative portrait of the Colorado experience — one thoroughly unconnected to reality. Of course, the right's oeuvre, whether selling TABOR, the Iraq War, federal tax cuts, school vouchers, Social Security privatization, and so on, invariably draws on the same set of well-honed tools of mendacity. Perusing reports about TABOR and Colorado from conservative outposts like the Heartland Institute, the Tax Foundation, the Reason Foundation, and the Independence Institute — all of which receive funding from some combination of the Scaife, Olin, Koch, and Bradley foundations — turns up many standbys from the movement's bag of tricks:

Repeat after me: up is down, right is left. A 2005 report by Chris Atkins of the Tax Foundation makes the following claim about the Colorado experience:

> [T]he impact of the revenue decline [during the 2001 recession] was mitigated by TABOR in the good years. Where most states spent all or nearly all available revenues, Colorado had to return surplus revenues to the taxpayers. Thus, the revenue decline in Colorado did not hurt as much because the state was not allowed to spend all the money it collected during the good times. In fact, had Colorado spent all surplus revenues, the budget deficit likely would have been much worse.[41]

Actually, it's hard to imagine how Colorado's budget deficit could have been much worse than it was in the wake of the recession. In January 2003, the National Conference of State Legislatures noted that Colorado's budget shortfall had reached 13.2 percent of the state's general fund—second highest in the nation. That number was so much larger than in most other states mainly because TABOR forced the state to pay tax refunds at a time of falling revenues and greater demand for public services like Medicaid.

The claim that "surplus revenues" in excess of the TABOR threshold refunded to taxpayers in the good years somehow mitigated the pain of the fiscal crisis that began in 2001 neglects the fact that TABOR forced public services to be cut significantly, as already described, throughout the 1990s. As David Bradley of the Center on Budget and Policy Priorities responded, "The idea of TABOR reducing the 'revenue deficit' in Colorado is the equivalent of saying a worker who has taken years of wage concessions to stay in her job is much better off when her job finally disappears, because the difference between her most recent salary and no income is much smaller than between her salary in previous years and no income."[42]

Omit inconvenient facts. Atkins wrote, "TABOR did not stop Colorado from saving money in a rainy day fund. Colorado already has several reserve funds at its disposal, including a statutory reserve equal to 4 percent of appropriations, to be used in case of revenue shortfalls (though the money has to be replaced in the future)."[43] While it is true that a statute—not TABOR—requires the state to set aside a reserve of 4 percent of the General Fund for each fiscal year, that annual replenishment amount counts as spending toward the TABOR limit. So, in effect, TABOR left the state with only a relatively small rainy day fund when it entered the recession by reducing the size of the overall budget below what it otherwise would have been over the course of the 1990s. Moreover, the legislature can waive the reserve requirement during times of fiscal stress, as it did in 2002 when it decided against appropriating any reserves at all. (TABOR also requires a separate emergency reserve, but it can be used only for non-fiscal emergencies such as natural disasters.)[44]

Don't worry, be happy! Atkins again: "Colorado ranks as the 13th healthiest state in the country, according to a 2004 survey conducted by the United Health Foundation. Prenatal care was one of 18 measures used to compile the total ranking—and it was the only measure on which Colorado was cited for needing improvement. In every other area of health measured by the rankings—obesity, smoking, crime, disease, poverty, etc.—Colorado ranked in the upper or middle tier of all states."[45] But most of those measures are closely connected to a population's broad demographic and economic traits. Compared to those factors, variations in public policies among states have only a marginal impact except for indicators like prenatal care, which directly relate to state governmental efforts. More than anything, Colorado's overall healthiness is attributable to its age profile. The state ranks fourth both in having the lowest elderly population and in the highest percentage of residents aged fifteen to forty-four years.[46]

Misrepresent authoritative sources. Referring to the near doubling of low-income children without Medicaid coverage in Colorado, the Tax Foundation's analysis says,

> [S]tudies by the Centers for Medicare and Medicaid Services (CMS) and the Kaiser Commission have concluded that the rise [in the percentage of uninsured children in Colorado from the early 1990s to 2002–2003] has nothing to do with tax and spending restrictions in TABOR. CMS attributes [the increase] to the fact that employers are dropping their coverage. The Kaiser Commission says many children are uninsured simply because their parents are not aware they are eligible for Medicaid coverage.[47]

Actually, both of those reports confine their analysis to general national trends and say nothing at all about Colorado in particular—much less about TABOR. The huge increase in uninsured low-income kids in Colorado occurred over a period when the national rate actually declined. TABOR was largely responsible, in part for a reason Atkins unwittingly alludes to.[48] A Colorado Department of Health Care study found that marketing and outreach activities for the state's children's health program were stopped, due to budget problems.[49]

Keep it short and oversimplified. The Tax Foundation's study says, "Colorado teachers are not underpaid by any reasonable standard." In support of that claim, it points to three accurate facts: the state ranked twenty-second in teacher salary in 2003, salaries increased 5 percent in 2002, and the state had the highest average instructional salary of any state in the Rocky Mountain region.[50] What those numbers don't convey is that hiring and retaining good teachers in any state occurs in the context of salaries paid by private sector employers for competing jobs. Colorado's average wages are eleventh highest in the nation—significantly higher than its teacher salary ranking. Much more important, the pay ratio of average teacher salaries to private sector earnings declined in Colorado since TABOR took effect, from thirtieth in the country to dead last. That's a "reasonable standard" for arguing that teachers have become underpaid in the state, thanks to TABOR, no?[51]

When all else fails, use imagination. In February 2005, the libertarian Independence Institute and Reason Foundation issued a report called "Priority Colorado," which promised to "demonstrate potential savings that Colorado lawmakers can utilize to address the current state budget deficit, while achieving greater results for the taxpayers." The report's premise is that "experience tells us that, despite our best efforts, there will always be waste, fraud, and abuse in organizations the size of Colorado's government."[52]

The Independence Institute and Reason Foundation's report concluded that between $347.5 and $615.15 million could be saved without imposing undue cost through strategies like "asset divestiture," "consolidation," "getting back to core functions," and "competitive sourcing."[53] Without ever identifying particular examples of "waste, fraud, and abuse," the report assumes throughout that the various strategies will provide savings of between 15 and 30 percent simply by declaring as "a rule of thumb" that any public organization is too large by that range. The joint budget committee staff (representing members of both political parties) reviewed the recommendations in "Priority Colorado," desperately hoping that they might be of use during the crisis. But, alas, the JBC staff concluded that many of those ideas had already been implemented, were only one-time stop-gaps, or were the results of simply misreading the law and budget documents.[54]

One of the remarkable aspects of the conservative movement's success has been its effectiveness at imposing a blur of confusion when it identifies a threat to its agenda created by readily discernable objective reality. Studies with misleading if not outright bogus claims are cranked out whenever facts emerge that contradict their belief system.

Journalists compelled by the mores of their profession to present both sides of issues usually quote with equal weight the "experts" of the right situated in their well-financed "policy institutes" alongside others who actually understand public policy and believe in effective government. It took thirteen years for a majority of the voters of Colorado to discern through that fog that TABOR really was causing serious harm to their state. But because the stakes for the right are so high nationwide in perpetuating the myth that TABOR is working in Colorado, the passage of Referendum C is just another inconvenient development to be processed through the movement's well-oiled spin machine.

Nowhere has a conservative owned up to the most obvious point. Even if you believe the argument that legislators aren't trying hard enough to cut the fat, you still have to admit that TABOR hasn't accomplished what Douglas Bruce, Grover Norquist, and the movement's well-financed think tanks continue to promise it will do: force legislators to cut the fat. Muscle, bones, and organs, yes, but somehow not the fat.

Déjà Vu

Of course, the state that Colorado supplanted as the right's favorite is California—the home to Ronald Reagan and Howard Jarvis. When Republican Arnold Schwarzenegger decided to run for governor there in 2003, a telling frisson of excitable indecision rattled leading conservatives pining for another charismatic actor to take command of the Democratic stronghold. Rush Limbaugh's memorable initial reaction was hostile:

> Hear me now and believe me later, my friends: all these conservative orgasms over Arnold Schwarzenegger are—like the "Gorbasms" liberals experienced over Mikhail Sergeevich Gorbachev— fake. I know that "R" next to Schwarzenegger's name excites the White House, but his own words prove he's not a conservative. I call this "The Hollywood Syndrome," and it happens every time some actor-type says anything remotely conservative. I'm not trying to cold shower anybody here, but don't look to anyone in Hollywood to validate your political ideas.

But Limbaugh reversed course a few days later, saying, "We got a golden opportunity out here in California if Schwarzenegger would simply be who he is. I think Schwarzenegger is a conservative."[55]

When Schwarzenegger recruited as an adviser Warren Buffett, widely regarded as the nation's most successful investor but someone utterly lacking in movement bona fides, further vacillation ensued. After Buffett publicly suggested that Proposition 13—the 1978 property-tax limit—"makes no sense," Schwarzenegger hurriedly tried to mollify conservatives: "My position is rock solid on that initiative. . . . I told Warren that if he mentions Prop. 13 one more time he has to do 500 sit-ups."[56] The supply-sider Lawrence Kudlow, a financial columnist in right-wing journals and a talking head on CNBC, applauded Arnold's take-down of "the sage from Omaha." (By the way, ask anyone on Wall Street whether Kudlow and Schwarzenegger have any business questioning Buffett's judgment on matters related to finance.) Kudlow especially liked this statement of Schwarzenegger's expressing sympathy for Californians: "From the time they get up in the morning and flush the toilet, they are taxed. When they go out to get a coffee, they are taxed. When they get in their car, they are taxed. When they go to the gas station, they are taxed. When they go to lunch, they're taxed. This goes on all day long. Tax. Tax. Tax. Tax. Tax."[57]

That sure sounds like Grover Norquist's tune, but Grover didn't support Arnold because Arnold wouldn't endorse the "no new taxes pledge"—the one that goes, "I will not raise taxes ever. Period." Schwarzenegger said he wouldn't make the pledge because "we don't know what kind of emergencies can come up. I have already made it clear that there could be things like terrorism or there could be disasters—any one of those things where we might have to look at that option. I would not increase taxes in order to get the financial situation improved because I think that is the wrong way to go." Norquist's reply: "Failure to sign the no-new-taxes pledge is the hole in the bottom of the Arnold Schwarzenegger boat. Schwarzenegger is not Ronald Reagan. Without the pledge, he's not the anti-tax candidate."[58]

Aside from the petulance, what's sordidly amusing about all the consternation among conservatives over the man who became California's governor was their complete indifference to the severe deterioration in governmental services and fiscal health that had already occurred over the course of the generation that followed Proposition

13. Without question, the story in California is far more complicated than Colorado's for many reasons. Proposition 13 itself, which imposed a property tax limit of 1 percent of the value of each parcel until it is sold, while rolling back assessments to their 1975 level, is fundamentally different from TABOR. It was enacted largely because homeowners were rebelling against rapidly escalating property taxes due to a boom in real estate values. The sequence of subsequently approved referenda in California constraining taxes and spending interacted with Proposition 13 in convoluted ways across the state's multiple, overlapping tiers of government. Those fiscal pressures were compounded by California's much larger and more diverse population—California is home to nearly eight times as many residents as Colorado—which evolved rapidly as large numbers of immigrants from an array of homelands took residence. And the differences between the political environments in California and Colorado approximate in complexity the differences between security threats in Iraq and Colorado.

Nonetheless, the bottom-line trends in the condition of public services are much the same in the two states—and in both cases the tax-and-spending constraints approved by voters were largely responsible. For example, a meticulous, assiduously balanced 216-page analysis by the RAND Corporation about the state's public K-12 schools—widely considered to be among the nation's best in the 1970s—concludes: "We found reason to be concerned about California's K-12 public schools. . . . Overall, the comparisons [to other states] are unfavorable to California more often than not. And in many instances, the results support the impression that California's relative standing in the nation has declined over the past three decades, and especially since the finance reform legislation in the 1970s."[59] Among the categories in which California's schools have fallen from above average or average in national rankings to well below average: per pupil expenditures, share of personal income devoted to public schools, student-teacher ratios (California ranks next-to-last nationally), per-pupil school construction expenditures, and National Assessment of Educational Progress (NAEP) scores (when differences in family backgrounds are taken into account, California's scores are the lowest in the United States).[60]

Other studies have documented deterioration in the state's roads and bridges, medical facilities, police and fire departments, prisons, and so on. The state lurches annually from one budget crisis to the next, each time banking on accounting gimmicks and dubious borrowing strategies to create the illusion of balancing revenues with outlays. As the *Paradise Lost* author and *Sacramento Bee* columnist Peter Schrag wrote after such a budget deal was reached in 2005, "It's yet another exercise of borrow, defer and fudge, a hold-your-nose compromise in an unworkable political system that couldn't be better designed to defeat rational policy-making and planning and foster responsibility."[61]

In November 2005, all four referenda that Schwarzenegger endorsed were decisively defeated. Those propositions included a spending limitation that was trounced by 24 percentage points and a plan to reduce the clout of public sector unions, which lost by 7 points. The governor's own poll ratings hovered in the 35 percent range. Schwarzenegger got the message, reached out to Democrats over the following year, restored funding to ravaged public services, distanced himself from President Bush, and won reelection in a landslide in November 2006. In explaining the dramatic turnabout, Mark Z. Barabak of the *Los Angeles Times* wrote, "This year he cut bi-partisan deals to fight global warming, boost the minimum wage, and reduce the cost of prescription drugs. He also made infrastructure—arguably the most eye-glazing topic on the planet—the center of his legislative focus, underscoring his new brass-tacks approach to governance."[62] Rebuilding from conservatism in California had begun.

An "Ideological Fetish"

In contrast to Grover Norquist, the conservative columnist George F. Will did not interpret Colorado governor Bill Owens's support for Referendum C's temporary TABOR reprieve as grounds for snuffing out Owens's political future. Reminding readers of what TABOR and the governor had accomplished for the state, Will effused, "TABOR has been spectacularly successful. Per capita spending has increased more slowly than in almost all other states, and Colorado ranks 50th in state taxes collected per $1,000 of personal income. Even though—actually, because—Gov. Bill Owens has cut taxes 41 times, revenues have surged, and in six of the last nine years taxpayers have received refunds, a total of $3.2 billion, about $3,000 per household."

As for the right's reprisals against Owens for supporting Referendum C, Will concluded, "Those now calling Owens an apostate from the church of conservatism need to answer two questions. Is one deviation from doctrinal purity sufficient grounds for excommunication? Is a political creed that is so monomaniacal about taxation that it allows no latitude for tacking with shifting fiscal winds a philosophy of governance or an ideological fetish?"[63]

Ponder for a moment the self-evident contradictions between those two paragraphs. On the one hand, "TABOR has been spectacularly successful" because it enabled Owens to preside over a state that now ranks last in taxes collected. On the other hand, Will chastises some of his brethren for being "monomaniacal about taxation" and adherents to "an ideological fetish"—that is, TABOR. In his voice of reason and moderation, it sure sounds like Will inadvertently described himself as a monomaniacal fetishist.

TABOR, like Proposition 13 before it, has become the embodiment of movement conservatism at the state level. To prefer limited government, lower taxes, or minimal safety nets is no longer sufficient to be characterized as conservative by those who have been largely responsible for the political success of the right in recent years. Ask Arnold Schwarzenegger. Rather, you must take the "no new taxes" pledge. And you must support TABOR. Without ironclad spending and tax constraints embedded into state constitutions, governors and legislatures have far greater discretion to operate under the conventional norms of republican governance—accountable to the public on election day if they want to retain their jobs. To the modern conservative movement, removing the discretion to govern is precisely the goal. In Colorado, the consequences are evident—and the right couldn't be happier with what happened there.

6

Sophisticated Sabotage
"Smart" Regulation

The most contentious Senate confirmation battle during President George W. Bush's first term resulted in the approval of John Ashcroft for attorney general by a margin of 58–42; the second highest number of "no" votes was the 37 registered against John D. Graham for his appointment to the vastly more obscure position of administrator of the Office of Information and Regulatory Affairs (OIRA), which is part of the White House Office of Management and Budget. That level of opposition obviously says a lot about Graham, but it also conveys how much a job that sounds so trivial actually matters.

OIRA was created in 1980 through the Paperwork Reduction Act signed into law by President Carter, but its first administrator was appointed under President Reagan, who sought to use the office to assert White House control over the explosion in regulations that had occurred throughout the previous decade, beginning in the Nixon administration. The blossoming of the regulatory era in the 1970s was an outgrowth of a deep political reaction to the visible harms that unfettered market forces had inflicted on the environment and public health and safety. New government institutions established during that period include the Environmental Protection Agency (1970), the National Highway Traffic Safety Administration (1970), the Occupational Safety and Health Administration (1971), the Consumer Product Safety Commission (1972), the Nuclear Regulatory Commission (1975), and the Department of Energy (1977). Every president from Nixon onward tried in one way or another to rein in the independence of the regulatory agencies, and OIRA under Reagan quickly became perceived to be a bottleneck or a black hole for agency-drafted rules that now required its review.[1]

The establishment of OIRA institutionalized a basic approach to regulation that is grounded in welfare economics and utilitarianism: government should intervene in markets only when the benefits of its involvement outweigh the costs. Much of the important legislation of the early 1970s, such as the Clean Air, Water Pollution Control, and Occupational Safety and Health Acts, made little or no reference to the costs associated with new rules. They required emissions levels to be limited using the "best available technology," and employers to provide safe workplaces "to the extent feasible."[2] As the decade unfolded, a consensus began to build that effort should be exerted to assess the relative costs of various interventions to minimize the expenses involved in complying with the law. Especially in the business community and academia, the idea of comparing for alternative rules the costs versus some sort of quantification of benefits took hold.[3]

Support for cost-benefit analysis as a valuable regulatory tool generally extended across the ideological spectrum. Schools of public policy such as Harvard's Kennedy School of Government and Princeton's Woodrow Wilson School of Public Policy—liberal in the sense that their missions are committed to the idea of good government—increasingly emphasized cost-benefit analysis in their curriculums. The very complexity of the cost-benefit methodology presented those schools with an opportunity to instill in their courses a new element of rigor of the sort associated with graduate schools of law, medicine, and economics. In the process, providing their students with those economic skills helped to clarify for the outside world how the schools were adding value to society. Its graduates, many of whom were expected to become leaders in government, were armed with the technocratic instruments that would help to ensure that future laws would be fair, just, and cost-effective. Moderate scholars like Supreme Court Justice Stephen Breyer and University of Chicago law professor Cass R. Sunstein have written books enthusiastically supporting cost-benefit analysis, arguing that it provides a concrete foundation for making decisions that otherwise would be arbitrary and potentially counterproductive in advancing the broader public interest. That said, they also acknowledged some of the limitations of the cost-benefit approach and the importance of factors that can't be readily quantified.

Over the course of the 1980s and 1990s, critics of the regulatory process increasingly used cost-benefit analysis to demonstrate that the costs of certain rules exceeded their benefits and that the bang per buck spent varied wildly from regulation to regulation. The seminal report along those lines was a ten-page article published in the obscure journal *Regulation* in 1986 by an OIRA economist named John F. Morrall III that, as Morrall himself wrote seventeen years later, included a table that became "both famous and infamous."[4] Morrall's chart ranked forty-four regulatory interventions by cost per life saved and showed that they ranged from a low of $100,000 (in 1984 dollars) for a rule providing steering column protections to $72 billion (yes, with a "b"!) for a proposed regulation controlling formaldehyde. Even setting aside the rejected or proposed rules in Morrall's table, the cost per life saved of the twenty-six final regulations that actually took effect varied by a mean average of $23 million and a median of $2 million—a range so wide that, Morrall argued, government was inefficiently and ineffectively going about the job of saving lives. It should do more of what's cost effective and less of what isn't. One of his further conclusions (which he reaffirmed in his later work) was that rules narrowly targeted at specific carcinogens are least cost-effective—often doing more harm than good—relative to other regulatory categories.

Cato, Heritage, the Mercatus Center at George Mason University, and numerous other outposts funded by the Scaife, Koch, Olin, and Bradley foundations and sundry industry associations, devoted enormous resources in the 1980s and 1990s to carrying the ball that Morrall handed off to them. Although Georgetown Law professor Lisa Heinzerling raised serious questions about Morrall's methodology in a 1998 article, as did University of Connecticut law professor Richard W. Parker in 2004, progressives throughout that period were almost completely unresponsive to the right's campaign to "scientifically undermine the regulatory system."[5] Next to no countervailing resources were systematically targeted toward rebutting the conservative movement's lines of attack until the creation in 2002 of the Center for Progressive Regulation, which operates on a shoestring by comparison to the conservative outposts.

One beneficiary of the right's largesse was Morrall's future boss, John D. Graham, who built his academic career in the 1990s largely on similar kinds of studies scrutinizing regulations from the standpoint of their costs and benefits. Widely regarded as a brilliant theoretician, Graham received tenure at Harvard when he was only thirty-two and shortly thereafter, in 1990, created the Center for Risk Analysis (CRA) at the university. His interest in regulatory matters emerged during his childhood, when "business was the talk of our household," Graham told *OnEarth* magazine's Steve Weinberg for an extensive 2003 profile titled "Mr. Bottom Line."[6] Graham's father, Thomas, was a leading executive in the steel industry who complained to the *Pittsburgh Post-Gazette* in 1977 about "the enormous cost burden placed on the industry by the environmental program. . . .The American steel industry is in serious danger of being jawboned, regulated, and legislated nearly to the point of oblivion." A 1995 *New York Times* profile of Thomas Graham described him as a contentious figure with so much enthusiasm for cutting costs and slashing jobs that his nickname was "the smiling barracuda."

John Graham's familial indoctrination into the grievances of regulated industries logically led him to energetically seek their largesse in support of his Center for Risk Analysis. According to Weinberg's examination of financial records, up to 60 percent of the center's budget came from corporations, including Dow Chemical, Exxon, General Electric, Monsanto, and Union Carbide. The concerns of outsiders about the influence those funding sources might have on the purported objectivity of the center's output failed to deter Graham's fund-raising voraciousness, and over the years the center's work was subject to more than the usual degree of criticism. In 1991, for example, Graham successfully solicited $25,000 in annual funding from the Philip Morris tobacco company in a letter that mentioned the center's "major projects underway in carcinogen classification." He added, "It is important for me to learn more about the risk-related challenges that you face." Graham's ties to the tobacco industry were decisive for some of the senators who opposed his nomination. His OIRA confirmation battle also wasn't helped by a CRA study paid for by the American Farm Bureau Federation, which concluded that eliminating the most toxic pesticides could disrupt the food supply and lead to a thousand premature deaths due to malnutrition—a finding that three Consumers Union scientists assessed as "not remotely credible."[7]

In his early years running the CRA, Graham wasn't bashful about adopting a rhetorical stance that openly expressed condescension toward supporters of strong regulations. A 1990 article in the journal *Public Interest* that Graham coauthored said that there was a "hypochondria raging among various consumer advocates and public interest groups, and among policy makers in the gamut of government agencies and commissions on health and safety." Restrictions on PCBs, saccharin, and nuclear power, Graham wrote, were outgrowths of that "flustered hypochondria."[8] But recognizing that stylistic stridency undercut his credibility as merely a number-cruncher who was following where the facts pointed, Graham's tone softened considerably over the course of the 1990s. Participating in a Heritage Foundation panel in 1996 at which other conservative speakers talked about the need for "regulatory relief," Graham counseled for a savvier rhetorical tack: "I think our message should be that we want smarter, more efficient regulation in order to get more protection at less cost. Therefore, the word 'relief' is entirely inappropriate."[9] Note the use of the pronoun *our* and the ingenious co-opting of a term—*smart regulation*—that President Clinton had adopted for an approach that would actually enforce laws in cost-effective ways. Consistent with that political acuity, Graham is often described as "charming" and "treats his critics with unflappable respect," according to Weinberg.

While at Harvard, Graham coined the phrase "statistical murder" to convey what he thought was wrong with the regulatory system. In a report for the National Center for Policy Analysis, a think tank supported by the Scaife, Koch, Olin, and Bradley foundations, Graham wrote:

> Spending $100 million per year on control of routine low-level releases of radiation from nuclear power plants might save one life-year each year [a life-year is a statistical measure of how much a lifesaving program increases the lifespan of a target population]. But the same amount of investment in cervical cancer screening and treatment is expected to save 2,000 life-years every year. . . . This perverse pattern of investment amounts to "statistical murder" of American citizens.[10]

The Lopsided Power Struggle

Just as hopeless bureaucrats are the central characters in the conservative narrative of how government works, the right's plotline owes everything to Franz Kafka. "The Regulatory State," as it is called, is a world in which average citizens are relentlessly subjected to oppressive constraints on their liberty, often involving absurd micromanagement of their everyday lives. Inexplicable, sometimes contradictory, rules govern every aspect of behavior, imposing on American families tedious reams of paperwork and onerous costs on their household budgets. The title of a report produced annually by the Cato Institute succinctly captures the right's portrayal: "Ten Thousand Commandments."

The Mercatus Center at George Mason University, which evolved from a think tank launched by the former head of the libertarian Koch Family Foundations, produced a "Primer on Regulation" in November 2005 that provides a tour of this world.[11] Written by Susan E. Dudley, the director of Mercatus's Regulatory Studies Program whom Bush would later nominate to succeed Graham, the report unfolds along these lines:

> From the moment you wake up until the time you go to sleep, regulations influence what you do. . . . Your day starts when your clock radio goes off in the morning. The Federal Communications Commission regulates not only the airwaves used by your favorite radio station, but also the content of the programming. Electricity provided by a utility that is most likely regulated by the Federal Energy Regulatory Commission and by state regulatory agencies powers the radio. The Consumer Product Safety Commission regulates the label on your mattress. The price of your cotton sheets is higher than it otherwise would be due to the U.S. Department of Agriculture's subsidy and price support programs for U.S. cotton producers, as well as quotas and tariffs for imported goods.
>
> The Food and Drug Administration regulates the content of your toothpaste, soap, shampoo, and other grooming products. The Environmental Protection Agency regulates the quality of the water coming out of your showerhead. Complying with EPA water quality standards can cost households over $300 per year, but you won't see this separate item on your water bill. . . . On your way out of the bathroom, you may have to flush your low-flow toilet twice, a result of mandates imposed by the Department of Energy's appliance efficiency rules. As you prepare your morning breakfast, you will check your FDA regulated labels for nutritional information. The FDA also regulates information about the health bene-

fits of foods so juice labels may not tell you about the latest research that links certain ingredients to the prevention or mitigation of certain diseases.

The primer continues on in this vein through a miserable day of commuting under the crushing weight of mandatory airbag requirements and working at a job in which "one-size-fits-all" employee benefit standards "prevent you from negotiating benefit packages that best suit employee needs, so you are unwittingly forced to accept lower wages in exchange for benefits you may not want."

If Mercatus's story sounds considerably less harrowing to you than Josef K.'s trial—the average American who is not self-employed or running a small business actually doesn't encounter much federal red tape—the right's more effective approach in conveying the evils of the regulatory state has been to tell anecdotes that do indeed boggle the mind. The signature work in that oeuvre is the lawyer Philip K. Howard's 1994 book *The Death of Common Sense: How Law Is Suffocating America*.[12] Howard describes, for example, how Mother Teresa gave up trying to build a homeless shelter in New York City because local codes required the installation of a costly and unneeded elevator in renovated multistory buildings. Other maddening tales in his book include an elementary school in a suburb of New York City that was required to remove children's art deemed to be a fire hazard from its walls; a Yorktown, Virginia, oil refinery whose legally mandated filters did little to prevent the actual source of the pollutants it continued to emit; and an Occupational Safety and Health Administration regulation that described sand as a "toxic substance." The libertarian ABC news correspondent John Stossel, the author most recently of *Myths, Lies, and Downright Stupidity: Get Out the Shovel—Why Everything You Know Is Wrong*, has pretty much made his TV career out of fomenting public fury over similar bureaucratic outrages.

Such stories have served the right well in stoking public animosity toward government while keeping supporters of environmental and safety regulations tongue-tied in the face of particular embarrassments that no one of sound mind can defend—although almost invariably the tales turn out to range from apocryphal to misleading.[13] But when it comes to debating how the U.S. regulatory system *ought* to work, not even the most vitriolic libertarian is so naive as to imagine that regulations will magically vanish. Philip K. Howard himself, who is actually a Democrat, notwithstanding the prominence of his book on conservative reading lists and its model for right-wing sequels, argues for allowing greater discretion on the part of civil servants in implementing regulations—letting them apply their own common sense. But that idea is obviously a nonstarter for the bureaucrat loathers on the right and an unwise proposal generally, given the abundant resources available to regulated companies to surreptitiously influence the judgments of particular officials.[14]

The real debates over regulatory policy boil down to a power struggle between the industries subject to government rules—represented by the conservative movement—and generally poorly funded groups supporting the broader public interest that prompted the legislation giving rise to regulations. Unfortunately, the ways in which those debates play out are genuinely Kafkaesque. Regulatory questions invariably focus on highly technical and obscure matters far beyond the comprehension, much less the interest level, of average citizens. Costs of alternative rules are compared to estimated benefits based on impenetrable calculations. Dollar values are assigned to the worth of a life—varying by several million bucks, depending on the agency—discounted at different interest rates on the not-crazy presumption that someone's death twenty years from now is less costly than a more immediate demise. Because such computations are so mind-bending from a moral as well as an economic standpoint, journalists rarely pay attention to regulatory issues—even when the stakes are high—unless something peculiar has happened, such as an injustice spotlighted on a Stossel segment. Or after people die, as in the cases of the Sago mine disaster or the outbreak of E. coli from tainted spinach. Beyond the minutiae of the myriad particular cases, even the debate over the broader framework for considering how to decide regulatory questions is complex and esoteric. In contrast to, say, abortion, most people don't have deeply held convictions about the uses of cost-benefit analysis.

But the battles over regulation are hugely important. Much of what the federal government does relates to developing and enforcing rules that implement legislative statutes. More than sixty agencies are involved in regulatory policy, collectively enforcing more than 144,000 pages of rules. According to the Office of Management and Budget, regulations adopted from 1993 to 2003 entailed costs between $34 and $38 billion annually, while all federal regulations combined amount to about ten times as much.[15] The lion's share of those regulations are intended to enforce missions supported by the vast majority of the public: environmental protections, workplace safety, fair investment markets, safe and effective drugs, untainted food, antitrust, low-risk transportation, and so on. In every last one of those realms, the record of progress in the United States attributable to regulations and their enforcement has been remarkable, notwithstanding the occasional failures, undeniable rigidities, extensive paperwork, and substantial financial costs that raise the right's hackles.

Because the overarching goals of regulatory systems are popular, and because overt efforts to undercut the progress they have achieved would be political suicide, the conservative movement has advanced its antiregulatory goals through a subtle collection of strategies that the authors Thomas O. McGarity, Sidney Shapiro, and David Bollier deconstruct in their book *Sophisticated Sabotage: The Intellectual Games Used to Subvert Responsible Regulation*. As they describe it:

> Responsible regulation necessarily requires a lot of technical expertise and analysis. This provides a crucial opening for the sophisticated saboteur intent on intellectual mischief. For example, by generating a large amount of quantitative data and analysis—material that is impenetrable to the layperson and too boring for the mainstream press to investigate—the sophisticated saboteur can "monkey-wrench" the regulatory process by requiring gratuitous mandatory studies. The predictable result: new procedures, research, and court challenges that delay government action for years, saving the relevant industry millions of dollars.
>
> The saboteur has a larger ambition, however: to commandeer regulatory debate and change the normative metrics for decision-making. This is especially strategic. Rather than having to fight one regulatory proposal after another, opponents can secure a more enduring polemical advantage (and favorable political outcomes) by changing the accepted categories for carrying on regulatory discussion.[16]

So here again, movement conservatives have redefined the public policy problem in a way that suits their broader purposes. The problem, they have largely convinced the public, is too much wasteful regulation that inefficiently drags down the economy and costs jobs. The answer is "smart" regulation, which ultimately amounts to advancements in the right-wing funders' mission of rolling back government, whatever the consequences.

A Moral Judgment in Statistical Disguise

Graham's argument that it would be more efficient for government to eliminate wasteful regulations while allocating greater resources toward more of the kinds of rules that have proved to be cost-effective is logical as an academic theory. It also has many adherents who are held in high esteem in the academy, including Robert Crandall of the Brookings Institution, the Harvard law professor W. Kip Viscusi, Breyer, Sunstein, and numerous mainstream economics and law professors. But the "statistical murder" argument has serious vulnerabilities beyond just implying slanderously that mindless regulators are implicitly killing people.

For one thing, costs of regulations are far easier to quantify than benefits are. Companies facing regulation are only too happy to provide extensive details about what they claim will be the impact on their cost structure of alternative new rules. Those numbers, in turn, can be readily punched into economic models that calculate what the ripple effects will be in terms of lost wages, price increases, reduced economic output, decreased tax revenue, and so forth—all of which are inherently defined in dollar terms. Those figures may ultimately turn out to be artificially inflated, but regulators tend to be deferential to the companies supplying them as long as there's some reasonable justification given. History has shown, though, that regulations can induce companies to innovate in ways that significantly reduce originally anticipated costs while yielding new technological advancements with broad economic benefits.[17]

Tabulating the benefits of any given regulation is a far squishier enterprise. By their very nature, regulations are intended to prevent harms that don't have a price tag on them. But cost-benefit analysis doesn't take you very far unless you can compare dollars to dollars. So, for one thing, a human life is assigned with a value so that the benefit of saving one can be computed. The number chosen matters a lot. For example, in the Environmental Protection Agency's analysis of the proposed rules for the Clear Skies initiative, it originally valued a life at $6 million, based on studies of wages for high-risk jobs and surveys asking people what they think a life is worth. In 2003, Graham's OIRA asked the EPA to slash that figure to $3.7 million—based on surveys alone—and reduce it by another 27 percent for people over seventy, based on a twenty-year-old British survey that found that older people valued their lives less than younger people did.[18]

Regulatory benefits also extend far beyond saving lives, in ways that are even more difficult—and sometimes impossible—to quantify. Yet many cost-benefit studies, including much of Graham's work, either ignore those qualitative benefits, give them short shrift, or approach them in ways designed to minimize their dollar value. For example, the public strongly supports laws discouraging pollution of the air, the water, and the soil not just because environmental degradation could kill them. The additional benefits of such regulation include avoidance of possible illness that may or may not be life-threatening, advancement of widely held values that respect and appreciate nature, reductions in unsightly and smelly smog and water pollution that many Americans viscerally abhor, encouragement of technological antipollution and medical advances that in themselves provide lasting economic payoffs, minimizing of potentially deleterious effects on the ecosystem, and reinforcing of public support for democracy by demonstrating the effectiveness of government in carrying out the public will.

Cost-benefit analysts sometimes try to come up with dollar figures for some of those benefits based mainly on surveys asking how much people would be willing to pay for various environmental improvements, as well as on data about the connection between different kinds of pollution, various illnesses, and the costs of medical treatment. But even most enthusiasts of cost-benefit analysis concede that such estimates are highly unreliable. The more general problem is that economics of this sort is ill-equipped to recognize what are essentially moral judgments expressed through the political process. Since hazardous waste sites most commonly arise near low-income populations, valuing in dollar terms what individual citizens would be "willing to pay" to clean them up doesn't adequately weigh the public consensus expressed through environmental legislation that such dumping grounds are morally unacceptable.

Compounding those enormous difficulties in calculating the potential benefits of regulations are uncertain relationships between cause and effect. In the EPA's highly controversial efforts to assess the costs and benefits of regulating arsenic in drinking water, for example, it estimated based on several imperfect studies that twenty-eight lung and bladder cancers a year could be prevented but declined to estimate the number of other kinds of cancers that could be avoided because doing so would be an "entirely speculative exercise"—even though the agency said it was confident that other cancers would be reduced. It also concluded that arsenic in drinking water was associated with noncancer ailments such as hypertension and diabetes, as well as adverse reproductive effects, but again did not quantify those outcomes because of inadequately reliable data. It noted, however, "If the Agency were able to quantify additional arsenic-related health effects and non-health effects, the quantified benefits estimates may be significantly higher than the estimates presented in this analysis."[19] Still, even the moderate Justice Stephen Breyer has argued that government cost-benefit analysts in the past have "erred on the side of safety."[20] But the arsenic case—and it is typical—demonstrates that the default position of cost-benefit analysis is to simply punt when it has insufficient research. That's entirely legitimate since there really is no other technical option, but it is by no means erring on the side of public protection.

Some liberals have argued that the shortcomings of cost-benefit analysis are so fundamental that the whole approach should either be scrapped entirely or relegated to a much less significant role. Unfortunately, the alternative frameworks that have been proposed for guiding how regulations ought to be implemented have their own shortcomings—though a few can constructively supplement cost-benefit analysis.

The fundamental problem is that all of the malleability inherent in cost-benefit analysis leaves it open to manipulation—particularly in the hands of extremely smart individuals who are predisposed to favor regulated companies, since costs are so much easier to count than benefits. Because the process is so complex, oversight from media and congressional watchdogs is even less likely than in other realms to deter abuses. Giving someone like John Graham so much power was especially dangerous, because his argument against "statistical murder" is deeply undemocratic. Congress enacted statutes aimed at limiting the exposure of the public to carcinogens because the public doesn't like the idea of being exposed to carcinogens. Experts might be correct that the risks posed by such exposures are much smaller than people think. But beyond doing whatever they can to educate people, and determining the most cost-effective ways to achieve mandated goals, eggheads in government are responsible for carrying out the laws of the land, rather than unilaterally deciding that the public is too stupid to decide what's good for it. Or determining on their own that the government should implement only rules costing less than what surveys show people would be "willing to pay" to experience sundry abstract benefits.

Graham is undoubtedly right that more cervical screening would be a highly efficient way to save lives. But his using that fact as a rationale to impede regulations like those intended to prevent radiation leaks from power plants isn't going to do anything to get one more woman to the gynecologist. Different laws were enacted to prevent different kinds of harms to the public. In a democracy, it really isn't up to a lone political appointee to decide which of those laws will be carried out and which won't. But that is the result that conservative ideology produced, along with untold damage to the environment and public health.

Smart Regulation in Action

In May 2000, after years of receiving complaints about tread separation in two models of Bridgestone/Firestone tires installed on Ford Explorers, the National Highway Traffic Safety Administration (NHTSA) opened a defect investigation into the matter. The problem appeared to be the cause of a number of car accidents, including some that resulted in fatalities. Lawsuits over defective tires had generally had mixed results, however, often because tire manufacturers successfully claimed that the car owners were responsible for failing to ensure that their tires were adequately inflated. That summer, in the face of the government's investigation, Bridgestone/Firestone and Ford recalled more than 14 million tires—a public relations disaster for the two companies. Congress responded to the outcry by enacting the

Transportation Recall Enhancement, Accountability and Documentation Act (called—what else?—the "TREAD Act") on November 1 of that year. The act imposed new defect-reporting requirements, enforcement measures, and this provision: "Not later than 1 year after the date of enactment of this Act [i.e., not later than November 1, 2001], the Secretary of Transportation shall complete a rulemaking for a regulation to require a warning system in new motor vehicles to indicate to the operator when a tire is significantly under-inflated. Such requirement shall become effective not later than 2 years after the date of completion of such rulemaking."

NHTSA proceeded to develop its proposed regulations for tire pressure–monitoring devices, drawing on its own research, as well as on data from other sources. It found in the process that underinflated tires are a significant, widespread problem. For example, it measured the air pressure of tires on about ten thousand passenger cars and light trucks and compared those levels to the vehicle manufacturer's recommendations and found that more than a third of the sample had underinflated tires. A separate survey determined that more than 70 percent of drivers check their tire pressure levels less than once per month.

As for the technology available to monitor tire pressure, NHTSA learned that there were two options: "direct" and "indirect" systems. Direct systems use pressure sensors located within each wheel. If the air pressure in any one of the tires falls below 20 percent, the direct monitor can alert the driver while specifying which particular tire, or tires, is underinflated.

Indirect systems are cheaper to install but also much less effective. They work only on vehicles equipped with antilock braking systems—which are more expensive to consumers and generally more profitable to auto manufacturers—and use wheel speed sensors to detect whether declining tire pressure is causing the rotational speed of the wheel to increase due to a reduction in the rolling radius. They operate by comparing the sums of the wheel speeds in diagonally opposed tires, so they can't detect underinflation when it occurs roughly equally in all four tires, two tires on the same side, or two tires on the same axle. All of those circumstances are common—occurring in about half the instances where at least one tire is underinflated. Moreover, indirect systems only detect underinflation levels of 30 percent or more, and they can also set off false alarms.

The proposed rules that NHTSA initially published included a summary of its cost-benefit analysis for two standards, both of which could be met by direct monitoring systems and neither of which could be fulfilled by indirect systems. Under the stricter of the two standards, 79 deaths per year would be prevented (counting only fatalities attributable to reductions in stopping distances but not crashes caused by blowouts or loss of control). That standard would also mitigate or prevent 10,635 injuries annually. The average net cost of that rule per vehicle would be $23.08, for a total net cost per year of $369 million. The all-important bottom line of net cost per "equivalent" life saved— a measure that weighs some unspecified number of injuries prevented as amounting to a life saved—came to $1.9 million. Car buyers don't haggle over an extra $23 for even the most trivial option, but, as we will see, the auto industry will fight like hell to avoid that burden even if it would prevent dozens of deaths and thousands of injuries.

After the comment period, NHTSA ended up putting forward a softened rule that required new vehicles to comply after a phase-in period with either of two standards, one of which temporarily allowed for indirect monitors. Following an additional phase-in period, the direct-system standard would be mandatory for all new vehicles.

Enter John Graham, whose agency responded with a "return letter" urging reconsideration. In that letter, OIRA argued that NHTSA should base its final rule on "overall vehicle safety" rather than limiting itself to "tire safety" concerns. The letter predicted that if NHTSA instead adopted the more relaxed standard allowing for indirect monitors as the ultimate, long-term requirement, automakers would have an additional incentive to install antilock brake systems—accelerating their adoption in new vehicles. OIRA claimed that "both experimental evidence and recent real-world data have indicated a modest net safety benefit from antilock brakes."

Notably, OIRA's arguments closely tracked those that had been submitted earlier to NHTSA by the Alliance of Auto Manufacturers, which includes DaimlerChrysler, Ford, the BMW Group, Fiat, Ford, General Motors, Isuzu, Mazda, Mitsubishi Motors, Nissan, Porsche, Toyota, Volkswagen, and Volvo. That was no accident. The public interest advocacy group Public Citizen found that OIRA's docket showed that Graham met on October 26, 2001, about tire pressure–monitoring systems with three representatives of the Alliance of Auto

Manufacturers, as well as with lobbyists for Toyota, Ford, Daimler-Chrysler, and Volkswagen of America.[21] That meeting was just before NHTSA submitted its revised rules in December and OIRA responded with its return letter in February.

In June 2002, NHTSA published its final rule, which responded to OIRA's letter by leaving in place the two standards but without any specification about what the long-term requirement would be—postponing that decision to March 1, 2005. NHTSA pointed out, though, that research about the effectiveness of antilock brakes in preventing fatalities was far from conclusive. Watering down the rule in response to OIRA's letter in essence freed auto manufacturers from any obligation to install direct monitoring systems—the only effective technology available. From a practical standpoint, the delay also meant that the first car model year when there might be any requirement to use direct systems would be 2006, and more likely later (if ever), given the way phase-ins typically work.

Three nonprofit advocacy organizations—Public Citizen, New York Public Interest Research Group, and the Center for Auto Safety—brought a lawsuit challenging the final rules as contrary to the intent of Congress when it enacted the TREAD Act. In August 2003, the U.S. Court of Appeals for the Second Circuit agreed in a caustic decision that all but ridiculed OIRA for its arbitrariness and capriciousness.[22] Referring to the inability of indirect monitoring systems to alert drivers who simultaneously have more than one underinflated tire, Judge Robert D. Sack wrote:

> Section 13 [of the TREAD Act] requires warning systems that indicate "when *a* tire is significantly underinflated." The TREAD Act's "*a* tire plainly means one tire, two tires, three tires, or all four tires, under the elementary rule of statutory construction that the singular ("a tire") includes the plural (more than one tire). . . . Obviously, if a vehicle has two tires that are significantly underinflated, then it has "a" tire that is significantly underinflated—indeed it has two instances of "a tire" that is significantly underinflated.

The judge ordered NHTSA to go back and come up with new rules that conform to the law. But it wasn't until April 2005—nearly five years after the TREAD Act's passage—when NHTSA ultimately finalized a rule requiring compliance with the stricter direct system standard. If nothing else, Graham had succeeded in buying the auto-makers valuable time. The monitors would not be required on all new cars and trucks until the 2008 model year, beginning with a phase-in with 2006 model vehicles. According to NHTSA's own research, the delay engineered by Graham in effect will have resulted in the loss of many dozens of lives and injuries numbering in the tens of thousands.

That's the sort of work that has made John Graham a hero to the conservative movement.

When the Fox Guards the Henhouse

The most important cluster of "reforms" that OIRA carried out under Graham were in connection with the implementation of the Data Quality Act of 2000. As the Clinton administration was winding down in 2000, Congress enacted a huge appropriations bill that included a short two-sentence rider inserted at the last minute, without debate or hearings, by Representative Jo Ann Emerson (R-Mo.) and Senator John Shelby (R-Ala.) at the behest of the Center for Regulatory Effec-tiveness—a lobbying outpost for regulated industries.[23] The Data Quality Act (sometimes referred to as the Information Quality Act) directed OMB to develop "rules providing policy and procedural guid-ance to Federal agencies for ensuring and maximizing the quality, objectivity, utility, and integrity of information (including statistical information) disseminated by Federal agencies, and information dis-seminated by non-Federal entities with financial support from the Federal government."

Graham seized on the opportunity and proposed through OMB a mind-bogglingly cumbersome set of new guidelines that enable regu-lated companies to challenge any data disseminated by agencies throughout every stage of their rule-making processes—not just after proposed regulations are published. His rules also required the agen-cies to respond to those outside challenges along the way and for OMB to become involved in disagreements, threatening to further bog down the already painfully slow regulatory process. Moreover, outside "peer review" would be required of "highly influential scien-tific assessments"—those that could lead to rules having a financial impact of more than $500 million a year—or if "the dissemination is novel, controversial, or precedent-setting, or has significant interagency interest." In other words, whenever OMB chooses to impose peer review. It remains unclear whether the courts will consider disputes arising over data quality to be judicially reviewable—so far, they haven't—but, if so, that could add an additional chilling effect on the regulatory process.[24] William Kovacs of the U.S. Chamber of Commerce told the *New York Times* about the act and OMB's implementation of it, "This is the biggest sleeper there is in the regulatory arena and will have an impact so far beyond anything people can imagine."[25]

In a 2004 analysis of data quality challenges submitted during the first year that the act was in effect, the advocacy and research organization OMB Watch found that 72 percent of the 185 requests came from regulated industries. Examples include a Chemical Products Corporation challenge to an EPA risk assessment of barium, seeking a higher threshold for the chemical in waste products, and a complaint by the Animal Health Institute (which represents manufacturers of animal drugs and biological products) questioning data about the potential dangers of using a particular antibiotic in poultry.[26]

Graham, in describing his own legacy, depicts himself as a hero not to industry but to good regulations. So, for example, he talks about the prompt letter he sent to the FDA encouraging it to expedite its labeling requirements for trans fats in foods. But in the small number of such cases where he seemed to lean toward the public's interest, the costs to the industries involved relative to what they were likely to have to spend anyway absent his intervention are negligible or close to it. Graham also likes to talk about how he made OIRA actions more transparent to the public, particularly by making information available on the Internet.[27] While that is true, and to his credit, the fact remains that the very complexity of the regulatory world inherently makes it anything but transparent—no matter how much information is visible for public review.

For liberal believers in cost-benefit analysis, Graham's tenure should be a wake-up call. Economic and scientific tools employed by genuinely impartial experts without question can be enormously useful, even indispensable, to the process of devising reasonable, cost-effective regulations. But in the hands of unchecked ideologues—especially those adept at disguising their antiregulatory agenda with slick public-relations tactics—those same tools can become pernicious instruments for eviscerating democracy. That is exactly what happened under John Graham and a conservative Republican Congress that demonstrated no interest in impeding the antiregulatory agenda. Unfortunately, simple adjustments to the tools themselves cannot fix what has gone wrong with the regulatory system. The only hope is a political solution, one that puts in place elected congressional overseers and regulators determined to tug the balance of power back from regulated industries and movement conservatives toward the general public interest. John Graham's enormous success in implementing conservative ideology, abetted by the Republican Congress, severely undermined the government's legal obligations to protect public health and safety. It remains to be seen whether the Democratic takeover of Congress in the wake of the November 2006 elections will significantly undo the damage.

Passive Aggression

While Graham's office served as the central locus for sabotaging public protections throughout the federal government, the Bush administration's departments and agencies themselves pitched in to further promote the conservative antiregulatory agenda. But in contrast to Graham's forceful initiatives, their efforts relied on passivity. Simply by withdrawing proposed regulations and dallying over others, curtailing enforcement of existing rules, and allowing industries to stop providing data essential to evaluating their impact on public health and safety, those agencies subtly but surely advanced the assault against safeguards.

Twice a year, agencies are obligated to declare their regulatory priorities, list timetables for accomplishing their plans, and announce the status of items from previously published agendas. OMB Watch combed through those reports for the Bush presidency through June 2004 and found that up to that point, work was simply abandoned on dozens of important regulations that previous administrations (including Bush I and Reagan) had identified as priorities. For example, the EPA withdrew ninety agenda items, most of which would have addressed Clean Air Act and Clean Water Act priorities; the FDA dropped sixty-two initiatives, including a proposed tracking system for notifying patients who received contaminated blood in the event of recalls; OSHA withdrew twenty-four, including a proposal that was on the verge of completion to protect workers from tuberculosis; and NHTSA abandoned a total of thirty-one. The agencies had explained those decisions by claiming that they wanted to refocus their energies on their own priorities. But the June 2004 progress reports showed that each one of those four agencies had failed to achieve 70 percent or more of its own benchmarks for the preceding six months.[28]

Relative to the recent past, the drop-off in productivity is stark. In the administration of George H. W. Bush, seventy-four "economically significant" rules were approved by those four agencies. The comparable numbers were fifty-five for the first Clinton term and fifty-one for the second. In George W. Bush's first term, just twenty-five significant rules emerged from those agencies. In the EPA alone, the major regulatory output dropped from forty in the first Clinton term to eleven under Bush.[29]

The downshift in drafting new rules coincided with a new approach to enforcing existing regulations that might be described as "not-so-tough love." Regulations, just like the laws we count on the police and the justice system to uphold, deter transgressions only if enforcement mechanisms are robust. If corporations are confident that they can safely violate rules without a significant chance of facing punishment, their bottom-line incentives will induce them to try to get away with their own form of statistical murder. Unsurprisingly, there's plenty of evidence that various Bush administration agencies have given short shrift to regulatory enforcement.

The EPA provides the clearest example of reduced policing, with a number of different studies that find compelling signs of Bush administration passivity. A report by the Environmental Integrity Project, a research and advocacy organization, found a 75 percent decline in lawsuits filed against polluters—from 152 down to 36—comparing the last three years of Clinton's presidency to the first three of Bush's. Lawsuits against energy companies, which are typically the biggest of all polluters, dropped a full 90 percent, from 28 under Clinton to 3 under Bush.[30] Similarly, an investigation by the *Philadelphia Inquirer* found that the monthly average of violation notices against polluters— widely considered to be the most effective enforcement tool—plummeted by 58 percent under Bush compared to the Clinton administration.[31] In fiscal 2004, the EPA's criminal enforcement program collected fines amounting to $47 million after falling relatively steadily from the $122 million it imposed in 2000.[32]

EPA administrator Michael Leavitt responded to the *Inquirer's* findings with language straight out of Graham's rhetorical script: "The agency has what we refer to as smart enforcement. Our focus is on enforcement that changes behavior in a positive way. The point of smart enforcement is that you use the best tool for each individual situation; compliance is the goal." J. P. Suarez, the EPA's enforcement chief, added that "Our upcoming numbers show that our pollution reductions are through the roof, the highest they've ever been, in almost every category," referring to quantities of treated contaminated soil and tainted water.

But the *Sacramento Bee* found good reason to question the reliability of the EPA's enforcement data. Its investigation uncovered that the agency had overstated its success in fighting polluters by lumping counterterrorism and narcotics cases led by other agencies into its environmental enforcement record. On April 26, 2003, Suarez issued a press release that said, "In fact, EPA's enforcement numbers in several categories are at an all-time high. The 674 enforcement cases initiated in 2002 was the highest ever." But as the *Bee* ferreted out, 190 of those cases were counterterrorism efforts not necessarily related to suspected crimes, let alone to pollution violations. Minus those cases, the tally drops to 484, which is historically typical. The paper went on to find that even that number and other enforcement statistics were inflated by changes in how the EPA accounted for what constitutes a case and a referral.[33] Similarly, the Transactional Records Access Clearinghouse at Syracuse University, an institution that gathers all kinds of unpublicized government data, issued a series of reports questioning the accuracy of the EPA's claims about its enforcement record. Those studies found that criminal charges for environmental violations dropped by about 30 percent under Bush compared to the second Clinton term, with even larger reductions in criminal filings under the federal hazardous waste management law, the Air Pollution Prevention and Control Act, and water pollution limitations.[34] Moreover, the EPA's own inspector general reported that the Bush administration's regulatory changes to the Clean Air Act's "new source review" program have "seriously hampered" enforcement efforts against power plants.[35]

There are indications that the not-so-tough-love enforcement approach may already be leading to deteriorations in environmental conditions. For example, an October 2004 Knight Ridder analysis found that over the course of the Bush administration, fish-consumption warnings for rivers doubled, fish-consumption advisories for lakes increased by 39 percent, beach closings rose by 26 percent, and Superfund cleanups of toxic waste declined by 52 percent.[36] Of the fourteen indicators reviewed, the only area of significant improvement was a decline of 9 percent in major air emissions from smokestacks and tailpipes—realms in which active regulatory enforcement is less essential because the long-established environmental rules that have produced such progress are structured in ways that require less energetic governmental policing.

Under the Bush administration, which arguably advanced the conservative cause further on the regulatory front than any other, the rule-making process has devolved into an exercise in perpetual procrastination. Acts of Congress are invitations to seek ingeniously complex rationales to avoid acting. The guiding philosophy for regulatory enforcement is that rules are made to be broken. It is a world where it is "smarter" and "more efficient" to prevent "statistical murder" by requiring the installation of tire pressure gauges that don't work half the time instead of the ones that almost always work. The language spoken is misinformation and doubletalk. And it all arose not from Kafka's imagination but from the conservative movement.

PART III

Ideas for Replacing Government "Monopolies" with Market Competition

7

"It Hasn't Worked Like We Thought It Would in Theory"

Marketizing the Schools

Since the mid-1950s, the libertarian Nobel Prize–winning economist Milton Friedman argued that public school systems should be replaced by government-financed vouchers that parents could use to pay for tuition at private schools, including those affiliated with religious institutions. His central claim: "Producers of educational services would compete to attract students. Parents, empowered by the voucher, would have a wide range to choose from. As in other industries, such a competitive free market would lead to improvements in quality and reductions in cost."[1]

Milwaukee might seem like an unlikely venue for the most complete manifestation in this country to date of Friedman's brainchild. How could such a direct challenge to public education take root in Wisconsin, the home to the progressive movement pioneer Robert LaFollette, countless reformers who followed in his footsteps, and residents with a long-standing commitment to robust government? In recent years, the state's experimental streak has shifted to more conservative causes, particularly under the leadership of Republican governor Tommy G. Thompson from 1987 to 2001. Thompson, who became most famous for state welfare reform experiments that helped to lead to the 1996 federal overhaul, initiated the push for school vouchers in

Milwaukee, drawing from Friedman's script when he argued at a 1989 White House policy conference, "Competition breeds accountability. Under the concept of parental choice, schools would be held accountable for their students' performance. Schools providing a high-quality education would flourish. Schools failing to meet the needs of their students would not be able to compete and, in effect, would go out of business."[2]

Milwaukee also happens to be home to the Lynde and Harry Bradley Foundation, which is deeply invested in the voucher idea and is one of the conservative movement's now familiar "big five" philanthropies. Led by the late libertarian firebrand Michael Joyce, who often said, "I don't think public funds should be used to support public schools at all," the Bradley Foundation in a variety of ways helped to launch, sustain, and stimulate the expansion of Milwaukee's voucher system in the late 1980s and 1990s.[3]

The centerpiece of Joyce's strategy at the outset was to create a think tank called the Wisconsin Policy Research Institute in 1987, which over the years issued report after report criticizing the public school system. From its inception through 1995, Bradley invested $4.4 million in the institute, whose staff regularly advocated on behalf of vouchers in the media while condemning the condition of the public schools.[4] John Witte, a political scientist at the University of Wisconsin who was assigned by the state to analyze testing results under the first years of the voucher program, said that WPRI's reports "were the kind where they clearly started with the headline and worked their way backwards. They were basically garbage." Nonetheless, released on weekends when news was slow, they often ended up on the front pages of local papers.[5]

Voucher Fever

The appetite for an idea as radical as vouchers in Milwaukee and other urban school districts arose from a grim reality that continues to this day: public school systems in U.S. cities are deeply troubled, without exception. Nationwide, although there are plenty of successful public schools situated in cities, there are no high-poverty school districts that perform at satisfactory levels. *Education Week*, in collaboration with the Pew Charitable Trusts, sought to identify a "solidly successful urban district, in which even extremely poor and minority children achieve at high levels," but concluded that "there are none."[6]

The conservative movement as a matter of practice misleadingly conflates the failures of city school districts with the condition of U.S. public education generally. Still, even some liberals and moderates have expressed a willingness to experiment with vouchers in cities simply because the down sides couldn't be much worse than the status quo. In 1990, the same year that Milwaukee launched its experiment, the Brookings Institution—commonly, if not always aptly, modified by the adjective "liberal"—published a book by two of its fellows, John E. Chubb and Terry M. Moe, that gave an enormous boost to the voucher movement. Titled *Politics, Markets and America's Schools*, Chubb and Moe argued that public schools are inherently doomed to fail because democratic, majoritarian institutions are irretrievably linked to bureaucracy and hierarchy, which bind schools in ways that keep them from achieving educational quality.[7]

Chubb and Moe's book, which received financial support from both the Bradley and the Olin foundations, went beyond Milton Friedman's theorizing in ways that added gravitas to the voucher idea. As the political scientist Jeffrey Henig has pointed out, Chubb and Moe's analysis gained enormous attention not only because they were legitimate academics housed at a respected, nonideological think tank, but also because they were the first voucher advocates to (1) link their proposal to a broad theory of politics and democracy that was compatible with the public-choice scholarship discussed in chapter 1; (2) anchor their plan in the existing empirical literature and their own original research; and (3) take pains to spell out a model in detail, rather than proposing a broadly worded call for greater choice.[8] In contrast to traditional school reformers who, humbled by experience, believed that there were no panaceas to fix urban schools, Chubb and Moe claimed that their voucher proposal would indeed cure all that ails public educational systems by short-circuiting the bureaucracies that they deemed to be the source of the problem.

Critics later found serious shortcomings with Chubb and Moe's analysis,[9] but the timing of their book's release on the eve of Milwaukee's voucher launch generated both enormous excitement on the right and trepidation among believers in traditional public schools.

Annette "Polly" Williams, an African American state representative whose district included part of Milwaukee, spoke at the Brookings book event about how vouchers created the possibility for poor urban blacks to attend the kinds of private schools that, according to Chubb and Moe, provided a better education than did public ones.[10] With black legislators, policy wonks at a liberal think tank, and Wisconsin reformers coalescing behind Milton Friedman's libertarian idea, the potential for a sea change in urban educational policy seemed real.

Then the experiment actually got under way. In its initial incarnation, the Milwaukee Choice Program was so small that all the fuss seemed more than a little excessive. In a district that enrolled nearly 100,000 students, the plan was originally set up to provide 1,000 low-income children with about $2,500 each to enable them to attend a nonsectarian private school. In the first year, only 558 applied and just 300 ended up enrolling in seven schools that agreed to participate. The program expanded a bit over time so that by the 1994–1995 school year, 771 students received $3,200 each to attend twelve non-religious private schools.[11]

Intensified Fighting

Upon the program's inception, the state assigned the University of Wisconsin's Witte with the responsibility for tracking the progress of the students. Witte concluded that from 1991 to 1995, students in the voucher program performed no better on state-sponsored tests than did children who remained in the public schools, after taking into account the socioeconomic backgrounds of the families involved (which are independently connected to test score differences). But in a reflection of how fervid the debate over vouchers had become over the same period, a battle royal over Witte's findings ensued—academic flame throwing that has continued to grow ever more intense and widespread whenever market-oriented school programs are evaluated.

Witte's principal antagonist was the Harvard University professor Paul E. Peterson, a voucher enthusiast whose educational research programs received more than $1 million in support from the Olin Foundation from 1994 through 2001.[12] A front-page *Wall Street Journal* article captured the duel between Witte and Peterson in all its vitriolic glory, noting that Witte referred to Peterson as "a snake" and that Peterson deemed Witte's work "lousy."[13]

In the case of Peterson, it's at least worth noting not only his ample support from the single-minded Olin Foundation and his position as senior fellow at the conservative Hoover Institution, but also that his voucher studies almost invariably conclude that the programs yielded meaningful test score improvements. Other scholars reviewing his Milwaukee findings, which were not peer-reviewed before their release, found them to be flawed, largely because the lion's share of both public and private school students whose performance was to be tracked dropped out of the study sample for various reasons.[14] In a subsequent analysis of the same Milwaukee data, Princeton's Cecilia Rouse landed somewhere in between Witte and Peterson, concluding that voucher students didn't do any better in reading but showed a slight-to-modest advantage in math.[15] The general consensus about Milwaukee's 1991–1995 experience, though, is that the program was too small and the time frame too limited to draw any meaningful conclusions from the scant data it provided.

The most important consequence of the academic tempest in the nation's brewing capital is that it played a role in causing the state legislature to drop testing requirements for the voucher program in 1995, when it voted to greatly expand the initiative to include religious schools. With the experiment scheduled to grow in size by more than tenfold, a systematic effort to gather and synthesize a much larger set of data presented an enormous opportunity to reach meaningful conclusions about whether the theory behind vouchers would actually work in practice. But Governor Thompson and other voucher supporters in the state legislature resisted the arguments of opponents that the private schools should be subject to the same testing requirements as the public schools. In addition to fears that the results may be as unimpressive as Witte found during the first phase, a legal concern may also have played a role. At that stage, there was a strong expectation that Milwaukee's broadened voucher program could end up in the Supreme Court over the question of whether providing public funds via vouchers to religious schools breached the constitutional church-state divide. Minimizing the government's entanglement with religious schools, which would be elevated with the imposition of public testing requirements, would help to reduce the risk of crossing constitutional boundaries in the eyes of the court.

The 1995 vote of the Wisconsin legislature, now with a Republican majority, to expand vouchers to religious schools led to three years of legal wrangling before the state Supreme Court ruled 4 to 2 that the plan was constitutional. The Bradley Foundation was intimately involved in those battles. It reimbursed the state of Wisconsin $350,000 for legal services to argue in favor of religious choice.[16] The state was represented in those efforts by the Kirkland and Ellis law partner Kenneth Starr, the conservative movement icon who was simultaneously the special prosecutor pursuing the Whitewater and Monica Lewinsky cases against President Bill Clinton. In addition, the Scaife Foundation paid hundreds of thousands of dollars in the 1990s to the Landmark Legal Foundation, an institution run by the voucher activist Clint Bolick, partly in support of its legal work defending Milwaukee's plan.[17] (The same cast was involved in defending Cleveland's voucher program before the U.S. Supreme Court, which in 2002 decided by a 5 to 4 vote that the plan did not violate the U.S. Constitution's provisions separating church from state.)

The Experiment Expands

After Bradley's side finally won in 1998, the first honest-to-goodness, large-scale voucher program in the United States involving religious schools finally got under way. To qualify, students had to come from families with incomes below specified income thresholds. By the 2005–2006 school year, about fifteen thousand students were enrolled in 125 schools in the program, at a cost of about $90 million. But, alas, there's no systematic way to assess whether it has been successful because of the state's decision against requiring the voucher schools to submit test scores that could be used to compare their performance with the public schools.

Fortunately, a team of reporters at the *Milwaukee Journal Sentinel* methodically conducted their own investigation into the program on the occasion of its fifteenth anniversary. As part of that undertaking, they visited all but nine of the voucher schools—those that refused to let in the reporters presumably didn't consider themselves to be the models of innovation that Friedman hypothesized—and published their findings in a fascinating seven-part series in June 2005.[18] Among the *Journal Sentinel*'s most significant conclusions (in the paper's own words):

- The voucher schools feel, and look, surprisingly like schools in the Milwaukee Public Schools (MPS) district. Both MPS and the voucher schools are struggling in the same battle to educate low-income, minority students.
- Based on firsthand observations and other reporting, at least 10 of the 106 schools visited appeared to lack the ability, resources, knowledge, or will to offer children even a mediocre education. Most of these were led by individuals who had little or no background in running schools and had no resources other than state payments.
- The voucher program has brought some fresh energy to the mission of educating low-income youth in the city by fostering and financially supporting several very strong schools that might not exist otherwise. There are at least as many excellent schools as alarming ones.
- Parental choice by itself does not assure quality. Some parents pick bad schools—and keep their children in them long after it is clear that the schools are failing. This has allowed some of the weakest schools in the program to remain in business. For example, Alex's Academics of Excellence, a school started by a convicted rapist, continued to enroll students for years even after facing two evictions, allegations of drug use by staff on school grounds, and an investigation by the district attorney. It was finally closed in 2004.
- Creating a new school through the choice program is easier than most people expected. Creating a good new school is harder than most thought it would be.

The *Journal Sentinel* reported that the marketplace theory, which held that parents would pull their kids out of bad schools or not choose them to begin with, did not pan out. "The reality is that it hasn't worked like we thought it would in theory," said Howard Fuller, a staunch voucher advocate who was one of the pioneers of the program and the Milwaukee superintendent from 1991 to 1995. Anneliese Dickman, a research director at the Public Policy Forum, a Milwaukee nonpartisan research organization, said, "Parents want to make choices based on measurable facets of school quality. But they are not getting that information and therefore make a choice based on something else. Unfortunately, what's troubling about this is that you really don't know if your choice has been a good one or not until you have invested a lot of time in your child's life at school."

In the absence of comparative test scores, it's impossible to discern whether Milwaukee's voucher plan has improved the education of the students participating in it relative to how they would have done otherwise. Although some researchers have attempted to draw conclusions about whether Milwaukee's public schools performed better because of the increased competition from vouchers—each student lost to a private school reduces the resources available to the public schools—methodological hurdles make it difficult to draw meaningful conclusions.

Most notably, Harvard University's Caroline M. Hoxby, who has received a grant from the Bradley Foundation and a fellowship from the Olin Foundation, published an analysis in the conservative Hoover Institution's *Education Next* quarterly claiming that competition from voucher schools produced better results in the city's public schools that were most directly affected by the challenge of losing students to private schools.[19] But Hoxby herself acknowledged that if the students who moved from the public schools to the voucher schools were below-average performers, that could be the cause of the test score improvements, rather than any benefits attributable to competition in and of itself.[20] Without test scores from all of the students at both the public and the private schools, even the most sophisticated analysis is basically speculation about the program's impact.

In any case, the *Journal Sentinel*'s diligent legwork calls into serious question fundamental aspects of the theory behind vouchers. If, in the real world, parents with vouchers choose schools based mainly on factors other than quality; if, in the real world, parents with vouchers keep their students even in schools that "lack the ability, resources, knowledge, or will to offer children even a mediocre education"; if, in the real world, parents have no access to reliable information such as test score performance to enable them to evaluate their choices; and if, even in the absence of oversight from government bureaucracies (purportedly the root cause of public school failure), most private voucher schools appear to be no more innovative than public schools, what justification remains for continuing to pursue this idea? None of what Milton Friedman, John Chubb, or Terry Moe promised would happen appears to be transpiring in the one place in the United States where their idea has been given a fair, ambitious shot. That hasn't stopped believers from continuing to make the same arguments. But unless the *Journal Sentinel*'s scrupulously fair reporters were hallucinating, it looks an awful lot like free market forces won't fix what ails urban schools.

The experience in Cleveland, the only other major city with an established government-sponsored voucher plan—albeit much smaller than Milwaukee's—has been similarly disappointing. There, though, analysts at Indiana University have actually tracked comparative test scores for about four thousand students—some who used a voucher to attend private schools and the rest who remained in the public system—who began kindergarten in the 1997–1998 school year through their sixth-grade year in 2003–2004. After accounting for racial and other differences (but not adjusted for income, due to data shortcomings), the researchers found no significant differences in overall achievement, reading, or math scores for sixth graders who had used vouchers throughout their academic careers compared to those who hadn't. The "scholarship" students did modestly better in language, science, and social studies but showed no difference from year to year in those subjects until the end of the sixth grade, so it remains to be seen whether even those results will hold. Without question, the bulk of the evidence over the seven years studied is that voucher recipients do no better than comparable students who remain in the public schools.[21] The bottom line: vouchers appear to be no more of a cure than the long line of school reforms that likewise have failed to overcome the daunting challenges facing city districts.

Holding Charter Schools Accountable

Many of the same purported virtues of vouchers have been ascribed to charter schools, which didn't exist as recently as 1990 but have rapidly proliferated to nearly four thousand across forty states and the District of Columbia. The basic idea is that individuals, groups, or organizations that come forward with a plan to create and manage a school that a state deems to be acceptable under its charter school law can be granted the opportunity to do so without having to adhere to the rules and requirements that conventional public schools face. Again, advocates claim that autonomy from the bureaucracy, which Chubb and Moe deemed to be the source of all problems with the public schools, creates new possibilities for innovation that will lead to improved educational outcomes. At the same time, most charter advocates argue that in exchange for autonomy, the schools must be held accountable for producing good results.

While many moderate Democrats are also enthusiasts of charters as a way of finding middle ground between vouchers and traditional public school reforms, conservatives have primarily fueled the rapid advance of the idea. They have generally been much more effective at connecting the concept to their broader beliefs about the virtues of market forces and the evils of bureaucracy—as well as the implacability of unions and their purportedly overpaid teachers—than progressives have been in tying charter schools to the goals of reducing inequality and promoting opportunity (though conservative charter advocates pay lip service to those values as well). In practice, the debates between the right and the middle/left over how charter schools should function mainly come down to battles over how much public accountability they should have. The Bradley and Walton Family Foundation–funded Center for Education Reform, which grades states based on what it judges to be the relative strength of their charter school laws, uses criteria under which less accountability and the absence of teachers' unions is always better.[22]

One of the most ambitious studies to date evaluating charter school accountability, by Bryan Hassel of the consulting firm Public Impact, found that of 506 "high-stakes" decisions about whether existing charter schools could remain open, 16 percent resulted in the closing of a school. While that figure demonstrates that there is some degree of accountability, Hassel also found that there was very little transparency and much confusion about the criteria for making a decision about whether to renew an existing charter school. Speaking at a 2004 event at the Brookings Institution, Hassel said, "It was very difficult to find out basic information about the expectations that were set, the data that was gathered, and the decisions that were made, and it was difficult for us—we had a research grant, we had trained researchers working on this. So I think it would be very difficult in many of these cases for a parent or a citizen to find out what was really going on in these processes."[23]

The most comprehensive and reliable evaluation of charter school performance to date was a 2006 analysis of National Assessment of Educational Progress (NAEP) test scores from three years earlier, produced by the National Study for Education Statistics, which is in the U.S. Department of Education. It compared fourth-grade reading and math scores from 150 charter schools relative to traditional public schools, taking into account variables such as income and race in the student bodies at each school. It found that traditional schools scored 4.2 points higher in reading and 4.7 points higher in math than the charters did on the 500-point test—a statistically meaningful advantage.[24] More studies that track students over time, such as the Cleveland voucher research, still need to be conducted to get a stronger read on whether different types of schools do better at boosting the progress of students. But the research to date is useful in showing that charter schools aren't obviously producing students who perform better on tests than public school pupils do.

To underline how the right uses academic work to confuse the public, it's worth noting that Harvard's Hoxby in 2004 produced a report that was widely trumpeted in conservative circles purporting to show that students in charter schools scored significantly higher on reading and math tests than did students in neighboring public schools with similar racial composition.[25] But Joydeep Roy and Lawrence Mishel of the Economic Policy Institute adjusted Hoxby's numbers to take into account parental incomes and a more accurate measure of racial characteristics for the children attending the schools. They concluded that the performance of the charter and the conventional public schools in Hoxby's study were actually statistically the same.[26]

Indeed, the socioeconomic backgrounds of students and their parents, as the sociologist James Coleman found back in the 1960s, are far and away the single most important factor in determining the performance of children at any given school and in the comparative performance among schools. A January 2006 study examining the scores on the 2003 NAEP test of more than 340,000 fourth- and eighth-grade students in more than thirteen thousand regular public, charter, and private schools called into question Chubb and Moe's long-standing claim that private schools are invariably superior to public ones. The researchers Christopher Lubienski and Sarah Theule Lubienski of the University of Illinois found that while overall test scores were higher at private schools, after taking into account the higher share of students from low-income backgrounds at conventional public schools, the public schools actually produced better results by a statistically significant margin in both grades.[27] A Department of Education study looking at the same data similarly found that for grade-four reading and grade-eight mathematics, there were no significant differences in test scores between public and private schools after adjusting for the socioeconomic characteristics of the students. The public schools produced better results for grade-four math, while the private schools had superior scores for grade-eight reading.[28] Again, such studies are "snapshots" that capture school performance at a point in time, rather than comparing the progress of individual students over a particular period, but they raise serious questions about the presumptive superiority of private schools. Because private schools only seem to do better because they have fewer low-income students, the new studies adjusting for those differences underline how right Coleman was that the socioeconomic composition of schools is far and away the most important factor in explaining educational outcomes.

Obviously, the new government studies—produced by the Bush administration no less, albeit with minimal fanfare—strike severe blows against the right's premises that the problems with public education reside in bureaucracies and teachers' unions. Less than three weeks after the Education Department released its report comparing public and private school test scores—an analysis that was years in the making with the involvement of a multitude of leading scholars— Olin beneficiary and voucher advocate Paul E. Peterson and his co-author Elena Llaudet issued a report questioning those findings.[29] Using alternative factors to control for variations in student characteristics—mainly by dropping most of the measures of socioeconomic difference used in the government's report—Peterson and Llaudet produced different models showing relatively higher scores for private school students. But the Lubienskis thoroughly demolished Peterson and Llaudet's transparent attempt to reach a sought-after conclusion: "By deleting variables that account for differences in the populations served by the public and private schools, and by not accounting for the missing data problems that arise [from Peterson and Llaudet's] inclusion of demonstrably inferior substitute measures of student demographics, [their paper] creates a strong bias that seriously undercounts the disproportionate number of disadvantaged students served by public schools."[30]

The Peterson and Llaudet response followed movement conservatism's tried-and-true tactic of blowing smoke that provides cover for their advocates to say, "Well, there are lots of studies on both sides, and it will be a long time before we really know for sure." But just as new drugs need to demonstrate their efficacy (and safety) in experiments before they gain acceptance, the burden of proof is on voucher and charter school proponents to show that their approach legitimately produces better results than public schools do after taking into account factors such as the family incomes of students. Public schools over the course of many decades have played a fundamental role in American society of assimilating immigrants and teaching children what it means to be an American. They are central to the ideal of the American dream because they provide all of the nation's children with an opportunity to learn, which improves their chances for realizing their economic and social aspirations. Thanks to universal public education, the share of citizens ages twenty-five to twenty-nine with a high school diploma has dramatically increased from 38 percent in 1940 to nearly 80 percent today.[31] That accomplishment has undergirded American democracy by providing some measure of unity to our extraordinarily diverse society, while contributing to the improvements in economic productivity that have enabled living standards to rise significantly over much of that period.

The bar should be set high for approaches that would use public funds to send children to schools that are less accountable to taxpayers. So far, notwithstanding all the hue and cry, the accumulating weight of the evidence is piling up decisively against the proposition that autonomy and market forces are the answer to what ails American education. It is also raising serious questions about the assertions that school bureaucracies and teachers' unions are mainly to blame— flawed though they undeniably are. The real problem seems to be the same as Coleman's diagnosis from the 1960s—schools with a high proportion of students from low-income families face enormous difficulties in producing an effective learning environment. Moving such students from one high-poverty school to another—whether they are public, private, or charter—can't get around those difficulties. Instead, resources and energy should be focused on alternative approaches that have demonstrated positive results, such as those that will be discussed at the end of this chapter.

Put to the Test

Unlike vouchers—at its core a libertarian idea, with most of its support coming from the right side of the political spectrum—the school standards movement is similar to charter schools in that it bridges the center. Its roots go back to the release of the 1983 report A *Nation at Risk*, which famously warned that America's educational institutions were being eroded by "a rising tide of mediocrity that threatens our very future as a Nation and a people."[32] In the years that followed, virtually every state, under the leadership of both Democratic and Republican governors, developed (1) new academic standards that specified what students are expected to know and be able to do in the core academic subjects in key grade levels; (2) tests that measured progress against those standards; and (3) accountability systems that, at a minimum, provided annual reports on school and district performance based on test scores.[33] President Clinton, who had implemented a standards program in Arkansas as its governor, pushed for federal standards-based reform with the Goals 2000: Educate America Act and the Improving America's Schools Act, both enacted in 1994.

Theories about the virtues of testing linked to some kind of accountability system, whether for students who are denied degrees because they scored low or for schools that face the stigma of being labeled as failing, rest on the presumption that threats provide effective incentives to perform better. No one disputes that setting clear standards and administering exams help to clarify what is expected of students and provide useful information about whether they have lived up to those aspirations. Traditionally, teachers have used test performance to help determine if students need more help in a particular area or if the teachers themselves need to do a better job of communicating material that doesn't seem to be getting through. But it very much remains an open question whether sanctions of one sort or another do anything to improve the educational process.

At the state level, the evidence remains far from conclusive about initiatives aimed at strengthening accountability through testing programs. For example, the Stanford University professors Martin Carnoy and Susanna Loeb conducted research in which they categorized all of the states based on how stringent their testing and sanctions systems on schools were from 1996 to 2000. They then compared state-level changes in fourth- and eighth-grade math scores on the NAEP math exams administered in those years. The researchers also took into account other performance measures, such as ninth-grade retention rates (the share of eighth graders who remained in school through ninth grade) and high school survival rates (the proportion of students who reached twelfth grade without dropping out). Carnoy and Loeb found a modest but significant relationship between states with stronger accountability systems and higher achievement gains at the eighth-grade level but no meaningful connections for fourth grade. Nor did they discern any relationship between accountability and retention rates in high school.[34]

Until George W. Bush became president, most of the enthusiasm among conservatives for tougher standards focused on state, rather than federal, efforts. The right's traditional view about schools is that the federal government should keep its paws off entirely. After the 1994 congressional elections, for example, when Republicans captured control of the House of Representatives for the first time in forty years, the newly anointed speaker Newt Gingrich told a gathering at the Heritage Foundation that "The difference between Bill Clinton and me is, I do not say, 'we need a Department of Homework Checkers at the federal level.'"[35] Gingrich also scrapped a bipartisan panel that Clinton had created to explore strengthening national standards. (For a brief while, Ronald Reagan himself had wanted to get rid of the Department of Education as well, but backed off when his own *Nation at Risk* commission raised its "rising tide of mediocrity" alarms.) Many conservative critics of the public school system at the time were strongly advocating state-level "high-stakes" tests that students would have to pass to receive degrees, tough standards for schools, and opportunities for families to move their kids out of "failing" schools to charter schools or to private schools through vouchers. But most were opposed to thrusting the heavy hand of the federal government into a process that was to a large extent happening anyway in the states.

As Texas governor, George W. Bush's most significant accomplishment was the implementation of a standards-and-testing system in that state's schools. Research into his Texas reforms, like cross-state studies of accountability systems, found some qualified signs of improvement (though the positive results were later discredited).[36] Bush trumpeted the favorable studies during the 2000 campaign and, upon becoming president, extended the same arguments he had used in Texas for stronger accountability in making the No Child Left Behind Act one of his foremost domestic priorities. Bush saw the legislation as a concrete manifestation of the "compassionate conservatism" theme that helped to catapult him, by the barest of margins, to the White House.

During the course of negotiations over the law, Bush was criticized by many on the right for his complicity with Senator Ted Kennedy (who himself was vilified by teachers' unions and others on the left for "making a pact with the devil"). But by and large, objections were muted because standards have substantial bipartisan support, Congress addressed the legislation shortly after the September 11 terrorist attacks, and the law had the endorsement of moderate and liberal groups such as the Democratic Leadership Council, the Citizens' Commission on Civil Rights, and the Education Trust. No Child Left Behind (NCLB) was decisively enacted in December 2001 by votes of 381 to 41 in the House and 87 to 10 in the Senate. As the University of Virginia law professor James E. Ryan wrote in 2004, "Who would have guessed, even ten years ago, that a Republican president, with huge bipartisan support, would enact the most intrusive federal education legislation in our nation's history?"[37]

Compassionate Confusion

Often, major legislation that incurs the ire of both conservative and liberal interest groups, while passing decisively, turns out to have a positive impact. Examples include the 1983 Social Security legislation, the Tax Reform Act of 1986, the 1990 replacement of Gramm-

Rudman-Hollings with more effective federal spending limits, and the welfare reform legislation of 1996. But the No Child Left Behind Act has little hope of entering that pantheon, even though it's too soon to fully evaluate its impact on student performance (notwithstanding the administration's claims that NCLB is responsible for modest test score improvements that mainly occurred before the law's implementation).[38] The problems with No Child Left Behind, which have become increasingly evident, derive from design flaws that induce actions that diametrically oppose the law's stated goals of increasing academic achievement, raising the performance of disadvantaged children, and attracting qualified teachers to every classroom. The flaws are not with the general concept of strengthening standards and accountability per se. Rather, as with the Medicare drug bill discussed in the next chapter, the shortcomings are an outgrowth of foisting conservative ideology onto an ambitious government initiative.

Under No Child Left Behind, states must conduct annual reading and math tests of all public school students in grades three through eight, and at least one more test in both subjects is required in grades ten through twelve. Beginning in 2007–2008, students must also take science tests at least three times between grades three and twelve. Scores on these tests must be tabulated under the law not only for every public school, but also disaggregated within each school for a variety of subgroups, including major racial, ethnic, and income categories, as well as for migrants, English-language learners, and the disabled. The act requires states to set what it deems to be a "proficiency" level on these tests for each grade and to tabulate the percentage of students—not just for each school but also for each subgroup—who are exceeding or falling below that benchmark. States must also set a proficiency goal for each year, with the percentage ratcheting up periodically until it reaches 100 percent by 2014. The first benchmarks for determining adequate yearly progress were based on test scores from the 2001–2002 school year.

No Child Left Behind requires all schools within a state that receive federal funding through Title I of the Elementary and Second School Act to make adequate yearly progress. (Nearly 60 percent of all schools in the country receive some Title I support, including many schools with low-income students in middle-class districts.[39]) The sanctions for schools that don't achieve adequate yearly progress escalate over time. In the first year of falling short of the adequate yearly progress benchmark, schools are identified as "in need of improvement." The news media invariably use the label *failing* for such schools, even though that word doesn't appear in the law itself. After two consecutive years of "failure," schools must develop a plan for improvement and are obligated to receive external "technical assistance." Students in such schools can choose another public school, including a charter school, within the same district. After three years, students in the school must receive either publicly or privately provided tutoring services. Among the penalties for four years of consecutive failure are the replacement of school staff and the implementation of a new curriculum. Five years in a row of falling below the threshold leads to one of several possible sanctions entailing "reconstitution," including the state's reopening it as a charter school or turning over its management to a private company.

With states having virtually unlimited discretion in establishing their own standards and tests, the act encourages them to make tests as easy as possible while setting the proficiency bar low. It also pushes them to delay significant elevations in the average yearly progress hurdle until as close as possible to the 2014 deadline, by which time the law might well be different. (Ryan likens that strategy to a "balloon mortgage.") Robert Linn, the past president of the American Educational Research Association, told the *New York Times* that the "severe sanctions" in the law "implicitly encourage states to water down their content and performance standards in order to reduce the risk of sanctions."[40] The conservative Massachusetts Board of Education member and standards advocate Abigail Thernstrom, the coauthor of *No Excuses: Closing the Racial Gap in Learning*, said the goal of 100 percent proficiency by 2014 is "ludicrous" and defines "proficiency way down . . . way, way down."[41] Although hardly anyone expects the 100 percent proficiency provisions to remain intact by then, if allowed to stand virtually every Title I school would be at risk of being "reconstituted"— including being replaced in the form of a private or a charter school.

One indication that many states are indeed defining proficiency down is that their passing rates have jumped enormously in the last couple of years after they revised their tests and proficiency thresholds. In Arizona, for example, the passing rates jumped nearly 30 percent after the state made changes to its tests and scoring cutoffs. The conservative education analyst Diane Ravitch, a proponent of national standards but a critic of NCLB's perverse incentives, noted that in 2005 there were large discrepancies between National Assessment of Educational Progress scores for each state compared to the states' reports about the proportion of students who were proficient on their own tests of reading and mathematics. For example, Tennessee reported 87 percent of its fourth graders proficient in math, compared to only 28 percent on NAEP. She found that only five states—South Carolina, Maine, Missouri, Wyoming, and Massachusetts—reported proficiency levels that aligned closely with NAEP results.[42] Inez M. Tenenbaum, South Carolina's superintendent of education, told the *New York Times*: "We set very high standards for our tests, and unfortunately it's put us at great disadvantage. We thought other states would be high-minded too, but we were mistaken."[43]

Similarly, No Child Left Behind's incentives are likely to further discourage good teachers from working in schools where they are most needed—in urban districts where test scores are lowest. Schools that don't make adequate yearly progress, even if they are improving over time or if just one of the subgroups falls short of the required proficiency level, are deemed to be failing—a stigma that extends to its teachers. Researchers in North Carolina found that schools with the lowest-performing students had even more difficulty retaining teachers after the introduction of the state's accountability system than before.[44]

The act also strongly discourages schools from admitting or retaining low-income and minority students, who are more likely to perform poorly on tests. Thomas J. Kane and Douglas O. Staiger found that schools with enough African Americans or economically disadvantaged students to qualify them as a subgroup under NCLB were much more likely to fail than were schools that do not have as many such pupils.[45] This incentive to shed such students directly undercuts what ought to be the overriding priority for genuinely leaving no child behind—that is, enabling more low-income and minority students to attend predominantly middle-class schools. Amy Stuart Wells and Jennifer Jellison Holme, who examined how testing systems affected the demographics of six relatively high-performing integrated high schools, found that parents became increasingly skeptical about the value of integration as they came to perceive their school less favorably than before in the context of focusing on its comparative test scores.[46] As a result, testing actually weakens public support for voluntary integration — the policy that holds out the greatest hope for improving the performance of low-income students.

The No Child Left Behind Act is less steeped in right-wing ideology than school vouchers are. Its inclusion of measuring sticks aimed at elevating the scores of underperforming subgroups of the population is admirable and enjoys bipartisan support. If it turns out that threats and sanctions actually do lead to improved test results, the most important challenge will be understanding how to sustain the changes in classrooms that might be enhancing the learning experience, assuming the improved outcomes aren't simply a product of finagling with numbers or inducing higher dropout rates. That's especially true for high-poverty districts. Still, as written, NCLB's perverse incentives and dependence upon labeling a large and growing portion of the public school system as a failure undergirds the right's overarching agenda of undercutting support for public schools while expanding vouchers and charter schools. When talking about No Child Left Behind, President Bush as a matter of course says that students in failing public schools should be given an opportunity to attend private schools at government expense.

NCLB's shortcomings also share some of the flaws of Colorado's TABOR amendment. In both cases, the ideologically driven reliance on rigid requirements to produce the desired results assumes that saying it shall be so, will make it so. In the real world, as most parents who have tried that strategy with their children will recognize, strict dictates, in and of themselves, rarely work and often backfire. Like TABOR, NCLB isn't so much about faith in markets as it is a mindset that government workers on their own have little incentive to perform effectively. As it turns out, predictably, ordering them to produce the desired result doesn't do much to lead to that outcome, at least not without producing unhappy consequences. If legislators in Colorado could have magically cut nothing but purported "waste, fraud, and abuse," and public school teachers could heroically improve student performance, democracy already provided plenty of incentives to produce those outcomes. All that inflexible strictures do on their own is create new problems while exacerbating the impression that government is failing — when it's really the conservative movement's ideas that are failing.

The Real Challenge

Conservative, market-based school reforms are failing for all kinds of reasons: the flawed premise that parents who choose schools for their children will behave like price- and quality-sensitive automobile shoppers; the unrealistic claim that clear, reliable information about schools will be readily available to parents; wishful thinking about connections between competition and educationally effective innovation; misguided scapegoating of teachers and administrators that distracts from the genuine challenges of providing a good education; and a lack of public accountability under the conservative movement's preferred approaches. But there's another, even more important explanation as to why vouchers, charter schools, and No Child Left Behind are showing little sign of yielding better results than past liberal reforms.

The fundamental flaw with all these ideas is that they don't even attempt to attack what is far and away the main problem with America's public schools: concentrated, persistent poverty in cities. That deeply entrenched reality has no easy answers or simple-minded panaceas, although a booming economy, such as that of the late 1990s, that raises wages across the board appears to be the best antidote by enabling poor families to move to better neighborhoods.[47] Now that welfare reform has largely shifted the public's attention elsewhere, both political parties generally perceive more peril than opportunity from talking about urban poverty. The topic is ill-suited to movement conservatism's orientation toward snappy, superficially appealing elixirs with political potency. And many Democrats, remembering the era when the right gained all kinds of mileage from attacking them over the failures of welfare and the shortcomings of the war on poverty generally, are understandably reluctant to raise the subject again. But the problem of systematically troubled urban schools remains, and the main reason why it is so intractable is that it's enormously difficult to teach effectively in classrooms and schools with large numbers of children from poor families.

Collectively, U.S. public schools perform roughly in the middle of the pack compared to other economically advanced countries based on testing results—that's been true for years, with no significant trend up or down.[48] But those overall averages for America's performance mask the extent to which suburban and rural schools in the United States are much better than city schools by any yardstick you want to choose. A comprehensive 1996 report by the National Center for Educational Statistics found "large differences between urban and non-urban schools and between high-poverty and low-poverty schools on most of the indicators of student background, school experiences, and student outcomes studied."[49] But the conservative movement, beginning when it latched onto A Nation at Risk, has been enormously effective at creating the impression that there is a pervasive public school crisis—the "rising tide of mediocrity" decried in that 1983 report. That claim is highly misleading, though, because suburban and rural schools—while uneven in quality and by no means perfect—measure up reasonably well compared to their international counterparts. The genuine crisis in the United States is in urban school districts.

Until far more is done to enable children now attending city schools with a high proportion of impoverished kids to enter schools with a large share of students from middle-class families, that crisis is almost certain to continue. Moving students through vouchers from one high-poverty public school in Milwaukee to a high-poverty private school doesn't help them very much, as the Milwaukee Journal Sentinel's series demonstrated. Nor will labeling those schools as failures. Earlier liberal reforms to increase funding, recruit better teachers, and cut class size in high-poverty schools proves that those strategies haven't been very effective either, although they can help at the margins. Raising the performance of U.S. students from the middle of the international pack to the top—along with much more ethnically and economically homogeneous countries like Japan and the Netherlands—seems improbable until the students being left behind in high-poverty urban schools have a chance at attending middle-class schools.

About 40 percent of urban students attend high-poverty schools (defined, depending on the study, as schools with more than 40 to 50 percent of students eligible to receive the free or reduced-price lunch). In contrast, just 10 percent of suburban students and 25 percent of rural students attend such schools. Research shows that high-poverty schools are much more likely to have unqualified teachers, poorly maintained facilities, disruptive classrooms, significant absenteeism, and high student-teacher ratios. Low-income children are also less likely to be "ready to learn" by the time they reach kindergarten age, and they face a range of other social and economic problems outside of the school.

But research also shows that when such students have an opportunity to attend schools with a sizable majority of children from middle-class families, they are significantly more likely to achieve at higher levels. For example, one study found that the average NAEP math score for low-income fourth graders attending schools with less than 25 percent of students eligible for free or reduced-price lunches was 218, versus just 204 for those attending high-poverty schools. That's a substantial difference, because 10 to 11 points amounts to a full grade level. The study showed that middle-class children attending high-poverty schools actually had a lower average score of 212 than did low-income students in predominantly middle-class schools.[50]

Conservatives such as Abigail and Stephan Thernstrom, both senior fellows at the Manhattan Institute, blame race rather than class as the principal source of test-score disparities.[51] And it's true that even middle-class African American and Hispanic students attending racially integrated middle-class schools have significantly lower test scores than their white counterparts do. It's a genuine, perplexing problem that we need to understand better so that the gap can be further reduced (it has declined somewhat in recent years), with the goal of eliminating it. But because the research is so clear that moving low-income students (whatever their race) from high-poverty to middle-class schools improves their performance without any negative impact on the students they join—and that high-poverty schools are almost preordained to be dysfunctional—as a matter of policy, voluntary socioeconomic integration can only help to reduce disparities by race.

What Works?

The political obstacles to systematically enabling more low-income urban children to cross district lines to attend middle-class schools in the suburbs are obviously big—some would say too formidable to make the idea practical. But various forms of the idea have been tried, with evidence of success. In Wake County, North Carolina, for example, the school board adopted a policy that no school should have more than 40 percent of its students eligible for free or reduced-price lunches, and no more than 25 percent of students reading below grade level. The district, which includes Raleigh and its surrounding suburbs, now has nearly 90 percent of its students reading at or above grade level. In

Wake, 63.7 percent of low-income students passed the 2005 High School End of Course exams, compared to less than 50 percent in counties without socioeconomic integration.[52] Additionally, 82 percent of Wake's students graduated from high school on time, compared to a national average of only 70 percent.

Similar approaches to promote socioeconomic school integration—often through public school choice and magnet school programs (not the court-ordered busing of the past)—are under way in San Francisco; LaCrosse, Wisconsin; Rochester, New York; San Jose, California; St. Lucie County, Florida; and Cambridge, Massachusetts. Other state programs in which suburban school districts elect to accept students from the city have been in effect for years in the metropolitan areas surrounding Minneapolis, Hartford, Boston, Rochester, and, yes, Milwaukee—where the Chapter 220 program has produced positive results.[53] The nation's largest interdistrict choice program is in the St. Louis area, where some twelve thousand city students are given the opportunity to attend suburban schools in sixteen districts. The program, originally begun as part of a court-supervised racial desegregation plan, was continued on a voluntary basis beginning in 1999 when business community leaders and others sought to preserve a system that had proved successful in raising the graduation rates and achievement of urban students who were educated in middle-class suburban schools.[54] Studies of Hartford's program, likewise, found that compared with control groups, the low-income students who attended suburban schools had higher career aspirations, were much more likely to attend college, had fewer incidents with the police, and were less likely to become teenage parents.[55] A related strategy involves enabling low-income families to move to mixed-income suburban housing though "fair-share" programs such as one in Montgomery County, Maryland. As former Albuquerque mayor David Rusk says, "Housing policy is education policy."

Based on real-world experience and evidence, those kinds of approaches have a much greater chance of making progress than do the ideologically driven reforms that have dominated debate in recent years. The central question about ideas for giving low-income children a chance to attend middle-class schools is not so much whether they will work educationally—evidence is plentiful that integration produces positive results—but whether they are politically feasible on a large scale in many locations. It will take genuine leadership and courage to persuade families living in the suburbs that they have a stake in seeing what happens if more low-income city kids get a chance to attend their middle-class suburban schools. Given the extent to which the conservative message about the virtues of markets has dominated in recent years, leaders may well be reluctant to take the leap required to talk about values rather than about supply and demand. But the nation is unlikely to make significant progress unless they do.

During the Social Security privatization debate, as we will explore in chapter 9, the conservative movement tried—largely without success—to convince the public that there was an imminent crisis that required fundamentally undercutting a successful government program. With public schools, the right has similarly adopted the strategy of sounding hyperbolic alarms and then imposing "solutions" that weaken the government's capacity to be effective. In this case, the purported public school crisis is actually a much narrower, though genuinely severe and urgent, problem with failing urban schools. The right's blanket indictment of public schools, along with the government administrators and the teachers' unions committed to public education, has in many ways diverted energy and resources from efforts that would actually improve student performance. The major school reforms pursued in recent years—No Child Left Behind and charters and, to a lesser extent, vouchers—have all been driven and shaped primarily by conservative philosophy and rhetoric, largely with the acquiescence and even enthusiasm of centrist Democrats. As a result, in contrast to the Social Security offensive that congressional Democrats uniformly opposed, conservatives have been far more successful politically in influencing education policy at all levels of government. And, as we have seen, it is very difficult to discern anything good that has come of it.

8

"Tough It Out"
Health Savings Accounts and Malpractice "Reform"

T hanks to overly generous medical coverage provided by private employers and the government, the right argues, average Americans consume medical services as voraciously as shoppers with all-you-can-buy gift certificates. In the process, the typical citizen's excessive demand drives up medical costs, wasting other people's money on doctor visits, tests, and drugs that do nothing for his or her health. When it comes to medicine, Americans are lucky duckies *and* hypochondriacs.

The right's solution to those purported problems? Make people pay more while reducing the obligations of employers and government. And while we're at it, we should make it more difficult for patients to sue for malpractice and collect sizable damages when health-care professionals negligently cause an injury or a death. The idea—as always in the conservative movement—is to get rid of government-induced "inefficiencies" so that the market for health care functions much like the markets for conventional consumer goods and services. A Cato Institute brief titled "Why Health Care Costs Too Much," by Stan Liebowitz, explained,

> No politicians are giving speeches blaming the average citizens of the country for overusing medical care. There are no fireside chats with the president asking citizens to stop seeing doctors so often, asking parents to have their children "tough it out" and not see the doctor for every little scratch, asking the elderly to give up that extra year or two of life. Politicians are not so foolish. But turning

a blind eye to the consumption of medical resources by patients is a mistake. If the country is overusing medical resources, patients must bear responsibility for much of that overuse. We cannot cut our medical expenditures without reducing our consumption of medical resources.[1]

The conservative movement's diagnosis and cure give short shrift at best to what just about everyone else recognizes as America's most significant health-care problem: the large share of the population that lacks medical insurance. But solving that problem can only be accomplished by more government. Better to change the subject by focusing on contrived concerns that could only be solved by less government.

The right's favored solution to what it believes to be wrong with the medical system is health savings accounts (HSAs). Hatched in the 1980s at a libertarian Dallas think tank called the National Center for Policy Analysis—funded, yes, by Scaife, Koch, Olin, Bradley, and assorted corporate foundations—the basic idea is to encourage citizens and employers to buy high-deductible insurance plans.[2] By definition, high-deductible policies require individuals to pay a substantial amount out of their own pockets for health-care expenses until those costs exceed a threshold when insurance payments begin to kick in. In 2006, the minimum annual deductible under the HSA legislation enacted two years earlier was $1,050 for individual coverage and $2,100 for family coverage. To induce people to elect those high-deductible policies, which generally—but not always—have modestly cheaper premiums than do plans with lower deductibles, the government offers the opportunity to open and manage tax-favored HSAs. The contributions of individuals to HSAs are tax deductible, investment earnings in the accounts accrue tax free, and any money withdrawn to be used for medical costs remains untaxed. Employers also receive tax breaks for any contributions they make to their workers' health savings accounts.

Is giving people more "skin in the game," as the right often puts it, the key to unleashing the healing virtues of capitalism on the medical system? Even if individuals consume "too much" health care, how can conservatives be confident that discouraging people through higher outlays from visiting doctors and taking medications won't be harmful to them? Will shifting a greater share of health-care costs onto households really undercut the forces that have produced the genuinely severe problem of persistently high rates of medical inflation? And how exactly are health savings accounts supposed to address the enormous flaw that is all but unique to the United States among industrialized nations, a failing that's largely attributable to the exorbitant cost of individual health insurance policies and reliance on employer-provided coverage: large and rising numbers of uninsured and underinsured citizens?

Health Care versus Haircuts

To buttress their central claim about the virtues of shifting health-care costs to individuals, advocates of HSAs over the years have recited like a mantra the results of a study conducted by the RAND Corporation in the 1970s. National Center for Policy Analysis president John C. Goodman, often called the "father of health savings accounts," boils the study down to this nugget: "A series of health insurance experiments conducted by the RAND Corporation in the 1970s found that people who paid a significant share of their health expenses consume about 30 percent less health care with little effect on their health."[3]

Let's look a little closer at the seminal RAND study because it is an essential pillar holding up the argument for HSAs. The report was actually commissioned by the Nixon administration, at a time when both private and governmental health insurance policies generally charged only modest deductibles and copayments, to find out what would happen if individuals had to pay more out of pocket. So RAND randomly assigned 5,809 people to insurance plans it created that either had no cost sharing, 25 percent, 50 percent, or 95 percent co-insurance rates. As it turned out, compared with free care, cost sharing reduced health care spending commensurately up the ladder, with individuals in the stingiest plans consuming about two-thirds of the amount expended on those with no copayments. That unsurprising finding indisputably validates the Economics 101 verity that higher prices reduce demand.

But what about the impact on the health of the participants? They consumed less medical care, but they were less healthy as a result. In a 1992 summary of the study, RAND's Emmett B. Keeler wrote, "People given free care had better results at the end of the study on blood pressure control, corrected vision and oral health (gums and filled cavities), especially for the poor and initially sick. . . . Regular medical screening (Pap smears, breast and rectal exams) was better with free care, but other health habits (exercise, diet, smoking) except for flossing were worse." Otherwise, though, RAND did not detect significant differences in health outcomes.[4] In 1993, the study's principal investigator, Joseph P. Newhouse, added that "Health among the sick poor— approximately the most disadvantaged 6 percent of the population— was adversely affected." The effects of reduced care in that group included higher mortality rates.[5] Another analysis of RAND's results found that the probability that low-income children in plans with cost sharing received effective medical services for acute conditions was 56 percent of that relative to those in plans with no cost sharing (and 59 percent for low-income adults). Higher-income children and adults in cost-sharing plans also had a significantly lower probability of receiving effective services.[6] In addition to those serious concerns that were submerged out of sight in the breezy summaries of the study provided by HSA advocates, there are other reasons for skepticism about their claims that reduced use of medical care had minimal health effects. Dr. Arnold S. Relman, the editor emeritus of the *New England Journal of Medicine*, points out, "Follow-up was limited to the relatively brief duration of the study, the population cited was relatively young (individuals aged 62 and older were excluded), and the methods of assessing health status were largely based on self-evaluation and relatively superficial physiological tests that easily could have overlooked serious underlying disease."[7]

One other important limitation of the RAND analysis in relation to current circumstances is that household out-of-pocket health-care costs today have become significantly higher than they were three decades ago, after taking inflation into account. In Keeler's 1992 synopsis of the research, he wrote, "The policies observed today in the market are very similar to the ones we have computed to be optimal in terms of limiting financial risk and of reducing overuse from insurance." That is, by 1992, insurance policies already had evolved to require individuals to contribute out of pocket what the RAND researchers had interpreted to be appropriate levels to discourage excessive consumption of health-care services. Needless to say, copayments and premiums have risen well above those thresholds in the years that have gone by and swallow an ever-larger share of family budgets. In 2003, 43 percent of nonelderly Americans were living in households with out-of-pocket expenditures on health care and health insurance premiums exceeding $2,000.[8] So the purported virtues of getting people to pay more for their own health care, at least to the extent that the RAND study has been used as a justification for more cost sharing, had long ago been achieved in the absence of HSAs. Americans already have more than enough skin in the game.

In a variety of ways, much research since the RAND analysis undermines the premise that requiring individuals to pay more for health services will transform them into sensible shoppers who buy only the care they need and little that they don't.[9] The fundamental problem is that the world of medicine is utterly different from markets for groceries, kitchen appliances, mutual funds, or any of the products and the services that *Consumer Reports* judges on behalf of the buying public. Not only do patients have little way of making astute decisions about their health care, to a distressing degree medical professionals themselves often act with little more than informed intuition about whether a particular test, procedure, or prescription will benefit a patient. Atul Gawande, a surgeon and a writer, put it this way:

> We look for medicine to be an orderly field of knowledge and procedure. But it is not. It is an imperfect science, an enterprise of constantly changing knowledge, uncertain information, fallible individuals, and at the same time lives on the line. . . . Spend almost any time with doctors and patients, and you will find that the larger, starker, and more painful difficulty is the still abundant uncertainty that exists over what should be done in many situations. . . . In the absence of algorithms and evidence about what to do, you learn in medicine to make decisions by feel. You count on experience and judgment. And it is hard not to be troubled by this.[10]

How on earth are average citizens supposed to make astute judgments about their health-care purchases? They have next-to-no information about distinctions in the ability, the expertise, and the track records of health-care providers; the reliability and usefulness of various tests under different circumstances; the relative merits of different medicines; and little clue as to whether a particular ache or pain is something to genuinely worry about. That's a lot different from choosing to get a haircut when you look shaggy at a barbershop you've been happy with in the past. Not to mention that a bad haircut will always grow back in. With health problems, you can't afford to take a chance and be wrong.

Comparative shopping for health care purely on the basis of prices, which would seem to be far easier to ascertain than information about quality, can be next to impossible. Anyone who doubts that should try calling a half dozen local doctor's offices, clinics, and hospitals to ask them how much they charge for, say, a chest X-ray. Expect to spend aggravating hours on the phone seeking information that is all but certain to prove to be inaccurate.

In the same Economics 101 class where students learn that higher prices reduce demand, they are also told that Adam Smith's "invisible hand" works magic only when a number of conditions are met—one of which is that consumers must have "perfect information" enabling them to make choices that will satisfy their desires. In health care, the information available to the public couldn't be much more imperfect. Nonetheless, the conservative movement insists that a higher dose of the market in the form of increased out-of-pocket costs won't harm public health. It's a testament to how successful the right has been in selling its belief system that such a threadbare claim so deeply disconnected from consistently observed real-world experience—not to mention economic theory—has become such a dominant force in the debate over health-care reform.

Another False Promise

The share of the U.S. national economy devoted to health-care spending has climbed inexorably for four decades, growing far faster than in other industrialized countries over that period. In 1970, total health-care spending per American was $1,313 (in 2002 dollars), or 7.0 percent of GDP; by 2002, those figures had soared to $5,267 per capita and 14.6 percent of GDP.[11] By comparison, the median for the countries in the Organization for Economic Cooperation and Development is $2,193 per capita and 8.5 percent of GDP.[12] Health-care prices are all but certain to continue to rise substantially faster than general inflation, consuming an ever-larger portion of the economic pie, particularly when the Baby Boomers add further demands on the system as they reach retirement age beginning in the next decade.

If that money were spent productively, improving public health and the quality of life for Americans, then the escalating cost burden would not be nearly as difficult to justify as it in fact is. After all, that largesse helps to create plenty of jobs, many of them good ones, while stoking the economy.[13] Unfortunately, most measures show that the performance of the U.S. health-care system lags well behind those of other advanced countries that spend far less per citizen. The litany is depressingly familiar: life expectancy here is lower than the average. Infant mortality rates are in the bottom fifth. Child immunization rates are below the median. And surveys show that Americans are considerably less satisfied with their health care than are citizens in many other countries. At more than $1,000 per person, health-care administrative costs are more than twice the level in most other advanced countries. And even with all of that additional money flowing into our system, about 15 percent of the population lacks health insurance, in contrast to the universal coverage almost everywhere else.[14]

So high, rapidly rising costs of medical care here are most definitely a big problem. But will HSAs, by making Americans foot more of the bill to discourage them from using health services, really do anything to diffuse those cost pressures as conservative advocates insist that they will? It's hard to see how.[15] The main reason why not is that the vast majority of health-care spending pays for costly procedures and treatments—often connected to serious illnesses or end-of-life care—that far exceed the deductibles that individuals are obligated to pay out of pocket. Health insurance covers all, or almost all, of those big-ticket costs under HSAs. Seventy percent of total health-care costs are spent on the top 10 percent of medical-care users. Nearly 80 percent of total medical outlays exceed the minimum HSA deductibles.[16] Those big bills are piled up by people who have major health problems. Since they have little or no skin in the game for those high costs—particularly considering that they are usually facing a medical crisis—why would they economize? In contrast, the bottom 50 percent of health-care users pay only 3 percent of total expenditures.[17] Although HSA advocates argue that some plans require patients to continue to make copayments for costs above the deductible threshold, thereby giving them an incentive to continue to be cost conscious for higher outlays, the law doesn't require those copayments of HSA-eligible plans. In any case, it's a reach to say that such marginal additional costs would significantly influence the decision making of patients with major health issues.

Basically, this means that any reduced spending induced by the higher deductibles required under HSAs would amount to little more than nickels and dimes saved in the mammoth health-care sector. The Congressional Research Service concluded that "it would be unreasonable to expect [HSAs] to produce a significant reduction in the nation's health care costs."[18] The employee benefits consulting firm Watson Wyatt argued that HSAs are unlikely to reduce employers' health-care costs because most corporate spending goes toward costs incurred by a small share of workers (and their family members) who have serious health conditions. The workers' higher deductibles would do little to change that.[19] The Bush administration's own actuaries at the Centers for Medicare and Medicaid Services argued that HSAs would have a relatively small net impact on health-care costs.[20]

Study after study has shown that U.S. health-care costs are so high primarily because our system constantly introduces ever more advanced, highly expensive technology that over time becomes available to more and more patients throughout the country.[21] Some of that technology produces significantly better results, while other innovations such as certain newly approved drugs improve only marginally at best over the status quo. The vast majority of individuals using those high-tech tests, procedures, and drugs are dealing with significant medical problems. It's difficult to see how HSAs will in any way alter the forces underlying the introduction and expansion of costly technology. Nor are HSAs tailored to address the other sources of rapid medical inflation, including high administrative costs. If anything, as we will see, the idea will only exacerbate those problems.

If HSAs are likely to induce some individuals to forgo medical treatment that they need, without reining in health-care inflation, what are they good for? Providing yet another windfall to the rich, if nothing else. All of the sundry tax breaks for individuals who contribute to health savings accounts are especially lucrative to those in the highest tax brackets. In 2006, President Bush proposed additional tax breaks for HSAs that would substantially raise the maximum that could be contributed to the accounts, add a new income tax credit of 15.3 percent of the amount contributed over and above the existing tax deduction, and expand tax breaks for individuals who buy their own insurance. (The tax credit is not "refundable," so it is unavailable to lower-income individuals who owe no income taxes.) Together, those changes would significantly enhance the appeal of the accounts to Americans with the highest incomes, without significantly increasing their attraction for middle- and low-income citizens.[22]

All of this might seem relatively harmless—just another convoluted way to further repay wealthy contributors to the Republican Party, as well as investment companies, insurers, and consulting firms that stand to profit from the new opportunities presented by HSAs. But actually the idea is more insidious than that. By encouraging rich and healthy workers to peel off from our already highly fragmented medical insurance system, it runs the risk of exacerbating the very problems that have produced high levels of uninsurance and inflation.

The U.S Social Security system, and the universal health-care programs of other countries, demonstrate that one thing governments do especially well is provide insurance. Only governments can guarantee that the entire population is covered—either by directly providing insurance or through laws requiring everyone to have a public or private plan—against risks of significant financial loss or hardship. When the entire population belongs to the same system of insurance, which is the case with "single-payer" systems, costs are minimized for everyone because the liability for the risks encountered by the minority is shared among the largest possible group. Administrative costs are relatively low because everyone is part of the same system, and there's no need for costly and wasteful activities like marketing and advertising. Of course, the right's rubric for universal health insurance, which has been devastatingly effective for many years in American politics, is *socialized medicine*. But that mindless terminology obscures the reality that almost every capitalist democracy other than ours guarantees health insurance for all its citizens, in most cases without direct government control of the provision of health-care services. Calling Social Security a "socialized retirement pension" or "socialized disability coverage" wouldn't change the reality that the program has proved to be enormously popular, cost-efficient, and effective in protecting all Americans for many decades.

HSAs in the Real World

It is much too soon to draw final conclusions about the impact of health savings accounts in the United States. Their tax advantages were enacted in December 2003, effective beginning in 2004. So there has been only a limited period of time for an HSA market to develop. (An earlier "demonstration" experiment with similar "medical savings accounts" demonstrated only that no meaningful market cropped up for them.)

But what do we know about the small number of HSAs in the United States so far?[23] A 2005 survey jointly sponsored by the Employee Benefit Research Institute (EBRI) and the Commonwealth Fund found that people with high-deductible health insurance plans, both with and without accounts, were far more likely than were individuals with lower deductibles to report dissatisfaction with the quality of their care, out-of-pocket costs, and the plans generally. Less than one-third said they would recommend the same coverage to a friend or a coworker.[24]

The impact of high-deductible plans and HSAs on the consumption of health care appears to be adhering to economic theory, while raising the red flags that opponents of the plans worried about. The EBRI/Commonwealth Fund survey found that one-third of the people in high-deductible plans, with and without accounts, had delayed or avoided getting health care when they were sick because of the cost. That's nearly twice the rate for individuals with lower deductibles. For people with health problems or income under $50,000 who had HSA-eligible plans, the rate of avoiding care was more than 40 percent. These individuals were also more likely to skip doses of their medications, in order to make them last longer, or not to fill their prescriptions at all. Individuals with health problems who belonged to high-deductible plans were most likely to skip their medications.[25]

Affirming the dubiousness of the claim that HSAs will transform consumers into informed health-care shoppers, the survey found that just 14 to 16 percent of insured adults—whether enrolled in a comprehensive or a high-deductible plan—had information from their insurers on the quality of care provided by their doctors or hospitals. Only 12 to 16 percent had information from their insurers about the cost and quality of health-care providers. About one-third of individuals enrolled in high-deductible plans checked in advance about the price of a doctor's visit or another health service.[26]

One other development, of little surprise, is that the emerging market for high-deductible plans tethered to HSAs is enormously complex; in some cases, HSA-eligible plans are actually more expensive than similar insurance coverage that does not meet the requirements needed to qualify for HSAs. The *Wall Street Journal* described the experience of Denice Carnahan, forty-eight, of Renton, Washington, who compared high-deductible options from Regence BlueShield. The HSA-eligible plan she looked at had a premium of $150 a month and a $2,500 deductible. Another plan that didn't meet the HSA requirements had both a lower price and a lower deductible: $127 a month, with a $1,500 deductible. Even though Ms. Carnahan was interested in opening an account, she asked, "Why would I pay more to take on more risk?" One reason for the discrepancy in that case was that the HSA-eligible plan covered some preventative care that wasn't provided under the non-HSA plan.[27] Larry Lutey, a vice president of human resources at Lutheran Social Services of Illinois, testified before the House Ways and Means Committee that some employees who had opened HSAs found the accounts "difficult to manage, difficult to understand, difficult to access, and have chosen to leave the plan for other alternatives."[28] Clearly, the myriad permutations of prices, benefits, and account-management options have added yet more layers of consumer befuddlement in a health-care world that already does more than its share to leave people mystified and stressed out.

It's too early for any meaningful assessment of the impact HSAs might ultimately have on overall health-care costs and the numbers of uninsured. So far, though, there's no sign of anything positive happening. How about in the two other countries that have much greater experience with the same basic idea?

Just as movement conservatives like to cite the experience in Chile with Social Security privatization as a model for the United States (see chapter 9), they often point to South Africa's experiment with HSAs as the beacon shining the way for America.[29] As with Chile, though, anyone other than a true believer who looks at the case closely will wonder why conservatives raised the example in the first place if they really want to help their cause.

About 15 percent of South Africans have private insurance, of whom half have medical savings accounts (MSA). These differ from their U.S. HSA counterparts in several ways, which include (1) a portion of monthly premiums is set aside in a special savings account, controlled by the insured, for buying health-care services; (2) the MSA is coupled with an insurance policy that has a high deductible for "day to day" medical care but no deductible for major medical costs, including medication for chronic conditions; and (3) only the balance available in the account is available for health-care costs at any given time, although the insured may borrow against future payments to the MSA for current medical expenses.

One of the most obvious upshots in South Africa, one that regulators there have relentlessly attempted to curb with minimal success, is that insurers have competed to recruit the healthiest citizens. For example, MSAs are often sold in tandem with plans that offer bonuses that include "access to a range of exclusive gyms and exotic holidays," a recruitment strategy far more likely to attract young healthy individuals than older and sicker folks. Timothy Stoltzfus Jost, a law professor at Washington and Lee University who has studied South Africa's health-care system, notes that the MSA advocate Shaun Matisonn's own data provide supporting evidence of such cherry-picking—younger people are more likely to choose MSA products, while older South Africans choose non-MSA schemes.[30] A 2002 Department of Health review of the system there concluded that MSAs were a nuisance rather than a constructive innovation: "The focus of health policy needs to be on risk sharing and cost containment. None of these key health policy objectives can be achieved through medical savings accounts."[31] The department's recommendation: phase out MSAs.

The other big experiment with HSA-type plans has been in the authoritarian country of Singapore, where "tough it out" could well be the government's motto. Beginning in 1984, Singapore has required all of its citizens to pay between 6 and 8.5 percent of their income into a "Medisave" account. Money accumulated in the accounts is used to pay for inpatient care and expensive outpatient care. Those accounts are supplemented by a voluntary catastrophic insurance fund called "Medishield" and a safety net for the poor called "Medifund."[32] The out-of-pocket costs for the citizens of Singapore are huge—in 1995, 57.7 percent of total health expenditure came directly from patients, with only 8.5 percent from the accounts.[33]

The government initially attempted to foster competition among health-care providers by requiring them to make price information readily available. But by 1993, costs were rising so rapidly, even with all of the right's vaunted mechanisms for curbing "excess demand" largely in place, that the government decided that the system wasn't working. It turned out that the health-care providers ended up competing successfully for patients not so much on the basis of price but by recruiting the best-known physicians with higher pay and by having the most advanced, most costly technology.[34] So the government intervened in a big way, actively regulating the system to hold down costs through controls on the introduction of technology, price caps on services in government hospitals, restrictions on the number of government hospital beds, and limits on the number of doctors.[35] Those changes have succeeded in significantly containing costs, but the heavy-handed response of the government to the failure of Medi-save accounts and price transparency is not exactly the outcome that free-market advocates had in mind. It sure isn't what they continue to promise will happen in the United States under their approach, despite clear evidence (albeit vague, given Singapore's secrecy) to the contrary.

The Medicare Drug Debacle

As we've seen, the conservative movement's ideas in their rawest forms often seem to lack the sort of compassion that President Bush promised in the 2000 campaign. To fill that politically precarious void, his administration has from time to time tried to shoehorn ideologically driven design features into reforms that superficially sounded like the kinds of government initiatives that used to make Democrats popular. Those competing forces explain much about the No Child Left Behind Act and came into play again with the 2003 enactment of a new prescription drug benefit for Medicare, which just about everyone across the ideological spectrum agreed was an even bigger mess.

When it came time for the Bush administration to work with the Republican Congress to fashion a bill, they relentlessly looked for ways to make it adhere to conservative free-market principles while minimizing its estimated projected cost. The legislation that ultimately emerged was a mishmash of nonsensical provisions almost certain to baffle elderly beneficiaries, escalate the plan's ultimate financial burden on the government, and leave large numbers of people at risk of owing far more out of pocket than they can comfortably afford. The drug benefit—called Medicare Part D—has been in effect only since January 2006, but already its flaws have become widely apparent. Those shortcomings, which were entirely avoidable, were an outgrowth of attempting to fit the right's ideological predilections into a major initiative that most Republicans didn't want to undertake in the first place. Three aspects of the law directly tied to the right's approach to government are particularly culpable:

1. *The "doughnut hole."* Under Part D, beneficiaries pay a conventionally modest deductible of $250 for their drug costs before insurance kicks in and pays 75 percent for payments owed above that threshold. But once a beneficiary's medication costs for the year exceed $2,250, insurance coverage disappears entirely for the next $2,850 in expenses. It isn't until the individual's total prescription costs top $5,100 that insurance resumes, now covering 95 percent above that benchmark for "catastrophic" bills. That substantial gap in coverage has become known as the "doughnut hole"—a gap that is scheduled to get significantly bigger in the years ahead.

   That structure obviously leaves older Americans who elect the drug benefit vulnerable to owing thousands of dollars for their prescriptions, and the law expressly prohibits them from buying supplemental coverage that would fill Plan D's cavernous gaps. Why? One reason is the same premise behind HSAs: high out-of-pocket spending, in the conservative worldview, discourages excessive consumption of unnecessary prescriptions while holding down overall costs. A report published with the final version of the bill noted that the doughnut-hole provisions keep beneficiaries from becoming "insensitive to costs."[36]

2. *No government leverage.* In conformance with the right's belief system that private markets are inherently more efficient than the public sector, Medicare Part D prohibits the government

from directly negotiating with drug companies. Beneficiaries who sign up for the benefit are obligated to choose from among the private participating insurers that have their own agreed-upon arrangements with pharmaceutical firms. The claim that disallowing governmental participation will reduce the overall costs of the plan is dubious at best. Because of its size relative to individual private insurers, the government can exert enormous negotiating leverage with pharmaceutical companies. The Veterans Administration's drug plan, for example, pays less than half of what Medicare Part D's private insurers do for comparable prescriptions.[37] The Congressional Budget Office assessed prescription drug prices in several other countries with national health insurance and found that their costs were between 35 percent and 55 percent less than in the U.S. private market, in part because of the negotiating leverage of those governments.[38]

3. *Shabby initial implementation* The months immediately before and after the January 1, 2006, launch of the Medicare drug benefit swamped journalists with a seemingly endless stream of stories about beneficiaries overwhelmed by the complexity of the choices confronting them, inadequate numbers of government customer service representatives, an abundance of inaccurate information, and pharmacies teeming with outraged and befuddled elderly people. To a large extent, those problems were an inevitable outgrowth of Plan D's reliance on the market, which led to more than two dozen insurers competing for beneficiaries with upward of fifty complicated plans that diverged from each other in myriad, often incomprehensible, ways. But even after taking those inherent difficulties into account, the Bush administration's hapless efforts to help people demonstrated more of the sort of ineptitude examined in chapter 1 arising from government run by people who disdain government.

The journalist Jonathan Cohn wrote an article for the *New Republic* contrasting the Bush administration's inept efforts at preparing for the implementation of Part D with the administration of President Lyndon Johnson's far more ambitious launch of the entire Medicare program itself in the mid-1960s. Cohn wrote:

[In 2005], experts repeatedly warned the Bush administration that it had inadequate contingency plans in place, culminating in a December Government Accountability Office report that predicted with eerie accuracy exactly what has happened at pharmacies around the country. . . . LBJ's team was far more cautious. Although confident that hospitals could handle any potential surges, it still drew up plans for transferring patients to overflow facilities, even lining up helicopters in Texas to provide speedy transport.[39]

Of course, you can always count on conservatives to heroically spin their own failures as a reaffirmation of their ideology—much as they blamed FEMA's incompetence after Katrina on the inherent flaws of public bureaucracies. Grace Marie Turner, the president of the Galen Institute—another health savings account advocacy group funded by the usual suspects—told the *National Journal* that the debacle in implementing the Medicare drug benefit was just another example of the inevitable ineptitude of government. "Private insurers would never have designed the rollout this way. With the government running the Web site and designing the package in the first place, the problem is still government overreach."[40] Never mind that "the government running the Web site and designing the package in the first place" was completely under the control of conservatives who see the world exactly as Turner does.

The Medical Malpractice Myth

Conservatives, in their cost-cutting zeal, habitually imagine colossal waste everywhere while singling out "obvious" targets for which the only possible explanation must be rampant profligacy. The best solution, they believe, is usually a simple but ironclad spending limitation, as in the case of the Taxpayer's Bill of Rights. Another example is "malpractice reform," which the right for years has insisted will prevent rising health-care costs attributable to what they call "defensive medicine" and soaring insurance premiums for medical professionals.

Here's an excerpt from a speech about the topic that President Bush delivered in January 2005, standing before bleachers full of cheering doctors in white coats, which word-for-word recites complaints crafted for years at conservative think tanks:

> What's happening all across this country is that lawyers are filing baseless suits against hospitals and doctors. That's just a plain fact. And they're doing it for a simple reason. They know the medical liability system is tilted in their favor. Jury awards in medical liability cases have skyrocketed in recent years. That means every claim filed by a personal-injury lawyer brings the chance of a huge payoff or a profitable settlement out of court. That's what that means. Doctors and hospitals realize this. They know it's expensive to fight a lawsuit, even if it doesn't have any merit. And because the system is so unpredictable, there is a constant risk of being hit by a massive jury award. So doctors end up paying tens of thousands, or even hundreds of thousands of dollars to settle claims out of court, even when they know they have done nothing wrong.[41]

The president's argument has been repeated so many times, not only by movement conservatives and doctors but also by a broad spectrum of commentators who have come to accept it as virtually indisputable, that a number of states have adopted legislation imposing the logical solution: making it more difficult for patients to sue for malpractice and putting a cap on the awards they receive in the event that a jury finds in their favor. But in a masterful 2005 book on the subject titled *The Medical Malpractice Myth*, the law professor and director of the Insurance Law Center at the University of Connecticut Tom Baker synthesizes an extensive body of research that consistently and decisively contradicts virtually every claim that Bush and malpractice reform advocates make.[42] It turns out that patients as a class are as innocent of excessive litigiousness as they are of driving up medical costs through hyperconsumption of health care.

One of Baker's most significant findings is that actual malpractice is a far greater problem than generally understood, with harms inflicted on patients that exceed by orders of magnitude the number of lawsuits. Extensive studies—nationally, within particular states, and in different health-care settings—all have drawn the same conclusion. One of the most revealing was conducted by the Harvard Medical Practice in the 1980s, published in 1990.[43] Extrapolating from their findings, the researchers concluded that there were at least 27,000 injuries from medical malpractice in hospitals in New York during 1984. By comparison, there were only about 3,800 claims filed in New York under malpractice insurance policies covering that year. That is, there were more than seven malpractice injuries for every malpractice claim.

What about "excessive" awards to malpractice victims? Yet another RAND report looked at the growth in malpractice awards between 1960 and 1999. The conclusion reads, "Our results are striking. Not only do we show that real average awards have grown by less than real income over the 40 years of the sample, we also find that essentially all of this growth can be explained by changes in observable case characteristics and claimed economic losses."[44]

The impact of "tort reform" in states that have adopted restrictions on malpractice lawsuits has been the subject of considerable research, though not yet enough to draw decisive conclusions. So far, however, the evidence generally shows that tort reform does not improve medical outcomes, and certain kinds of malpractice restrictions may have a detrimental effect on health.[45] A 2004 Congressional Budget Office study, which looked at the effect of state tort reform on per patient spending by Medicare for a variety of illnesses, found "no effect of tort controls on medical spending."[46] In any case, tort reform is a solution to an imaginary problem and a distraction from the real issue of how to prevent high levels of negligent health care.

Genuine Health-Care Reform

Although most of the public recognizes that the biggest problem with the U.S. health-care system is that far too many citizens lack medical insurance, the conservative movement continues to relentlessly hype its claims that the country should focus on how overinsured Americans spend too much on medical care and on how excessive malpractice lawsuits drive up costs. Its preoccupation with health savings accounts and malpractice reform has accomplished little besides diverting debate away from another try at universal coverage. But mere distraction, in and of itself, is an enormous accomplishment for movement conservatives, while a continuing source of harm to the country generally, as well as to large numbers of Americans.

Repairing America's deeply flawed health-care system is the nation's most urgent domestic challenge.[47] Devoting such a large and rapidly growing share of our economic pie toward an inefficient and all-too-often ineffective medical industry threatens to further bog down living standards while leaving tens of millions of uninsured citizens at great risk to their finances and health. Achieving universal health insurance will be enormously difficult to accomplish not only because the problems are so complex and severe, but because the political forces in this country have proved time after time to be stacked in favor of inertia. From a policy standpoint, there is no shortage of models in other countries to draw from in designing a system that works better than ours. By guaranteeing that everyone in the population is covered by health insurance in one way or another, universal systems are far more efficient because of economies of scale, risk-pooling, and the absence of the extensive fragmentation that produces such high administrative costs here. The more forceful federal role also presents a variety of additional opportunities for controlling costs, depending on the system, whether through the exertion of leverage in negotiating prices or setting standards for approving payments only for effective treatments. Overall, Americans already spend far more than would be necessary to cover everyone. But getting from here to universal coverage requires the money to come out of different pockets, producing winners and losers in the process. And the potential losers will do anything in their power to prevent change. The conservative movement can be counted on to continue to help the opponents of reforms that would tackle the real problems.

That said, one set of constructive reforms where both the left and the right have found common ground relates to improving the quality of health care through greater public transparency and information sharing. A wide range of initiatives have proved to be successful along these lines, many of them spearheaded by Donald Berwick of the Institute for Healthcare Improvement. One example is Berwick's "100,000 Lives Campaign," in which participating hospitals adopted a short checklist of steps to take when treating patients under particular eventualities that commonly lead to avoidable deaths. Items on the checklist include automatically deploying rapid-response teams for emergency care of patients whose vital signs suddenly deteriorate, and giving aspirin and beta blockers to all heart attack patients shortly after admission and before they are discharged. Over the first eighteen months of the program, hospitals documented that 122,300 lives were saved.[48] Another example is an effort by the Colorado Health and Hospital Association to make available to consumers online information about the performance of twenty-seven Denver area hospitals with respect to eleven common medical procedures. Based on data compiled from hospital billing information, the association posted for each category and institution a grade indicating whether the mortality rate was above, below, or equal to the state average—after adjusting for factors such as age, gender, and illness severity.[49] One other case in point was the effort by the American Society of Anesthesiologists in the late 1980s to examine malpractice claims that had contributed to the profession's especially high rate of lawsuits. Based on those efforts, the society developed ways to reduce errors and now has one of the highest safety ratings in the profession, with its malpractice insurance premiums falling back to their 1985 levels.[50]

Conservatives and progressives will differ about how much the government should actively push for, or even require, such initiatives and whether financial incentives should be offered to health-care providers to encourage them to be more forthcoming in making information available about the quality of health care they provide. But just about everyone, outside of the health-care profession itself, agrees that quality will improve if more data are disclosed about patient outcomes and if best practices are widely shared and followed. The right isn't wrong about everything.

9

"A Sure Loser"
Social Security Privatization

For many years, the Cato Institute employed José Piñera as co-chairman of its Project on Social Security Choice/Privatization. What made Piñera such a crowd pleaser at Cato luncheons was his experience in privatizing Chile's pension system in 1981, when he served as labor minister to the former dictator Augusto Pinochet. During the 2005 Social Security debate, President Bush pointed to Chile's system as a "great example" from which the United States can "take some important lessons." The *CBS Evening News* even ran a laudatory segment about what it labeled "a success story," claiming that many Chileans had benefited from high rates of return on their investment accounts.

But with Social Security privatization, there's always more than meets the hype. For example, a 2004 report from the World Bank, which once enthusiastically promoted pension privatization in Latin America, noted with disappointment that "more than half of all workers [are excluded] from even a semblance of a safety net during their old age."[1] Stephen J. Kay of the Federal Reserve Bank of Atlanta studied Chile's experience and found that investment accounts of retirees are much smaller than originally predicted. One reason is that investment commissions and management fees in Chile and other Latin American countries with similar systems in many cases run more than twenty times Social Security's administrative costs, swallowing up a significant share of whatever returns workers earn. Kay also found that the transition costs to the government of shifting to a privatized system were far higher than originally projected. Many younger workers stayed out of the system entirely, finding it too cumbersome and costly, which only leaves more of tomorrow's elderly unprotected while adding to the future burden on the government.[2]

In January 2006, one of the few areas of agreement between the two opposing candidates for Chile's presidency was that the country's privatized pension system was in serious trouble. Of particular interest is that one of those candidates was José Piñera's brother Sebastian, in his own right a billionaire businessman and a conservative. In a debate, Sebastian Piñera said, "Chile's social security system requires deep reforms in all sectors, because half of Chileans have no pension coverage, and of those who do, 40 percent are going to find it hard to reach the minimum level." The *New York Times*, which provided excellent reporting on the problems with Chile's pensions throughout the U.S. Social Security debate, noted that Cato's Piñera would not respond to requests for an interview about his brother's criticism of the pension system he had created under Pinochet.[3]

Another model that Cato once extolled but that ultimately betrayed the right was the United Kingdom's privatized pension scheme. Beginning in 1985, Margaret Thatcher, second only to Ronald Reagan in the pantheon of conservative movement heroes, oversaw a fundamental transformation in her country's retirement support system. After she and her Conservative Party imposed reductions in guaranteed government benefits, they enacted legislation that allowed workers to "contract out" of the national system by setting up personal pensions instead. During the first five years after the changeover, about ten times as many workers as originally projected contracted out—a huge "take up" rate that was originally hailed as one of the triumphs of the Tory government. But in the late 1980s and early 1990s, in what was called the "mis-selling scandal," it became evident that a large percentage of those individuals had been lured by unscrupulous investment brokers into arrangements that would leave them far worse off than if they had simply remained in the government system. Over the course of eight years, the government imposed fines of about 12 billion pounds to compensate 1.7 million people.[4]

Even after reforms were instituted, the British pension system remains deeply troubled. High commissions and fees continue to eat into the returns on investment accounts. Large numbers of citizens are at high risk of impoverishment in their retirement. Meanwhile, in

2004 alone, 500,000 people chose to abandon their private pensions and return to the government system. Norma Cohen, a senior corporate reporter at the *Financial Times* who wrote a piece for the *American Prospect* detailing the problems with the U.K.'s privatized pension system, noted that even some conservatives there have been looking more and more kindly on American Social Security as a model for reform. Christine Farnish, the chief executive of the National Association of Pension Funds, which represents employers who sponsor the largest private pensions, told Cohen, "It's actually cheaper for the state to carry the risk. It doesn't have to make a profit, and it delivers efficiencies of scale that most companies would die for."[5]

America Avoids the Same Fate

Undaunted by the unhappy experiences in Chile and the United Kingdom, the conservative movement launched a full-bore effort to support President George W. Bush's call to do much the same thing to America's Social Security system. Ultimately, though, Bush's push to partially privatize the retirement, disability, and life insurance program flopped despite months of extensive personal campaigning for the top domestic priority of his second term.

An October 20, 2005, front-page postmortem in the *Wall Street Journal*, headlined "How a Victorious Bush Fumbled Plan to Revamp Social Security: A Divided Republican Party, Strong Opposition Derails Push for Private Accounts," attempted to explain what went wrong. The story documented a litany of political roadblocks that arose in rapid-fire succession, beginning almost the moment after Bush pronounced at his first post-reelection news conference: "We'll start on Social Security now." That stunning statement meant that he was going to press for a fundamental change to the nation's most successful and popular federal program, diverting a portion of the taxes that finance the system into individual investment accounts. Right off the bat, many Republicans in Congress recoiled. The *Journal* quotes Senator Lindsey Graham of South Carolina, a Republican who strongly supports privatization, as saying that Bush "jumped out with a very big idea that he ran on, but he didn't lay the political groundwork in the Senate or the House. He ran on it. We didn't. He's not up for election again. We are."

Other obstacles: insufficient advance warning to enable right-wing advocacy groups to fully mobilize at the outset behind privatization; the quick galvanization of labor, AARP, and other opponents of the idea; the success of Harry Reid of Nevada, the new leader of the Senate Democrats, in managing to sustain uncharacteristically united opposition from his flock against the president's plan; and irreconcilable divisions that emerged on the Republican side. Ultimately, privatization ended with a whimper because Republicans who insisted on combining the president's proposed new accounts with Social Security benefit cuts—"the pain caucus"—couldn't find common ground with the "free lunch" conservatives who wanted just the accounts without any other changes, regardless of the fiscal ramifications.[6] The *Journal* might also have mentioned, but didn't, the role in privatization's demise of polls showing declining support for the president's plan as his campaign progressed, media coverage that increasingly highlighted the proposal's risks, and effective Internet-based efforts to rally the public against the idea.

All of those observations about what went wrong politically are accurate, as far as they go. But they miss the underlying explanation for the failure. The real reason that Social Security privatization unraveled is that the idea itself is an utter fraud.

Sink or Swim

Most major public policy proposals that reach the point where they become seriously considered by Congress have evident strengths, weaknesses, and uncertainties connected to them about what their actual impact will be. That's true of virtually all plans that emanate from across the ideological spectrum, regardless of whether the subject is health care, welfare, the environment, taxes, and so on. Legislation that ends up before Congress has already been fairly well baked in the sense that debate over it centers on whether the benefits from the plan in advancing its stated goals will outweigh its costs, taking into account guesses about unexpected consequences that might arise.

But proposals to partially privatize Social Security—all of them, regardless of the particulars—are less than half baked. That is, the changes that privatization plans would set in motion would directly and inevitably undercut the purported goals of the legislation. All privatization proposals inherently weaken, rather than strengthen, Social Security, the federal budget, and the retirement security of Americans. Those fundamental flaws are matters of mathematics—rather simple mathematics at that. Dismantling Social Security—not "saving" or strengthening it—is precisely the reason why conservatives support privatization. It's the reason why the libertarian Cato Institute has for more than two decades spent untold resources trying to spread fear about the existing system and imparting egregiously misleading claims about private accounts. To pass the political laugh test, privatization proponents have to try to fool people into thinking that somehow their plan will bolster Social Security and the retirement prospects for tomorrow's elderly. But as long as the laws of subtraction and multiplication remain sound, their proposals would inherently do the opposite. That's why Social Security privatization—far and away the conservative movement's highest domestic aspiration—was a political failure in 2005 and would inevitably be a policy failure if, save us, it ever became law in the future.

For years, privatization advocates have been partial to the *Titanic* as a metaphor for Social Security. Someday government's big ocean liner is going to ram into an iceberg and sink, they like to say, taking all of us down with it. One could indulge them and respond by noting that a few minor midcourse corrections could steer the program and all of us clear of those distant dangers, which is true.[7] But the much more important point is that privatization amounts to descending into the hull and tossing around a few hand grenades. Its intent is to destroy. The grenade throwers, however, will say anything to get you to think they're just trying to transfer people to a leaner, faster vessel when the only possible outcome would be to leave the vast majority of working Americans much farther out to sea than they otherwise would be.

It's not difficult to understand why privatization is a fraud—though journalists compelled to report on the subject from the standpoint of "balanced neutrality" rarely came right out and told their readers and viewers what should have been fairly obvious. Start with forecasts of what will happen to the program if nothing is done to it. The most commonly used projections are developed by the Social Security Trustees, who annually assemble a 200-plus-page report describing everything anyone could possibly want to know about the state of the system and its future prospects. Privatization supporters don't really dispute anything in it.[8]

The 2005 report's "intermediate" forecast—the one based on assumptions roughly halfway between its "high-cost" (pessimistic) and "low-cost" (optimistic) scenarios—showed that the program will be able to continue paying all currently promised benefits in full until the year 2041. After that point, the payroll taxes funding the system will be sufficient to pay 74 percent of promised benefits, declining gradually to 68 percent by 2079. The total shortfall between promised benefits and projected revenues amounts to 1.92 percent of all the expected future payroll income subject to the Social Security tax.[9] The reason why Social Security's costs will gradually rise, of course, is the coming retirement of the Baby Boom generation—those born between 1946 and 1964—and declining fertility rates.

Just to provide a sense of scale, the financing gap could be bridged by raising the existing 6.2 percent Social Security payroll tax that both workers and employers currently pay to 7.2 percent. Increasing the combined rate 2 percentage points from 12.4 to 14.4 would be more than enough to cover the 1.92 percent shortfall. Deducting a few hundred more dollars annually from the paychecks of already struggling Americans is obviously a nonstarter politically, but it demonstrates that the problem is far from insurmountable. Another way to think about the size of the gap: all of Bush's tax cuts since 2001, if made permanent, amount to nearly three times as much as the Social Security shortfall.[10]

Today, payroll taxes are more than sufficient to finance all the benefits owed to current retirees, disabled workers, and families of deceased workers. Roughly nine out of every ten payroll tax dollars collected each year go right back out the door to beneficiaries. The remaining dollar is credited to Social Security's trust fund, which is invested entirely in U.S. Treasury securities and loaned back to the government. When the overall federal budget was in surplus late in the 1990s, the Social Security trust fund provided the resources to pay down the national debt; now that the overall budget is in deficit, the money is used to finance government outlays while reducing the amount of government borrowing from the public that would otherwise have to take place.

So Social Security's problem is a genuine but manageable long-term financing shortfall based on highly uncertain seventy-five-year forecasts. Not incidentally, the Congressional Budget Office issued its own projections, which even more optimistically showed that the Social Security trust fund would hold out until 2052, after which pay-roll taxes would be sufficient to pay 78 percent of promised benefits.[11] Keep in mind that seventy-five years ago, the country was in the early stages of the Great Depression, when no one imagined even the advent of Social Security, much less World War II, the broadly shared economic prosperity that followed, the civil rights movement, space travel, personal computers, the Internet, and so on. Acting rashly today based on predictions extending three-quarters of a century into the future would seem to be less than prudent.

Worse Than Nothing

What would privatization do to solve Social Security's long-term financing problem? News reports throughout the debate often said, in effect, "nothing." But that's wrong. Privatization would actually make Social Security's financing shortfall *worse*—more immediate and more severe. It has to. By diverting substantial tax revenues now ear-marked to the program into personal investment accounts, privatiza-tion deprives the system of the money that would otherwise go to pay benefits over time. Creating new personal accounts would not change the amount of revenue that the government collects, but it would increase federal spending a lot because the accounts would have to be financed while payments owed to current and future Social Security beneficiaries ages fifty-five and older (the president promised) would be honored in full.

The upshot: under the personal accounts proposal that the presi-dent endorsed, the date when Social Security's trust fund would be exhausted would move up from 2041 to 2030. The date when the sys-tem would have to begin drawing from the interest on the assets in the program's trust fund would be pushed forward from 2017 to 2011. And, in the process, the federal government would have to borrow about $5 trillion over the first twenty years alone of the plan's imple-mentation. By 2050, Social Security privatization would increase the federal debt by about 19 percent of the Gross Domestic Product—roughly half as much as today's entire national debt.[12]

When the point is made, privatization advocates either change the subject or resort to the old smoke and mirrors.[13] They invariably end up going back to their extreme exaggerations about how the existing system is going, as the president repeatedly said, "Bust, bankrupt, flat-out broke." The mischievous implication is that if the thing is going to fall apart eventually anyway, why not dismantle it now?

The biggest selling point for privatization advocates has always been that their approach would provide a much better deal for future retirees than Social Security would. Cato's Social Security Web site famously provides a calculator that magically generates high six-figure and even seven-figure lump sums under privatization, almost regardless of your financial circumstances. But it turns out that claims about higher rates of return, too, are demonstrably—not just theoretically—false. Even conservative economists like Gary Becker, Robert Barro, Olivia Mitchell, and former Bush chief economic adviser N. Gregory Mankiw have acknowledged that private accounts wouldn't make future retirees better off.[14]

There are three main reasons why the rate-of-return argument for privatization is bogus. One of those explanations is that Social Security is fundamentally an insurance program, as opposed to an investment plan. It protects all workers and their families against a number of risks that can befall people throughout their lives. If you become disabled, Social Security provides benefits to you and your family—unlike investment accounts. If you die, Social Security provides benefits to your survivors. About a third of the program's beneficiaries receive disability and/or survivor's insurance payments. Moreover, upon retirement, Social Security protects you against inflation by indexing its benefits to increases in living costs—unlike investment accounts. Social Security also protects you against outliving your assets, unlike investment accounts, because its payments continue to you and your surviving spouse until you both die. Those insurance protections, which would be costly in the private marketplace if you could even find comparable products, have substantial, real value that rate-of-return measurements don't fully capture.

When you buy homeowner's insurance, your hope is that it will yield a low rate of return; you get a big payoff from it only if something bad happens to your property, such as a flood or a robbery. Taking into account Social Security's insurance protections, taxpayers across the income spectrum receive far more value than just the retirement payments they can expect to receive. Investment accounts do not provide insurance protections, and privatization would almost inevitably dilute Social Security's existing insurance coverage despite claims to the contrary.

Second, the huge borrowing required to create the new accounts eventually has to be paid off, which significantly cuts into rates of return. Under the president's proposal, workers who elected to open investment accounts would, in effect, only be allowed to keep returns that exceeded the rate of inflation plus 2.7 percent. Individuals whose accounts earned less would receive no premium from their investments and would end up with less than if they hadn't opened accounts in the first place. That so-called clawback provision reflects the fact that the government in effect is making a loan to workers to enable them to create their accounts—and the loan must be repaid when they draw upon the accounts in their retirement. Neither the Cato calculator nor the many other pro-privatization PowerPoint presentations extolling the magic of compounding interest came clean with the public that the costs of making the transition to the new system would have to be subtracted from the pocketbooks of workers in their golden years.

Third, higher investment returns can be attained only by bearing greater risk. For that reason, the Congressional Budget Office and even the Bush administration's own Office of Management and Budget incorporated the cost of the added risks associated with the stock market when they projected what rates of return will be. In effect, that "risk-adjusted" rate of return amounts to the same 2.7 percent above inflation that Treasury securities historically provide. Even though stocks have provided higher returns over time on average, investors must be willing to accept a greater degree of risk that they will end up worse off than if they keep their money in the safest investment. Economists adjust for the cost of bearing additional risk in making projections about the future by assuming that returns to investors in the aggregate will amount to the expected return on the safest option—U.S. Treasury securities.[15]

Taking into account those three factors, combined with cuts in guaranteed benefits under the "progressive price indexing" approach[16] that the president endorsed, projections of what workers would ultimately receive under his proposal show that all except individuals with the lowest incomes would end up with much less than they would receive under the current system.[17] For example, average wage workers (earning $36,600 in 2005) who retire in 2045 at age sixty-five are scheduled to receive $19,837 annually from Social Security (in 2005 dollars); under progressive price indexing, their Social Security benefit would be $16,584 — 16 percent less. Workers with higher earnings would end up with even deeper reductions. Those cuts apply to everyone, whether or not they elect personal accounts. Workers who opted for private accounts would have their guaranteed benefits reduced further, reflecting the fact that they will have to pay back the government for its loan to open the accounts. The only chance of ending up better off would be if their investment returns happen to significantly exceed the 2.7 percent real rate of return. Obviously, retirement prospects for workers would be much less secure than if relatively modest adjustments were implemented, along the lines of Robert Ball's plan, to sustain the current system.

Let's now go back to President Bush's 2005 State of the Union address to hear his key phrases about his plans for Social Security:

> One of America's most important institutions — a symbol of the trust between generations — is also in need of wise and effective reform. Social Security was a great moral success of the 20th century, and we must honor its great purposes in this new century. [Applause.] The system, however, on its current path, is headed toward bankruptcy.

Actually, on its current path, significant benefit cuts would be required in several decades, but payroll taxes contributed by future workers would still be sufficient to pay about three-fourths of promised benefits.

> And so we must join together to strengthen and save Social Security. [Applause.]

In fact, as we have seen, diverting payroll taxes to finance private accounts would inherently weaken Social Security and threaten to unravel the program entirely.

> As we fix Social Security, we also have the responsibility to make the system a better deal for younger workers. And the best way to

reach that goal is through voluntary personal retirement accounts. [Applause.]

Again, even conservative economists have conceded that private accounts would not improve rates of return. In fact, because of the huge government borrowing required to pay for the accounts and the risks associated with them, the lion's share of workers would be worse off.

> The goal here is greater security in retirement, so we will set careful guidelines for personal accounts.

Today, about one-fifth of retirees depend on Social Security for all of their income; nearly two-thirds of beneficiaries rely on the program for more than half of their income.[18] Dramatically reducing those promised benefits, as the president proposed, would inevitably—no ifs, ands, or buts—make Americans less secure in their retirement.

How could such a half-baked idea possibly have reached the point where the president of the United States stood before the nation and endorsed it with rhetoric that is demonstrably untrue? It's one of the modern conservative movement's great success stories.

The "Leninist Strategy" Is Born

Back in 1981, Social Security really was on the verge of a crisis. The system's trust fund, which historically had been adequate to provide a cushion of only a few months' to a year's worth of benefit payments, faced a deficit by the summer of 1983. Without changes, beneficiaries faced a disruption in the processing of their checks until additional revenue could be found to cover the gap.

President Ronald Reagan, who had expressed hostility toward Social Security as "a sure loser" from the 1950s onward, initially assigned David Stockman, the director of the Office of Management and Budget, with the task of responding to the problem. Stockman deeply shared the contempt of his boss for big government and saw an opportunity in the looming shortfall, crafting a package of benefit cuts. Eligibility rules for collecting disability benefits would be tightened. A new cap would be placed on the total Social Security benefits in certain categories that a single family could receive. Payments to particular kinds of dependents would be eliminated. And, most important, benefits to workers who retire before age sixty-five would be reduced by about a third. Under Stockman's plan, assembled with only a handful of others, the penalty for leaving the workforce between the ages of sixty-two and sixty-five would be boosted from 20 percent of the normal Social Security benefit to 45 percent. The changes would take effect almost immediately after enactment, meaning that workers approaching retirement suddenly would discover that they would receive substantially less than they had been expecting. In his book *The Triumph of Politics*, Stockman describes with a curious sense of pride how he conveyed the proposals to the president in a background paper written in "perfectly incomprehensible Social Security Administration format and jargon which obscured almost everything." The cover memo "explained almost nothing." When Stockman presented the plan directly to Reagan, who was still recuperating from John W. Hinckley Jr.'s assassination attempt just a few weeks earlier, "Only 60 minutes had been allotted for that meeting on May 11 with the president—not much time to review a plan which in both philosophy and detail reversed 45 years of Social Security history."[19]

Reagan signed off, word got out, and the country went nuts. A little more than a week after the May 11 meeting, the Republican-led Senate voted 96 to 0 for a resolution rejecting Stockman's Social Security cuts. The political debacle sent Reagan's poll ratings into a tailspin and, in the words of the Reagan biographer Lou Cannon, ended "any major assault against the basic premises of the federal budget."[20]

Chastened, Reagan in late 1981 appointed a bipartisan panel chaired by the Wall Street economist Alan Greenspan, who had served as head of the Council of Economic Advisers under President Ford, to come up with ideas to improve Social Security's finances. The National Commission on Social Security, as it was called, had more clout than most such blue-panel groups because it included four sitting U.S. senators. But after deliberating through December 1982 (and dismissing out of hand a proposal by the conservative Stanford economist Michael Boskin to convert the program into a system of private accounts), the commission reached an impasse with the shortfall now approaching just a few months away.[21] The Republican members wanted benefit cuts, while the Democrats wanted to rely mainly on tax increases, and no one was inclined to compromise.

At that point, White House aide Richard Darman told Robert Ball, the former commissioner of Social Security and a pivotal Democratic member of the panel, that top administration officials were making plans to seize the offensive if no agreement was reached. Martin Feldstein, the chairman of Reagan's Council of Economic Advisers, was gaining traction in the White House with recommendations to put big Social Security benefit cuts before Congress. Darman said he believed that if no agreement was reached, Reagan could be convinced to launch an educational campaign to convince the public that the program should be phased out or greatly reduced.[22] Ball took the threat seriously and put together a plan that, in part, delayed cost-of-living adjustments for six months, accelerated previously scheduled payroll tax increases, taxed a portion of the benefits of upper-income retirees, and required all newly hired federal workers and employees of nonprofit institutions to pay Social Security taxes. The jump-started negotiations ultimately resulted in an agreement by January 15, which Congress approved virtually without change within weeks.

The 1983 reforms went far beyond the immediate task of simply deferring another Social Security shortfall for a few years. Anticipating the retirement of the Baby Boom generation beginning nearly thirty years in the future, the Greenspan Commission struck an explicit bargain with workers. Their payroll taxes would be significantly increased to finance a large trust fund guaranteeing that benefits would be paid to them when they retired many years down the road. In effect, this approach meant that the added cost of paying benefits to retired Baby Boomers ultimately would be financed by a slice of the income taxes owed by future workers. Just as a portion of today's income tax revenue goes toward interest and principal owed to holders around the world of U.S. Treasury securities, in the future a share of income tax revenue would end up, by way of the trust fund, financing Social Security benefit checks.

The Greenspan Commission's solution placed part of the added burden of financing the retirement of the Baby Boom generation on the shoulders of the future workers who will be most able to afford to pay. Income taxes, in contrast to Social Security payroll taxes, are progressive; that is, workers with the highest earnings pay a substantially larger share of their incomes to the Internal Revenue Service than do middle- and low-income families. The Baby Boomers themselves also bear their own share of sacrifice because the Greenspan Commission both increased their payroll taxes—raising national savings in the process—and gradually raised the age when they could collect full benefits to sixty-seven by the year 2022. By addressing the long-term challenge of sustaining Social Security well into the next century with changes that distributed the costs fairly, the 1983 reforms were widely hailed as a reasonable and courageous political compromise.

At the signing ceremony, Reagan proclaimed, "This bill demonstrates for all time our nation's ironclad commitment to Social Security. It assures the elderly that America will always keep the promises made in troubled times a half a century ago. It assures those who are still working that they, too, have a pact with the future. From this day forward, they have our pledge that they will get their fair share of benefits when they retire."[23]

But during the 2005 debate over Social Security privatization, time and again President Bush and advocates of private accounts talked about the retirement of the Baby Boom generation as though no one had ever before noticed the inevitable demographic changes facing the country—the very changes that the Greenspan Commission's reforms addressed with remarkable success. Twenty-two years after Reagan signed those adjustments into law, without any significant intervening legislation, the Trustees' forecasts showing that the next shortfall isn't due until 2041 demonstrated just how effective the 1983 reforms had been. Nonetheless, at one point Bush even went to the Bureau of the Public Debt in West Virginia as a photo-op before a speech in which he said, "A lot of people in America think there is a trust—that we take your money in payroll taxes and then we hold it for you and then when you retire, we give it back to you. But that's not the way it works. There is no 'trust fund'—just IOUs that I saw first hand."[24] In other words, Reagan's "ironclad commitment" was a ruse pulled on the American people. Tarnishing the reputation of the conservative movement's foremost icon is a small price to pay for the right's ultimate prize of tearing down the government's biggest, most successful program.

President Bush's line of attack derives directly from a blueprint that was published in the *Cato Journal* just a few months after Reagan signed the 1983 reforms into law. Written by Stuart Butler and Peter Germanis of the Heritage Foundation, the article was called "Achieving a 'Leninist' Strategy."[25] Butler and Germanis wrote that because "it will be a long time before citizen indignation will cause radical changes to take place" to Social Security, the conservative movement should follow the path of Lenin, who believed that capitalism (like Social Security, in the eyes of the authors) was doomed by its inherent contradictions. "Unlike many other socialists at the time, Lenin recognized that fundamental change is contingent both upon a movement's ability to create a focused political coalition and upon its success in isolating and weakening its opponents." Butler and Germanis went on to describe a strategy of "guerrilla warfare against both the Social Security system and the coalition that supports it," particularly emphasizing the importance of convincing already skeptical young workers that the program would be long gone by the time they retired.

The plan that Butler and Germanis pointed to as a model for reform had been developed by the libertarian Peter J. Ferrara, who had written a paper while attending Harvard Law School that outlined how Social Security could be converted into a web of private investments. The irony, of course, is that Ferrara's proposal and the varying incarnations that succeeded it in the years that followed never managed to resolve their own genuinely inherent contradictions. None of them—not one—ever figured out how to simultaneously sustain existing benefits for current retirees and finance new accounts without creating much bigger fiscal problems than Social Security's long-term shortfall. None of them—not one—ever managed to explain convincingly how the retirement security of Americans would be improved by exposing them to greater market risk. None of them—not one—ever demonstrated how workers would end up financially better off in their retirement after taking into account transition costs.

For years, those fundamental problems with privatization kept the idea from being taken seriously outside of libertarian circles, with the exception of periodic articles about Social Security by journalists who by and large didn't understand what they were writing about. The presidential candidate Pierre S. "Pete" DuPont IV (R-Del.) endorsed the idea in 1988, but few people took him seriously either.[26]

During the 1990s, though, the privatization concept slowly but surely gathered steam. The single most important factor was the bull market, which was providing annual returns to investors in the double digits, particularly in the second half of the decade. As stocks soared, right-wing foundations and investment companies seeded an assortment of new pro-privatization outposts to supplement the efforts of Cato and Heritage in peddling purportedly big payoffs from investing Social Security taxes in the market. With names like For Our Grandchildren, the Alliance for Worker Retirement Security, the Third Millenium, and Generations Together, they honed a marketing pitch that bubbled with all the excitement of infomercials hawking no-money-down real estate and AbBlasters.[27] Americans enviously watching investors get rich and journalists looking for something new to write about started to pay more attention.

Another factor was heightened recognition that the aging of the population was becoming more imminent, combined with a growing drumbeat on the part of some opinion leaders that the demographic changes would be "unaffordable" for the country. Some of the alarmist arguments, particularly about the risks posed by rapidly increasing health-care costs as the population ages, were legitimate. But in regard to Social Security, their claims that the country could not adapt to the program's gradual growth from 4.6 percent of GDP a year today to about 6.4 percent annually by around 2030 were hyperbolic. Nonetheless, the escalating sense of concern about the retirement of the Baby Boomers in general and about Social Security in particular increased the appetite for an "outside-the-box," unconventional idea to "reform" the program.[28]

A less commonly recognized but crucial factor in privatization's emergence was the role played by Harvard professor Martin Feldstein, the economist who had earlier encouraged Reagan to push for big cuts in Social Security benefits. Throughout the 1990s, especially in the second half of the decade, Feldstein published studies, edited volumes of academic papers, and wrote op-eds that supported privatization. Unlike the eccentric Ferrara, who had no background in economics and little credibility in academic circles, Feldstein has long been widely regarded as one of the grand pooh-bahs of the economics profession. It is difficult to exaggerate his influence, which was comparable to the role that the Brookings scholars John Chubb and Terry Moe played in lending scholarly cover to the idea of school vouchers. One of the original supply-siders discussed in chapter 4, Feldstein since 1977 has been president (with one brief break) of the National Bureau of Economic Research, which publishes research papers that come out well in advance of publication in academic journals. In that role, he shapes the research agenda for the profession and guides the work of individual economists, forming relationships with many of its leading lights. For years, Feldstein has also had an opportunity in his Ec10 introductory economics class at Harvard to indoctrinate large lecture halls filled with tomorrow's leaders about the insidious effects of taxes.[29]

Because Feldstein ended up proposing a number of different privatization plans over the years, critiquing each one in detail would be tedious. But they all had similar flaws: failing to account sufficiently for the risks associated with higher potential stock returns; comparing future retirement benefits under his proposals, which entailed large infusions of additional money from unexplained sources, with Social Security scenarios in which no supplemental funding arises; and assuming without any basis in fact that private accounts would boost savings generally, producing greater economic growth.[30] Feldstein was especially creative in trying to surmount the challenge of transition costs, which he sometimes simply assumed out of existence. For example, Peter R. Orszag and Jonathan M. Orszag offered this analysis[31] of one of Feldstein's more recent proposals, which he published with Jeffrey Liebman in January 2000:[32]

> In presenting their data and conclusions, [Feldstein and Liebman] do not incorporate the cost of moving from the current pay-as-you-go Social Security system to the individual account system. The authors are well aware of the transition costs associated with such a shift but choose to exclude them from the calculations in their paper. They write that their analysis "deals with only the long-run situation in which the demographic change has increased the cost of the pay-as-you-go system and the alternative plans are fully phased in. In practice, of course, it would be necessary to go through a transition period in which the population is aging and the new funding system is gradually put into place." In effect, the comparisons that Feldstein and Liebman undertake are similar to a comparison between buying a home and renting an apartment in which the unrealistic assumption is made that the mortgage on the home is already paid off. . . . By assuming away a key cost—the mortgage payments—the analysis would be misleading and highly biased toward one option.

The shortcomings of Feldstein's work flew way over the heads of most noneconomists. The general presumption, in light of his stature, was that any questions about the validity of his conclusions must be nothing more than the usual academic quibbling that always arises over policy proposals. But when the number crunchers at the White House Office of Management and Budget, the Social Security Administration, and the Congressional Budget Office assessed the impact of Social Security privatization during the 2005 debate, they implicitly concluded, in effect, that Feldstein all along had been assuming away the fundamental flaws of the idea.

Social Security privatization doesn't add up. It never has and never will. But the conservative movement believes it can sell anything.

Spin Cycle

Ever since Franklin Delano Roosevelt signed the Social Security Act into law in 1935, conservatives have recited a litany of grievances against the program that sound much the same from decade to decade. In a superb *New York Times Magazine* article, Roger Lowenstein catalogued the depth of the right's long-standing hostility toward Social Security as a "socialistic scourge":[33]

> Playing on the fact that each worker was to receive a government number, the Hearst papers published front-page illustrations of a man wearing a chain with a dog tag. Henry Ford said Social Security could cost Americans their basic freedoms, like the right to change jobs or to move from one town to another. . . .
>
> Alfred Landon, the Republican who ran against Roosevelt in 1936, called it "a cruel hoax" on the American people. . . . His platform . . . stated, "The so-called reserve fund is no reserve at all, because the fund will contain nothing but the government's promise to pay."

Milton Friedman wrote that Social Security "involves a large-scale intrusion into the lives of a large fraction of the nation without, so far as I can see, any justification that is at all persuasive, not only on liberal principles, but almost on any other."[34] Barry Goldwater, who said programs like Social Security transform a recipient into a "dependent animal creature," proposed repealing it entirely.[35] Note that the objection is purely ideological. Conservatives and libertarians have no problem dismantling an immensely popular, fair, and effective program—one that has much to do with the decline in poverty among the elderly from more than 35 percent before 1960 to about 10 percent today—simply because it doesn't conform to their convictions of how the world ought to work.

Still, Reagan and Stockman's bruising experience in trying to impose cuts on the program in 1981 reinforced Social Security's reputation as the "third rail of American politics." The Republican president Dwight Eisenhower had recognized as much when he wrote, "Should any political party attempt to abolish social security, unemployment insurance, and eliminate labor laws and farm programs, you would not hear of that party again in our political history. There is a tiny splinter group, of course, that believes you can do these things. . . . Their number is negligible and they are stupid."[36]

So the conservative movement had no illusions that attaining the crowning achievement of bringing down Social Security would be anything other than a political high-wire act. Shortly after President George W. Bush took office in 2001, he gingerly stepped out on the tightrope by appointing a sixteen-member "President's Commission to Strengthen Social Security." Unlike past Social Security blue-panel groups, and there have been many, the individuals chosen for Bush's commission were prescreened to ensure their openness to the idea of diverting payroll taxes to private accounts. A key staff member was Andrew Biggs of the Cato Institute. Treasury Secretary Paul O'Neill, a privatization advocate, believed it was a mistake to stack the commission with like-minded members. He later told the author Ron Suskind, "If you're certain you're right—and I think we are on private accounts—you shouldn't be afraid to include the opposing voices at your table."[37] One of the commission's guiding principles was that "modernization must include individually controlled, voluntary personal retirement accounts, which will augment Social Security."[38]

Just before the end of 2001, the commission produced a unanimous report that put forward three alternative privatization plans. But its release only three months after the September 11 terrorist attacks, when Congress and the country generally were preoccupied with the challenge of preventing future terrorism, and in the wake of the stock market collapse, caused barely a ripple. As the *Los Angeles Times* reporter and Pulitzer Prize–winner Michael A. Hiltzik noted in his excellent book *The Plot against Social Security*, the next day's newspapers buried the story—on page 27 in the *New York Times*, page 33 in the *Washington Post*, and page 20 in the *Wall Street Journal*. Hiltzik wrote, "Most coverage interpreted the three-option package as a retreat from President Bush's original mandate that the commission produce one plan to be railroaded through Congress on a single vote."[39]

The commission report sat dormant until the president resumed his privatization push in 2005, but it lay in wait as a potentially useful political prop when the debate began in earnest after the State of the Union address. Always armed for rhetorical warfare, privatization advocates and the Republican leadership in Congress assembled a playbook of a hundred-plus pages, replete with talking points, polling data, sample constituent letters, op-eds, suggested speeches, a PowerPoint presentation, and other resources. Thumbing through that document underlines the extent to which the right was determined to remain on the offensive in undercutting public support for Social Security—the Leninist strategy still very much alive—while making misleading claims, at best, about the impact of privatization.[40]

In fact, the very word *privatization* itself was one that the playbook strongly admonishes its readers against invoking. In the chapter titled "Communicating Social Security Reform," the first item under "key recommendations" reads as follows:

> *"Personalization" not "privatization"*: Personalization suggests increased personal ownership and control. Privatization connotes the total corporate takeover of Social Security; this is inaccurate and thoroughly turns off listeners, who are very concerned about corporate wrongdoing.

Of course, it was the conservative movement itself that invested so much over many years in popularizing the concept of Social Security *privatization*, using that very word at every opportunity. Cato's effort was labeled the "Project on Social Security Privatization" from 1995 until stealthily transforming into the "Project on Social Security Choice" in 2002 after focus group results came in. (Its Web site now inaccurately says that the effort was inaugurated in 1995 as the "Project on Social Security Choice.")

Leaving aside the conservative etymology of *privatization*, the term is also a more precise description of what the president proposed than the "personal accounts" construction that the conservative poll-ster Frank Luntz and his followers demanded be invoked. The "-iza-tion" suffix conveys that Social Security would be fundamentally transformed from its existing state into something different. The phrase "personal accounts," in contrast, fails to communicate that the program would be changed. President Clinton also had a "personal accounts" proposal, but his plan would have supplemented Social Security rather than shifting funds away from it into accounts. While the terminology wars were largely fought over the difference between "private" and "personal" accounts, it was really the right's largely suc-cessful push to get the media to stop using the word *privatization* that misled the public. A proposal for either private accounts or personal accounts sounds far less threatening than what the president actually wanted to do: partially privatize Social Security.

The centerpiece of the "Saving Social Security" playbook is the theme tracing back to Alf Landon that the system's trust fund is noth-ing but an empty promise. With forecasts showing that the program can continue to pay benefits in full until the year 2041, generating the sense of urgency required to produce immediate change left privatiza-tion advocates with no other choice than to undercut public faith in the assets that will sustain the program that long. So here's the script provided by the playbook, one that the president and supporters of pri-vatization recited with only minor variations and flourishes through-out the debate:

> One argument for doing nothing goes like this, "The Social Secu-rity trust fund can tide us over." After all, these people say, this trust fund contains billions of dollars in government bonds. Unfor-tunately, no, the trust fund doesn't help at all. Some say that the Social Security trust fund has been looted. But the real problem is that the "Social Security trust fund" is an empty promise.
>
> You see, the trust fund is filled with government bonds. These are an excellent, stable investment under most circumstances. But in this particular case, the bonds are IOUs written by the govern-ment to the government. That's the problem. Think of it this

way—normally a bond works like loaning money to a friend. Let's say you lent $100 to your friend Joe. You trusted Joe to repay you, so for 20 years, you carried around an IOU from him. When it came time to finally get the cash, you just turned that piece of paper over to Joe, and he gave you the money. Clean and simple.

But now suppose, instead of loaning that money to Joe, you had decided to just spend that $100. And let's say you wrote yourself an IOU, promising to pay yourself back for the money you'd spent. You carried it around for 20 years, and then one day you found that you needed cash. Bad news—having that IOU from yourself to yourself doesn't help. If you needed more cash, you'd have to go out and earn it.

And this is exactly the problem with the Social Security trust fund. It's really just one giant IOU. The money that was in the trust fund has been spent by the rest of the federal government. In order to put that money back into Social Security when it's needed, the government will have to borrow money, make cuts somewhere else in the budget, or raise taxes. And we're talking here about massive amounts of money. The trust fund does not delay the need for action by a single day or reduce the cost of paying benefits by a dollar.

Here again, the privatizers are playing three-card monte. Since the nation's founding, the federal government has issued debt both to the public and to particular government agencies. All of that debt, including the U.S. Treasury securities held in the Social Security trust fund, are backed by the full faith and credit of the United States. Not once has the federal government ever come close to defaulting on a single bond or note, even when the nation's gross debt load was vastly higher—with the peak of 122 percent reached toward the end of World War II, compared to about 64 percent today. The government's annual budget every year allocates a portion of tax revenues to pay the interest on outstanding debt—the debt held by both the public and different government accounts—as well as retiring any securities that mature. Nothing about Social Security's trust fund differs from that long-standing set of accounting procedures. Unlike individuals who exchange IOUs, the government has the power to tax to meet its obligations—and paying the interest and the principal in the future on the trust fund's securities presents no unusual challenge, in and of itself.

The assets are real and will be honored, enabling future retirees to collect their promised benefits decades into the future even if no changes are made.

There is one legitimate cause for concern, however, that the administration's representatives rarely if ever mentioned. The gross debt of the United States as a share of GDP, which declined from more than 67 percent in 1996 to 57 percent by 2001, rose back up by 7 points during the first five years of the Bush administration, with that figure sure to escalate on the current path. The reason for that increase has nothing to do with Social Security, whose surpluses actually keep the federal deficits lower than they would otherwise be. The main cause has been the significant cuts in income taxes, primarily to the benefit of the highest earners, while federal spending has risen somewhat. If the trend toward growing federal debt continues to rise, this means that an increasingly large share of each year's budget will have to be devoted to interest payments rather than to public services. Social Security privatization, by significantly adding to the federal debt, would further weaken the overall budget and escalate future interest obligations. That, combined with significantly reduced benefits under privatization, would really be "bad news" for "Joe" and his children.

Very high federal debt levels put upward pressure on interest rates, dampening economic performance. Slower economic growth would be harmful for many reasons, one of which is that less tax revenue would be available to pay future Social Security beneficiaries in full for as long as is currently projected. In that scenario, the danger isn't that government would default on the trust fund assets but that the securities would have to be drawn down more rapidly than anticipated. The best way to strengthen Social Security is to take steps to improve the prospects for strong economic growth, which would increase the revenues available to pay future benefits. You don't need to follow the double-talk of the privatizers to understand that.

The Bottom Line

So here again, the right contrived a problem—in this case, what they claim erroneously to be Social Security's impending bankruptcy. They say that such a radical problem requires the radical solution of, in essence, phasing out the program before it's too late. To make their case, they have woven together one calumny after another—the wonderful experience in Chile, the worthless trust fund IOUs, the promise of superior future returns, and so on. And if they had been successful, Social Security, the personal finances of most American families, and the government's financial condition all would have been much worse off, but the right would have finally won its seventy-year war against the nation's most successful government program.

Ultimately, all of the furious spinning about Social Security's purportedly fatal flaws and the virtues of privatization unraveled like a ball of yarn. Journalists, opponents of the plan, neutral number crunchers, and the general public chewed it over until it became all too obvious that privatization, not Social Security's trust fund, was the empty promise.

Despite the decisive defeat, don't expect the conservative movement to abandon its eternal quest to bring an end to Social Security. In a November 21, 2005, *New York Sun* op-ed, just weeks after the president conceded that his Social Security plan was dead, Cato's Michael Tanner was back at it. He wrote, "Because of the failure to reform Social Security this year, the program's future unfunded obligations have increased by $660 billion. That amounts to a debt of more than $2,200 for every man, woman, and child in the United States. This comes on top of a previous unfunded obligation of $12.8 trillion."[41] Actually, the Trustees' forecast projects that the present value of the seventy-five-year shortfall is $3 trillion, and the Center on Budget and Policy Priorities' Jason Furman's always scrupulous calculations show that the cost of delaying a year amounts to $160 billion.[42] But leaving aside Tanner's relentlessly dubious math, he might also have mentioned that implementing privatization in 2005 would have cost the Treasury far more than doing nothing would.

This fight won't be over until the right stops spinning, which is to say never.

10

America's *Real* Problem—and How to Overcome It

In each of the preceding nine chapters in this book, one of the root causes of the government's failures was always the same: conservative ideology. With sincere apologies to fans of President Reagan: today, in the United States, conservatism is not the solution to our problem; conservatism is the problem.

It was movement conservatism's approach to public management that caused FEMA to revert from a model agency to a turkey farm, producing the inept response to Hurricane Katrina that appalled all Americans. Movement conservatism gave us the unitary executive doctrine, which, in its disparagement of historical precedent and consensus constitutional scholarship, contributed mightily to the horrors of Abu Ghraib and elsewhere—undermining America's long-standing moral authority while exacerbating the risk of future terrorism against us. The conservative movement's advocacy of "benevolent hegemony" offered a philosophical justification for invading Iraq even in the absence of indisputable evidence that it was building and stockpiling weapons of mass destruction. Conservatism falsely promised, again, that large tax cuts for the rich would produce broadly shared economic benefits without leading to large federal deficits. A conservative idea for constraining state taxes and spending caused public services to deteriorate dramatically in Colorado—an outcome that hasn't stopped the movement from peddling the same idea in other states. Conservative regulatory policy has significantly curtailed the enforcement of laws intended to protect public health and the environment, with harmful consequences. Conservative school reforms, which have shown little sign of working, have sidetracked efforts to pursue other ideas that have demonstrated success. The conservative remedies for what ails the health-care system, which don't even broach the huge problem of uninsured and underinsured Americans, are more than anything a diversion intended to stave off universal coverage. And, finally, conservatism continues to advocate killing Social Security to save it.

The right's ideas, one after another, have failed. Often they have failed in vivid ways that a large swath of the public reacts viscerally against—the debacles of FEMA, Iraq, Abu Ghraib, and Social Security privatization. The core reason why conservatism is failing is also easy to explain. The job of elected officials is to *govern*. But the modern conservative movement, which flourished from the seeds of deep hostility toward government, produced ideas implicitly designed to weaken the public sector. The right paid lip service to goals like fiscal responsibility, better schools, health care, retirement security, and so on, but that rhetoric's purpose was mainly to generate political support for actions that would have the effect of rolling back government—the movement's overriding priority. You have to actually believe that government *can* work to make it work effectively.

Some conservatives will reply that the failures that occurred in the Bush administration weren't the outgrowth of their ideology. Instead, they will blame the incompetence of particular individuals, as in the case of Donald Rumsfeld's prosecution of the Iraq War; or the inherent fallibility of government, they insist, demonstrated by FEMA's response to Katrina; or an inadequate commitment to "true conservativism," which explains the growing deficits, rampant pork-barrel spending, and deeply flawed "big government" initiatives such as the Medicare drug bill and No Child Left Behind; or inept salesmanship, which purportedly is the reason why Social Security privatization melted down in Congress. By all means, let's have debates over such excuses, because they are just that—excuses for failures. Back in the day, liberals were the ones always on the defensive trying to explain why one policy or another didn't work out as hoped. Conservatives weren't particularly merciful in allowing for mealymouthed explanations about how, say, the disastrous policy of constructing huge low-income housing projects didn't count as an example of "true liberalism." The recent damage was done by people who proudly and loudly wore the conservative label, and that, bottom line, is the basis on which voters should be encouraged to assess accountability.

To date, relatively few leading Democrats or progressives have seized on the opportunity to aggressively redefine conservatism as the ideology of government failure, much as the right successfully campaigned for decades to discredit liberalism. The dots remain mostly unconnected, with Democrats falling into the trap of talking about the incompetence of individuals on an issue-by-issue basis, rather than the interrelated fiascoes arising from the right's belief system and policies. Before, opponents of conservatism could only warn about the dangers of its ideas. Now, after those ideas have been put into practice, progressives can make a much more concrete and compelling case that conservatism equates with government failure. Compared to the liberalism of the 1960s, the conservatism of recent years has provided even more raw material for telling a story that the public won't like about adherents to an ideology. The right doesn't have a single notable policy success for which it can legitimately claim exclusive responsibility.

In recent years, Republicans largely succeeded in making the case to the public that theirs was the party of ideas while Democrats were wishy-washy flip-floppers. But most of the conservative movement's big ideas have now been tried, and they have failed miserably. Today the right has nothing left to fall back on, other than the same flawed ideas, because their ideology doesn't allow for adjustments to real-world results. For example, they certainly aren't going to start saying that tax cuts for the rich are bad for the federal budget and unhelpful to the economy, even though the evidence at this point couldn't be much clearer. If Democrats can help the public to recognize that so much of what has gone wrong in recent years is attributable to the rigidities of conservative ideology, their historical orientation to try whatever works to achieve progress ought to sound a lot more appealing to voters.

It's Security and Opportunity, Stupid

Two words, *security* and *opportunity*, capture a great deal about what Americans have sought in the past from their government, and which government in the twentieth century made great strides in delivering.

Security from enemies beyond our borders and from crime within. Security from excessive governmental incursions on personal privacy and liberties, fulfilling the promises of freedom embedded in the U.S. Constitution. Security against severe impoverishment, malnourishment, and preventable disease. Security against harms caused by unchecked market failures. Security against discrimination. And with those protections—to a large extent as an outgrowth of them—have come opportunities for more and more Americans to attain good educations, pursue happiness at work and at home, and enjoy better living standards. Progress in improving security and opportunity was often painful and difficult, and the gains often came with significant costs. But particularly from the time of World War II through the year 2000, the United States became a country in which a far greater share of its citizens could safely enjoy freedom, prosperity, and opportunity. Government was integral to that progress, and Republicans as well as Democrats share the credit.

Today, the nation's most significant problems—as opposed to those conjured up by the conservative movement—directly relate to a lack of security and opportunity. The Iraq War, the torture horror, and the right's share-the-spoils approach to homeland security have left us much more vulnerable to terrorism than we should be. All but the wealthiest Americans face greater economic risks—experiencing wider year-to-year income fluctuations and weaker protections from employer-provided health insurance and pensions than in the past.[1] Negligent conservative governance has exacerbated that economic insecurity. Likewise, undermining regulations and deprofessionalizing public sector management have left Americans less secure against dangers such as natural disasters, environmental pollution, unsafe food and drugs, and, as chapter 6 showed, seemingly obscure but largely preventable risks such as underinflated tires.

Strengthening the security of Americans enhances their flexibility to pursue their dreams. For example, universal health-care coverage would enable workers to feel confident that they could move from one job to the next—or start a business of their own—without having to worry about losing medical insurance.[2] Sound educational and economic policies, as demonstrated in the past, help to empower citizens with knowledge and skills to pursue a wider range of better jobs throughout their careers, while bouncing back more quickly after setbacks. Public health and safety protections enhance the probability that individual Americans and their families will be able to enjoy long, healthy lives.

Largely because of the conservative movement's effectiveness in shifting the terms of the debate over the role of government, most Democrats remain either tongue-tied or excessively verbose when they try to explain what they stand for. The one lesson Democrats can learn from the right is that sticking to a clear, coherent message that encompasses an agenda that will resonate with Americans is politically effective. This message should be that Democrats will improve security and opportunity for everyone by pursuing and building on public policies that have proved to be effective. Period end.

Getting Back on Track

Democrats took three detours during an otherwise admirable Clinton administration, initially with some justification, that since then have made it more difficult to regain their sense of direction.

One of those detours was accepting the right's preoccupation with the size of government as the main basis for judging success or failure. The framework of "limited government," comfortingly intoned on every occasion by President Reagan and a de rigueur plank of conservative mission statements, elegantly recasts the antigovernment agenda of the world's Scaifes, Koches, and Coorses as an unobjectionable banality. Small implicitly equates with good, and big with bad, leaving no reason to investigate whether the government, whatever its size, is effectively fulfilling its democratically assigned missions. President Clinton, in his determination to distance himself from traditional liberalism, served movement conservatism well when he declared in his 1996 State of the Union Address that "the era of big government is over." A president who ultimately achieves universal health insurance won't be able to repeat Clinton's boast but will improve lives for Americans.

The mindlessness of the obsession with size has been laid bare as large numbers of ideologues on the right insist that the main problem with President Bush is that he is a "big government conservative." They bemoan the Medicare drug bill and the No Child Left Behind Act, as well as his negligible efforts to stop excessive congressional earmarks for pet projects, simply because they make the government bigger. But they miss the point that two conservatives writing for the *Weekly Standard*, Ross Douthat and Reihan Salam, at least partially get:[3]

> After all, Ronald Reagan, the man whose legacy Bush has supposedly betrayed, presided over a federal government that consumed 23.5 percent of GDP in 1984. Granted, this was at the height of the Cold War defense build-up, yet the figure far surpasses spending under President Clinton, which reached a low of 18 percent of GDP in 2001. Under Bush, spending has inched over 20 percent of GDP, a definite increase from the era of the peace "dividend." But spending is still far from Reagan-era levels. And the post-9/11 defense buildup (defense spending has increased by roughly 40 percent over 2001 levels, to nearly half a trillion dollars) accounts for the bulk of the increased spending. When you factor out spending on homeland security, domestic discretionary spending has barely budged under Bush.

Judging by federal spending alone, why wouldn't the right consider Bill Clinton to be more conservative than George W. Bush, who in turn must be more conservative than Ronald Reagan?

Much more important than size, per se, is the bang government delivers in achieving popular goals for the taxpayer's buck. As chapter 4 showed, the Republican presidencies beginning with Reagan greatly increased federal deficits, while the opposite happened under Clinton. High and rising deficits mean that a greater share of each future tax dollar will have to go toward paying interest on the federal debt, crowding out resources that can be devoted to productive activities. All other factors being equal, that's wasteful and potentially damaging to the overall economy. Conservatives upset about government spending levels under Bush often fail to acknowledge that it was his massive tax cuts, which the right applauded, that produced those deficits far more than the much smaller increases in nonmilitary spending. Moreover, if "limited government" leads to the transformation from FEMA under Clinton to FEMA under Bush, how exactly is that supposed to be a good thing? Colorado's state government was "limited" in the extreme. That hasn't turned out so well, either. Why are Democrats continuing to share the fixation on government's size when they should be talking about getting the most effective and efficient results for taxpayers?

A second, related detour is the "third way," centrist rhetoric that served a useful purpose in the early 1990s but that now boxes too many of today's Democrats into squishy positions that sound like "conservatism lite." Holding fast to the center was constructive from the standpoint of both politics and policy when the midpoint between conservative and liberal amounted to an agenda with enough ambition to include universal health insurance, which Clinton's administration unsuccessfully pursued. But movement conservatism's dominion over the federal government throughout this decade has, in essence, shifted policy debates much further to the right than they were as recently as the 2000 presidential campaign. In the process, the center has moved so far toward starboard that some "third way" Democrats shy from even acknowledging that the Iraq War was a mistake, while voting for legislation, widely criticized by top former military brass, that gives the president authority to reinterpret the Geneva Conventions' ban on torture. Some centrist Democrats voted for Bush's tax cuts, as well as for a bankruptcy bill that did the exact opposite of strengthening security and opportunity for Americans.

What was once a perfectly legitimate and constructive inclination to find the middle ground has now amounted in many cases to complicity in the failures of movement conservatism. Depending on the particular Democrat, stubborn centrism can be attributed in varying degrees to the difficulty of shedding a once tried-and-true strategy, a relatively conservative predilection in the first place, or sheer political fear propagated by hypercautious consultants and pollsters. But it's worth noting that the most significant political success that Democrats had during the first six years of the Bush administration was their united opposition to Social Security privatization, which was a stand for principle rather than yet another cowering concession in the name of centrist compromise. The Clinton era was good while it lasted, but these times demand greater Democratic unity, assertiveness, and initiative in highlighting the extremism and consequent failure of the ideologues in power—and a policy agenda explicitly tied to building on past governmental successes rather than to some squishy notion of a third way.

The third detour has been to neglect the most important lesson of the welfare reform act of 1996, which replaced the New Deal era's Aid to Families with Dependent Children program with a system that imposed new work requirements and time limits on recipients of government welfare benefits—almost entirely single mothers. That legislation, which was strenuously opposed by many liberals and groups that traditionally support Democrats, produced far better results than progressives anticipated. Most significantly, it led to dramatic reductions in welfare rolls, while poverty rates among single mothers declined during the booming economy of the late 1990s. A leveling off in the rate of out-of-wedlock births may also be at least partly attributable to welfare reform. One of the law's other virtues was disarming conservatives of a bludgeon that they had relentlessly used to whack government and liberals. Welfare reform didn't do much to alleviate America's persistent poverty problem, as vice presidential candidate John Edwards argued so powerfully during the 2004 campaign, but it did improve government by overhauling an outdated program that was ineffective and poorly designed.

On balance, most Democrats seem to have come out of the welfare reform experience mainly with a sense of relief that it's behind them, and that they can now safely ignore the politically difficult issues posed by urban poverty. But that's not only cowardly, it's an abandonment of the Democratic Party's heritage and an abdication of government's responsibility to improve the lives of all the nation's citizens. Chapter 7 discussed some ideas on that front that deserve far more attention, and many more Democratic candidates should follow Edwards's leadership in refocusing the nation's attention on what remains an unacceptable failure in the globe's wealthiest country.

The real lesson that Democrats should take from welfare reform is to be more assertive in proposing major overhauls or even the elimination of other clearly ineffective programs, tax breaks, or policies. Jonathan Rauch's books *Demosclerosis* and *Government's End* document the pervasiveness of programs and write-offs whose public purpose, if there ever was one, has long since passed. The political constituencies supporting them are forever fierce and entrenched, so trying to clear away useless but deeply rooted detritus like the Targeted Exports Program or wool and mohair subsidies might seem to be little more than an exercise in futility. Clinton budget director Leon Panetta, after hearing criticism that the administration's National Performance

Review proposed eliminating only fifteen relatively inconsequential programs in 1993, said, "I would kiss the ground and thank God if we could eliminate fifteen."

But if Democrats are going to seize on the opportunity presented by conservative failures to clearly define themselves as crusaders for effective government, they need to embrace welfare reform as an example of their willingness to cast aside past ineffective practices while creating meaningful accountability mechanisms for new policies. For example, reforming the income tax code along the lines of Reagan's 1986 legislation, which simplified the system and made it fairer by eliminating large numbers of inefficient write-offs and shelters, is one idea that progressives should revisit.

A 2005 Government Accountability Office report about job-training programs headlined "Substantial Funds Are Used for Training, but Little Is Known Nationally about Training Outcomes" describes exactly the kind of wastefulness that Democrats would have far more credibility in repairing than conservative ideologues would. Establishing transparent assessments of whether laws, regulations, programs, and tax incentives are accomplishing what they were intended to do would further help to underline the differences between today's progressives and conservatives. That strategy will require a fundamental cultural change, which can happen if Democratic leaders come to recognize how the big-picture political benefits can greatly exceed the costs of infuriating particular interest groups. They might take note that New York City mayor Michael Bloomberg, a pragmatic Republican, has become enormously popular in a Democratic city largely because of his boldness in reforming city government programs while focusing on results.

One additional benefit of such an approach is that it can free up squandered governmental resources for much more productive purposes. As Rauch, a moderate, wrote:

> As long as the government keeps doing everything that it ever did, and keeps trying to do every possible sort of thing at once, it cannot function well, and so the public will continue to resent it. That means people will resent its champions, who happen to be liberals. . . . To change the political culture so that housecleaning becomes a routine part of governing, liberals will need to take the

lead in scouring for programs to eliminate, rather than merely launching the occasional symbolic attack on "corporate welfare" and blowing raspberries at conservatives.[4]

In Our Hands

Notwithstanding the failures of conservatism as a governing philosophy, many of the movement's thinkers have held true to form, unremittingly continuing their onslaught against the liberal menace. The titles of three recent books by authors associated with the *National Review* speak for themselves. *The Party of Death: The Democrats, the Media, the Courts, and the Disregard for Human Life*, by Ramesh Ponnuru; *Women Who Make the World Worse: And How Their Radical Feminist Assault Is Ruining Our Schools, Families, Military, and Sports*, by Kate O'Beirne; and *Liberal Fascism: The Totalitarian Temptation from Mussolini to Hillary Clinton*, by Jonah Goldberg. One other notable book, published in 2006 by the American Enterprise Institute, is the libertarian Charles Murray's *In Our Hands: A Plan to Replace the Welfare State*. Murray is perhaps most famous for coauthoring, with support from the Bradley Foundation, a widely criticized and deeply flawed tome titled *The Bell Curve* (with Richard J. Herrnstein, 1994) that elaborately attempted to convince readers that blacks were genetically predisposed to having lower IQ scores than whites. In his new book, Murray proposes what he calls "The Plan," which would entirely scrap Social Security, Medicare, Medicaid, the Earned Income Tax Credit, unemployment insurance, food stamps, college loans and grants, low-income energy assistance, and Head Start, plus other "welfare programs, social service programs, agricultural subsidies, and corporate welfare." In their stead, the government would provide to every adult age twenty-one or older an annual check for no more than $10,000 — scaling downward as individual incomes rise above $25,000 a year.

Murray deserves credit for candidly coming out and putting forward what really has been movement conservatism's underlying plan all along, just without all the subterfuge and spin. Eviscerating government is the name of the game. Messrs. Scaife, Coors, Koch, and Olin would surely have signed up for his proposal in a second. Would you?

Back in 1996, Michael Lind, a former protégé of William F. Buckley Jr. who became disillusioned with the right over its increasingly hyperbolic attacks on taxes, welfare, and liberal values, wrote a prescient book called *Up from Conservatism: Why the Right Is Wrong for America*. Lind concluded it by writing, "It is too late to rescue American conservatism from the radical right. But it is not too late to rescue America from conservatism."[5]

Tick . . . tick . . . tick . . .

NOTES

Introduction

1. *Creating Solutions. Getting Results: The Heritage Foundation 2003 Annual Report* (Heritage Foundation, 2004), www.heritage.org/About/upload/63116_1.pdf, last accessed March 9, 2007.

2. The Senate shifted from Republican control to Democratic when Vermont's Jim Jeffords switched from the Republican Party to become an Independent in May 2001. But it went back to the Republicans after the 2002 elections.

3. Paul Glastris, "Editor's Note," *Washington Monthly* (December 2004), www.washingtonmonthly.com/features/2004/0412.glastris.html, last accessed March 9, 2007.

4. Reagan preceded that famous line with the phrase "In this present crisis," referring to the economic conditions at the time. But his message resonated throughout the conservative movement and the country, in ways that were not constrained by any particular context. George H. Nash, the author of the authoritative *The Conservative Intellectual Movement in America*, wrote that by the end of the 1980s, conservatism had evolved to encompass five distinct impulses: libertarianism, traditionalism, anticommunism, neoconservatism, and the Religious Right. Reagan, Nash wrote, "performed an emblematic and ecumenical function. Much of Reagan's success as a spokesman for conservatism derived from his embodiment of all these impulses simultaneously." See George H. Nash, *The Conservative Intellectual Movement in America* (Wilmington, Del.: Intercollegiate Studies Institute, 1996, 1998), p. 332.

5. George F. Will, "Transformation's Toll," *Washington Post*, July 18, 2006, p. A19.

6. Bruce Bartlett, *Impostor: How George W. Bush Bankrupted America and Betrayed the Reagan Legacy* (New York: Doubleday, 2006).

7. Andrew Sullivan, *The Conservative Soul: How We Lost It, How to Get It Back* (New York: HarperCollins, 2006).

8. Andrew Ferguson, "Older & Wiser? A *Weekly Standard* 10th Anniversary Symposium," *Weekly Standard*, September 19, 2005, www.weeklystandard.com/content/Public/Articles/000/000/000/051byxff.asp, last accessed March 9, 2007.

9. Rick Perlstein, "The Conservative Movement: Its Past, Present and Future" (remarks at Princeton University's conference on this topic, December 2005), www.huffingtonpost.com/rick-perlstein/i-didnt-like-nixon-_b_11735.html, last accessed March 9, 2007.

10. Andrew Rich, *Think Tanks, Public Policy, and the Politics of Expertise* (New York: Cambridge University Press, 2004), pp. 53–54.

11. James A. Smith, *The Idea Brokers: Think Tanks and the Rise of the New Policy Elite* (New York: Free Press, 1991), pp. 221–222.

12. Many other conservative foundations have played a crucial role. They include the Earhart, Smith Richardson, W. H. Brady, Philip M. McKenna, and JM foundations. But from the standpoint of influence and impact, the general consensus is that the foundations associated with the five families discussed here have been far and away the most important.

13. Russell Kirk, *The Conservative Mind: From Burke to Eliot*, 7th rev. ed. (Washington, D.C.: Regnery, 2001), p. 8.

14. Barry M. Goldwater with Jack Casserly, *Goldwater* (New York: Doubleday, 1988), p. 121.

15. William Safire, *Safire's New Political Dictionary* (New York: Random House Reference, 1993). For further discussion of definitions of conservatism, see John W. Dean, *Conservatives Without Conscience* (New York: Viking, 2006), pp. 1–19.

16. See Robert G. Kaiser and Ira Chinoy, "Scaife: Funding Father of the Right," *Washington Post*, May 2, 1999, p. A1.

17. Edwin J. Feulner Jr., "Waging and Winning the War of Ideas" (address to the Public Relations Society of America 39th National Conference, Washington, D.C., November 12, 1986), www.heritage.org/Research/PoliticalPhilosophy/HL84.cfm, last accessed March 9, 2007.

18. Movement conservatism's opposition to abortion and affirmative action doesn't fall within the scope of this book because the law of the land to a large extent continues to support those practices. The goal here is to see what has happened after conservative ideas have been implemented (with the notable exception of Social Security privatization, discussed in chapter 9, which mathematically could not have delivered what advocates promised).

1. "A Heckuva Job"

1. *Hurricane Katrina: A Nation Still Unprepared*, special report of the Senate Committee on Homeland Security and Governmental Affairs, May 2006, http://hsgac.senate.gov/_files/Katrina/FullReport.pdf, last accessed March 9, 2007.

2. William A. Niskanen, "The Peculiar Economics of Bureaucracy," Papers and Proceedings of the Eightieth Annual Meeting of the American Economic Association, *American Economic Review* 58, no. 2 (May 1968): 293–305.

3. The historical summary of federal politicization comes from a draft of a forthcoming book on the subject by the Princeton University political scientist David E. Lewis.

4. Joel D. Aberbach and Bert A. Rockman, with Robert W. Copeland, "From Nixon's Problem to Reagan's Achievement: The Federal Executive Reexamined," in *Looking Back on the Reagan Presidency*, Larry Berman, ed. (Baltimore: Johns Hopkins University Press, 1990), pp. 175–194.

5. Paul C. Light, *The Changing Shape of Government* (Policy Brief no. 45, Brookings Institution, 1999).

6. See Steven Kelman, *Unleashing Change: A Study of Organizational Renewal in Government* (Washington, D.C.: Brookings Institution Press, 2005).

7. Brian Friel, "Gore Issues Call for Performance-Based Pay," GovExec.com (January 14, 1999), www.govexec.com/dailyFed/0199/01149952.htm, last accessed March 9, 2007.

8. *Urgent Business for America: Revitalizing the Federal Government for the 21st Century* (report of the National Commission on the Public Service, January 2003), p. iv.

9. Ibid., p. 20.

10. Gardiner Harris, "Drugs, Politics, and the FDA," *New York Times*, August 28, 2005, p. 1.

11. Dan Eggen, "Civil Rights Focus Shift Roils Staff at Justice," *Washington Post*, November 13, 2005, p. A01.

12. Stephen Barr, "Agency's Reorganization Results in Accusations, Employees Leaving," *Washington Post*, March 18, 2005, p. B02.

13. David Lewis provided me with the data from his forthcoming book.

14. Paul C. Light, *Fact Sheet on the Continued Thickening of Government* (Brookings Institution, July 23, 2004), www.brookings.edu/views/papers/light/20040723.htm, last accessed March 9, 2007.

15. Patrick S. Roberts, *Reputation and Federal Emergency Preparedness Agencies, 1948–2003* (paper prepared for delivery at the 2004 Annual Meeting of the American Political Science Association, September 2–5), p. 10, www.training.fema.gov/emiweb/downloads/RobertsPfema%208%2020%2004%20apsa.pdf, last accessed March 9, 2007.

16. Roberts, *Reputation and Federal Emergency Preparedness Agencies*, pp. 11–13.

17. Ibid., p. 14.

18. James N. Baker, Howard Manly, and Daniel Glick, "The Storm after Hugo," *Newsweek*, October 9, 1989, p. 40.

19. Roberts, *Reputation and Federal Emergency Preparedness Agencies*, p. 15.

20. Ibid., p. 15.

21. Larry Van Dyne, "Perfect Places for Those Hard-to-Place Contributors," *Washingtonian* (November 1992).

22. William Claiborne, "Cultures Being Clubbed," *Washington Post*, May 20, 1993, p. A21.

23. National Academy of Public Administration, *Coping with Catastrophe: Building an Emergency Management System to Meet People's Needs in Natural and Manmade Disasters*, February 1993, pp. ix, 64–66.

24. Roberts, *Reputation and Federal Emergency Preparedness Agencies*, p. 19.

25. R. Steven Daniels and Carolyn L. Clark-Daniels, *Transforming Government: The Renewal and Revitalization of the Federal Emergency Management Agency* (PricewaterhouseCoopers Endowment for the Business of Government, April 2000), p. 13.

26. NAPA, *Coping with Catastrophe*, pp. 42–43.

27. Roberts, *Reputation and Federal Emergency Preparedness Agencies*, p. 19.

28. Jerry Ellig, *Learning from the Leaders: Results-Based Management at the Federal Emergency Management Agency* (Mercatus Center, George Mason University), March 29, 2000, pp. 18–19.

29. Council for Excellence in Government, *FEMA Reborn* (undated), p. 1.

30. See Ellig, *Learning from the Leaders*, and Daniels and Clark-Daniels, *Transforming Government*.

31. "Mastering Disaster," GovExec.com, February 1, 1999, www.GovExec.com/gpp/0299fema.htm, last accessed March 12, 2007.

32. Council for Excellence in Government, *FEMA Reborn*, p. 4.

33. "Mastering Disaster."

34. Eric Klinenberg and Thomas Frank, "Looting Homeland Security," *Rolling Stone* (December 15, 2005), www.rollingstone.com/politics/story/8952492/looting_homeland_security, last accessed March 12, 2007.

35. *Hurricane Katrina: A Nation Still Unprepared*, p. 214.

36. Mark Murray, "FEMA Director Has a Tough Act to Follow," GovExec.com, June 5, 2001. Witt said at the time, though, that it was appropriate for Allbaugh to strengthen FEMA's capacity to respond to terrorism—which it had done effectively after the Oklahoma City bombings.

37. Joseph M. Allbaugh, Testimony before the Senate Appropriations Committee, May 16, 2001.

38. Jason Peckenpaugh, "Tall Order," GovExec.com, July 1, 2003, www.GovExec.com/features/0603/ots03s1.htm, last accessed March 12, 2007.

39. Shane Harris, "Cuts to Disaster Mitigation Program Questioned in Wake of Hurricane Response," GovExec.com, September 16, 2006, www.GovExec.com/dailyfed/0905/091605njl.htm, last accessed March 12, 2007.

40. Murray, "FEMA Director Has a Tough Act to Follow."

41. Committee on Government Reform—Minority Staff, *Waste, Fraud, and Abuse in Hurricane Katrina Contracts*, U.S. House of Representatives, August 2006.

42. "That's a BIG Scoop You've Got There, Paul," *National Journal* (July 21, 2001).

43. Klinenberg and Frank, "Looting Homeland Security."

44. *Hurricane Katrina: A Nation Still Unprepared*, p. 216.

45. Letter from Pleasant Mann, president, AFGE Local 4060, to Senator Hillary Rodham Clinton, June 21, 2004.

46. Stephen Barr, "Morale among FEMA Workers, on the Decline for Years, Hits Nadir," *Washington Post*, September 14, 2005, p. B02. For more on FEMA's decline, see Jon Elliston, "Disaster in the Making," *Independent*, September 22,

2004, http://www.indyweek.com/gyrobase/Content?oid=oid%3A22664, last accessed March 12, 2007.

47. Spencer S. Hsu, "Leaders Lacking Disaster Experience," *Washington Post*, September 9, 2005, p. A01.

48. *Hurricane Katrina: A Nation Still Unprepared*, p. 214.

49. Ibid., pp. 214–215.

50. Megan O'Matz and Sally Kestin, "State Records Show Bush Re-Election Concerns Played Part in FEMA Aid," *South Florida Sun-Sentinel*, March 23, 2005, p. 1.

51. Transcript of Senate Homeland Security and Governmental Affairs Committee Hearing on FEMA Response to Florida Hurricanes, May 18, 2005.

52. Robert Dreyfuss and Jason Vest, "The Lie Factory," *Mother Jones* (January/February 2004), www.motherjones.com/news/feature/2004/01/12_405.html, last accessed March 12, 2007.

53. George Packer, *The Assassins' Gate: America in Iraq* (New York: Farrar, Straus and Giroux, 2005), p. 106.

54. Dreyfuss and Vest, "The Lie Factory."

55. Karen Kwiatkowski, "The New Pentagon Papers," *Salon*, March 10, 2004, http://archive.salon.com/opinion/feature/2004/03/10/osp_moveon/index.html, last accessed March 12, 2007.

56. See Packer, *The Assassins' Gate*; Dreyfuss and Vest, "The Lie Factory"; and Kwiatkowski, "The New Pentagon Papers."

57. Kwiatkowski, "The New Pentagon Papers."

58. Paul R. Pillar, "Intelligence, Policy, and the War in Iraq," *Foreign Affairs* 85, no. 2 (March/April 2006): 17–19.

59. David E. Lewis, "Political Appointments, Bureau Chiefs, and Federal Management Performance," pp. 7–8, available at www.wws.princeton.edu/research/papers/09_05_dl.pdf, last accessed March 12, 2007.

60. Ibid., p. 11.

61. Ibid., pp. 20–21.

62. Aimee Curl, "Careerists Make Best Managers," *Federal Times*, October 10, 2005, www.federaltimes.com/index.php?S=1160661, last accessed March 12, 2007.

63. David Brooks, "The Best-Laid Plan: Too Bad It Flopped," *New York Times*, September 11, 2005, p. 14.

64. David Boaz, *Catastrophe in Big Easy Demonstrates Big Government's Failure* (Cato Institute, September 19, 2005), available at www.cato.org/pub_display.php?pub_id=4819, last accessed March 12, 2007.

2. The Nixon Doctrine

1. An article in *Slate* on February 13, 2006, by David Cole titled "The Nixon Doctrine" first developed the connection between the Bush administration's claims about executive power and Nixon's assertion. Cole's piece is available at www.slate.com/id/2136057/, last accessed March 12, 2007.

2. Jane Mayer, "The Hidden Power," *New Yorker,* July 3, 2006, www.newyorker .com/fact/content/articles/060703fa_fact1, last accessed March 12, 2007.

3. Ibid.

4. Ibid.

5. Jerry Landay, "The Federalist Society," *Washington Monthly* (March 2000), www.washingtonmonthly.com/features/2000/0003.landay.html, last accessed March 12, 2007.

6. Jeffrey Rosen, "Power of One," *New Republic* (July 24, 2006), p. 8.

7. Ron Chernow, *Alexander Hamilton* (New York: Penguin, 2004), pp. 258–259.

8. See, for example, Lawrence Lessig and Cass R. Sunstein, "The President and the Administration," *Columbia Law Review* 94, no. 1 (January 1994), available at www.lessig.org/content/articles/works/thepresident.pdf, last accessed March 12, 2007.

9. Mayer, "Hidden Power."

10. Jess Bravin, "Judge Alito's View of the Presidency: Expansive Powers," *Wall Street Journal,* January 5, 2006, p. A1.

11. Ibid.

12. John Yoo, *The Powers of War and Peace: The Constitution and Foreign Affairs after 9/11* (Chicago: University of Chicago Press, 2005).

13. Cass R. Sunstein, "The 9/11 Constitution," *New Republic* (January 16, 2006), p. 21. See also David Cole, "What Bush Wants to Hear," *New York Review of Books,* November 17, 2005.

14. Cole, "What Bush Wants to Hear."

15. Transcript and audio available at www.informationclearinghouse.info/article11488.htm, last accessed March 12, 2007.

16. Phillip Carter, "The Road to Abu Ghraib," *Washington Monthly,* November 2004, www.washingtonmonthly.com/features/2004/0411.carter.html, last accessed March 12, 2007.

17. Address by President George W. Bush at the U.S. Army War College, Carlisle, Pennsylvania, May 24, 2004, available at www.whitehouse.gov/news/releases/2004/05/20040524-10.html, last accessed March 12, 2007.

18. The transcript of Schlesinger's August 24, 2004, briefing to reporters is available at: http://transcripts.cnn.com/TRANSCRIPTS/0408/24/lol.04.html, last accessed March 12, 2007.

19. ACLU, *Army Documents Show Senior Official Reportedly Pushed Limits on Detainee Interrogations* (May 2, 2006); links to the government documents confirming the abuses are available at www.aclu.org/safefree/torture/25406prs20060502 .html, last accessed March 12, 2007.

20. Associated Press, "27 Detainees Dead in U.S. Custody," March 25, 2005, www.msnbc.msn.com/id/7297209/, last accessed March 12, 2007.

21. *USA Amnesty International's Supplementary Briefing to the U.N. Committee against Torture,* May 3, 2006, web.amnesty.org/library/print/ENGAMR510612006, accessed March 12, 2007.

22. Lawrence Wilkerson, "Dogging the Torture Story," *Nieman Watchdog*, July 11, 2006, www.niemanwatchdog.org/index.cfm?fuseaction=Ask_this.view&askthisid=214, last accessed March 12, 2007.

23. All of the memos discussed in this section are available at the *New York Times* Web site "A Guide to the Memos on Torture," www.nytimes.com/ref/international/24MEMO-GUIDE.html?_r=1&oref=slogin, last accessed March 12, 2007.

24. Jane Mayer, "The Memo," *New Yorker*, February 27, 2006, www .newyorker .com/fact/content/articles/060227fa_fact, last accessed March 12, 2007.

25. Douglas Jehl, "Files Show Rumsfeld Rejected Some Efforts to Toughen Prison Rules," *New York Times*, June 23, 2004, p. 10.

26. Mayer, "The Memo."

27. Neil A. Lewis, "Fresh Details Emerge on Harsh Methods at Guantanamo," *New York Times*, January 1, 2005, p. 11.

28. Mayer, "The Memo."

29. Major General George R. Fay, *Investigation of the Abu Ghraib Detention Facility and the 205th Military Intelligence Brigade*, August 23, 2004, p. 112, available at http://fl1.findlaw.com/news.findlaw.com/hdocs/docs/dod/fay82504rpt.pdf, last accessed March 12, 2007.

30. Carter, "Road to Abu Ghraib."

31. Daniel Klaidman, Stuart Taylor Jr., and Evan Thomas, "Palace Revolt," *Newsweek*, February 6, 2006, www.msnbc.msn.com/id/11079547/site/newsweek/, last accessed March 12, 2007.

32. Mayer, "The Memo."

33. Adam Liptak, "The Court Enters the War, Loudly," *New York Times*, July 2, 2006, The Week in Review, p. 1.

34. Heather MacDonald, "How to Interrogate Terrorists," *City Journal* (Winter 2005), www.city-journal.org/html/15_1_terrorists.html, last accessed March 12, 2007.

35. See detailed rebuttals to MacDonald by Georgetown University Law professor Marty Lederman at http://balkin.blogspot.com/2005/01/heather-macdonalds-dubious-counter.html, and http://balkin.blogspot.com/2005/01/heather-mac-donalds-few-bad-apples.html, last accessed March 12, 2007.

36. Charles Krauthammer, "The Truth about Torture," *Weekly Standard* (December 5, 2005), www.weeklystandard.com/content/Public/Articles/000/000/006/400rhqav.asp, last accessed March 12, 2007.

37. *Report of the International Committee of the Red Cross on the Treatment by the Coalition Forces of the Prisoners of War and Other Protected Persons by the Geneva Conventions in Iraq during Arrest, Internment, and Interrogation*, February 2004, www.globalsecurity.org/military/library/report/2004/icrc_report_iraq_feb2004.htm, last accessed March 12, 2007.

38. "Son of Al Qaeda," *Frontline*, PBS television broadcast, April 22, 2004; transcript available at www.pbs.org/wgbh/pages/frontline/shows/khadr/interviews/khadr .html, last accessed March 12, 2007.

39. Christopher Cooper, "Detention Plan: In Guantanamo, Prisoners Left to Languish in Sea of Red Tape," *Wall Street Journal*, January 26, 2005, p. 1; Tim

Golden and Don Van Natta Jr., "U.S. Said to Overstate Value of Guantanamo Detainees," *New York Times*, June 21, 2004, p. 1; also, for an excellent detailed examination of the Guantanamo experience, see Joseph Margulies, *Guantanamo and the Abuse of Presidential Power* (New York: Simon & Schuster, 2006).

40. Joseph Lelyveld, "Interrogating Ourselves," *New York Times Magazine*, June 12, 2005, p. 36.

41. Anne Applebaum, "Tortured Credibility," *Washington Post*, March 20, 2007, p. A19.

42. Transcript available at www.washingtonpost.com/wp-dyn/content/article/2006/09/06/AR2006090601442.html, last accessed March 12, 2007.

43. Michael Kinsley, "Torture for Dummies," *Slate*, December 13, 2005, www.slate.com/id/2132195/, last accessed March 12, 2007.

44. Liptak, "Court Enters the War."

3. "We Will, in Fact, Be Greeted as Liberators"

1. Patrick E. Tyler, "U.S. Strategy Plan Calls for Insuring No Rivals Develop," *New York Times*, March 8, 1992, p. 1.

2. Patrick E. Tyler, "Lone Superpower Plan: Ammunition for Critics," *New York Times*, March 10, 1992, p. 12.

3. William Kristol and Robert Kagan, "Toward a Neo-Reaganite Foreign Policy," *Foreign Affairs* (July/August 1996), www.carnegieendowment.org/publications/index.cfm?fa=view&id=276, last accessed March 13, 2007.

4. A video of Fukuyama discussing how Kristol believed that Republicans did best politically when the United States had an enemy to fight is available at http://bloggingheads.tv/?id=81&cid=271&in=04:59, last accessed March 13, 2007.

5. The text of the January 26, 1998, letter is available at www.newamericancentury.org/iraqclintonletter.htm, last accessed March 13, 2007.

6. George Packer, *The Assassins' Gate: America in Iraq* (New York: Farrar, Straus and Giroux, 2005), pp. 40–41.

7. Ibid., p. 41.

8. See Fareed Zakaria, "We Had Good Intel—The U.N.'s," *Newsweek*, February 9, 2004, available at www.msnbc.msn.com/id/4122113/, last accessed March 13, 2007.

9. William Kristol and Robert Kagan, "The U.N. Trap," *Weekly Standard*, November 18, 2002, available at www.carnegieendowment.org/publications/index.cfm?fa=view&id=1133, last accessed March 13, 2007.

10. Cheney speech at VFW 103rd Convention, August 26, 2002; transcript available at www.whitehouse.gov/news/releases/2002/08/20020826.html, last accessed March 13, 2007.

11. Jonathan Weisman, "Iraq's Alleged al Qaeda Ties Were Disputed before the War," *Washington Post*, September 9, 2006, p. A01.

12. Jonathan S. Landay, "Doubts, Dissent Stripped from Public Version of Iraq Assessment," Knight Ridder Newspapers, February 9, 2004, www.commondreams.org/headlines04/0210-02.htm, last accessed March 13, 2007.

13. Seymour M. Hersh, "Selective Intelligence," *New Yorker*, May 12, 2003, www.newyorker.com/fact/content/?030512fa_fact, last accessed March 13, 2007.

14. Paul R. Pillar, "Intelligence, Policy, and the War in Iraq," *Foreign Affairs* (March/April 2006), www.foreignaffairs.org/20060301faessay85202/paul-r-pillar/intelligence-policy-and-the-war-in-iraq.html, last accessed March 13, 2007.

15. The Downing Street Memo was first revealed by the *Sunday Times* of London on May 1, 2005, available at www.timesonline.co.uk/article/0,,2087-1593607,00.html, last accessed March 13, 2007.

16. James Fallows, "Declaring Victory," *The Atlantic* (September 2006), p. 70.

17. The most recent allied casualty figures in Iraq can be found at: http://icasualties.org/oif/, last accessed March 13, 2007.

18. Sabrina Tavernise, "Iraqi Death Toll Exceeded 34,000 in 2006, U.N. Says," *New York Times*, January 17, 2007, p. 1.

19. The best estimates of Iraqi civilian casualties are available at: http://www.iraqbodycount.org/, last accessed March 13, 2007.

20. One survey of Iraqi physicians overseen by epidemiologists at Johns Hopkins University's Bloomberg School of Public Health, using a controversial technique called "cluster sampling," estimated that about 600,000 more violent deaths attributable to the war occurred in the country since March 2003. It was published in *The Lancet*, a British medical journal.

21. See Matthew Yglesias, "The Price Is Wrong," *American Prospect*, July 5, 2006, www.prospect.org/web/page.ww?section=root&name=ViewPrint&articleId=11646, last accessed March 13, 2007.

22. Joseph E. Stiglitz and Linda Bilmes, "The Economic Costs of the Iraq War: An Appraisal Three Years after the Beginning of the Conflict," paper prepared for presentation at the Allied Social Science Associations meetings, Boston, January 2006, www2.gsb.columbia.edu/faculty/jstiglitz/cost_of_war_in_iraq.pdf, last accessed March 13, 2007.

23. See T. Christian Miller, *Blood Money: Wasted Billions, Lost Lives and Corporate Greed in Iraq* (New York: Little, Brown, 2006).

24. Daniel Benjamin and Michele Flournoy, "Won't Deploy? Can't Deploy," Slate.com, September 14, 2006, www.slate.com/id/2149684, last accessed March 13, 2007.

25. Lawrence Korb, Max Bergmann, and Peter Ogden, "Tapped Out," *New Republic Online*, September 13, 2006; www.tnr.com/doc.mhtml?i=w060911&s=bergmannkorbogden091306, last accessed March 13, 2007.

26. Benjamin and Flournoy, "Won't Deploy?"

27. The National Security Advisory Group, *The U.S. Military: Under Strain and at Risk*, January 2006, available at merln.ndu.edu/merln/mipal/reports/US_Military_Under_Strain_and_at_Risk.pdf, last accessed March 13, 2007. That report, which was assembled under the chairmanship of former defense secretary William J. Perry by a group consisting mainly of former Clinton administration officials, draws primarily from government sources.

28. National Security Advisory Group, *The U.S. Military*.

29. Korb et al., "Tapped Out."

30. Thom Shanker, "Army and Other Ground Forces Meet '06 Recruiting Goals," *New York Times*, October 9, 2006, p. 19.

31. "Equipment Shortfalls Hurt Army Readiness," *USA Today*, July 27, 2006, www.usatoday.com/news/washington/2006-07-27-army-readiness_x.htm, last accessed March 13, 2007.

32. *America's Image Slips. But Allies Share U.S. Concerns Over Iran, Hamas*, Pew Global Attitudes Project, June 13, 2006, available at http://pewglobal.org/reports/display.php?ReportID=252, last accessed March 13, 2007.

33. Francis Fukuyama, *America at the Crossroads: Democracy, Power, and the Neoconservative Legacy* (New Haven, Conn.: Yale University Press, 2006), p. 111.

34. National Counterterrorism Center, *Report on Incidents of Terrorism 2005*, April 11, 2006, available at http://wits.nctc.gov/reports/crot2005nctcannexfinal.pdf#search=%22national%20counterterrorism%20center%20and%20country%20reports%20on%20terrorism%20%22, last accessed March 13, 2007.

35. The Memorial Institute for the Prevention of Terrorism makes its data available on a Web site that viewers can analyze according to a variety of criteria. It can be accessed at: www.tkb.org/Home.jsp, last accessed March 13, 2007.

36. Peter Bergen and Paul Cruickshank, "Iraq 101: The Iraq Effect—The War in Iraq and Its Impact on the War on Terrorism," *Mother Jones*, March 1, 2007, www.motherjones.com/news/features/2007/03/iraq_effect_1.html/, last accessed March 13, 2007.

37. Fallows, "Declaring Victory," p. 62.

38. Ibid., p. 69.

39. Robert A. Pape, *Dying to Win: The Strategic Logic of Suicide Terrorism* (New York: Random House, 2005), p. 39.

40. Robert A. Pape, *What We've Learned about Suicide Terrorism since 9/11* (Cato Institute, September 12, 2006), available at www.cato.org/pub_display.php?pub_id=6679, last accessed March 13, 2007.

41. "The Logic of Suicide Terrorism," *American Conservative*, June 18, 2005, www.amconmag.com/2005_07_18/article.html, last accessed March 13, 2007.

42. Dana Priest and Josh White, "War Helps Recruit Terrorists, Hill Told," *Washington Post*, February 17, 2005, p. A01.

43. "The Logic of Suicide Terrorism."

44. Anthony M. Cordesman, *Patterns in Iraq's Evolving Insurgency* (Center for Strategic and International Studies, February 3, 2006). See especially pp. 19–29, available at: www.csis.org/media/csis/pubs/060203_iraqicombattrends.pdf, last accessed March 13, 2007.

45. Dana Priest and Ann Scott Tyson, "Bin Laden Trail 'Stone Cold,'" *Washington Post*, September 10, 2006, p. A01.

46. David Rohde, "An Afghan Symbol for Change, Then Failure," *New York Times*, September 5, 2006, p. 1.

47. Yochi J. Dreazen and Philip Shishkin, "Growing Concern: Terrorist Havens in 'Failed States,'" *Wall Street Journal*, September 13, 2006, p. 1.

48. See, for example, William Kristol, "And Now Iran," *Weekly Standard*, January 23, 2006, www.weeklystandard.com/Content/Public/Articles/000/000/006/585tdlqf.asp?pg=1, last accessed March 13, 2007.

49. Kim R. Holmes and John Hillen, "Misreading Reagan's Legacy: A Truly Conservative Foreign Policy," *Foreign Affairs* (September/October 1996), www.foreignaffairs.org/19960901faresponse4230/kim-r-holmes-john-hillen/misreading-reagan-s-legacy-a-truly-conservative-foreign-policy.html, last accessed March 13, 2007.

50. William Kristol and Lawrence F. Kaplan, *The War over Iraq: Saddam's Tyranny and America's Mission* (New York: Encounter Books, 2003).

51. Ken Jowitt, "Rage, Hubris, and Regime Change: The Urge to Speed History Along," *Policy Review* 118 (April–May 2003): 33–42, www.policyreview.org/apr03/jowitt.html, last accessed March 13, 2007.

52. George F. Will, "Transformation's Toll," *Washington Post*, July 18, 2006, p. A19.

4. Lucky Duckies

1. From a transcript of Armey's appearance on *CNN News*, August 2, 1993.

2. Federal News Service transcript of a Republican press conference following House passage of the bill, August 5, 1993.

3. Congressional Record, *Omnibus Budget Reconciliation Act—Conference Report* (Senate), August 6, 1993.

4. David E. Rosenbaum, "Clinton Wins Approval of His Budget Plan as Gore Votes to Break Senate Deadlock," *New York Times*, August 7, 1993, p. 1.

5. Congressional Record, *Omnibus Budget Reconciliation Act—Conference Report* (Senate), August 6, 1993.

6. Ibid.

7. Alan S. Blinder and Janet L. Yellen, *The Fabulous Decade: Macroeconomic Lessons from the 1990s* (New York: Century Foundation Press, 2001), p. 1.

8. Alan B. Krueger and Robert Solow, "Introduction," in *The Roaring Nineties: Can Full Employment Be Sustained?* (New York: Russell Sage Foundation and Century Foundation Press, 2001), p. xvii.

9. Rebecca M. Blank and Matthew Shapiro, "Labor and the Sustainability of Output and Productivity Growth," in *The Roaring Nineties*, p. 333.

10. J. Bradford DeLong, "Time for the *Washington Post* to Retire Robert Samuelson," *Brad DeLong's Semi-Daily Journal*, February 8, 2006, www.delong.typepad.com/sdj/2006/02/time_for_the_wa.html, last accessed March 13, 2007.

11. Blinder and Yellen, *The Fabulous Decade*, p. 5.

12. Ibid., pp. 17–19.

13. Federal Open Market Committee transcript, July 6–7, 2003, p. 66.

14. See Stacey Tevlin and Karl Whelan, "Explaining the Investment Boom of the 1990s," *Journal of Money, Credit and Banking* 35, no. 1 (February 2003): 1–22, available at http://www.federalreserve.gov/pubs/feds/2000/200011/200011pap.pdf, last accessed March 13, 2007.

15. Blinder and Yellen, *The Fabulous Decade*, p. 6.

16. Ibid., p. 82.

17. Ibid., p. 83.

18. Robert L. Bartley, "Checking in with the Frontrunner," *Wall Street Journal*, December 1, 1999.

19. Richard W. Stevenson. "At Bush's Ear, a Supply-Sider with a Heart," *New York Times*, December 12, 1999, section 3, p. 1.

20. Bruce Bartlett, *Impostor: How George W. Bush Bankrupted America and Betrayed the Reagan Legacy* (New York: Doubleday, 2006), p. 49.

21. N. Gregory Mankiw, *Macroeconomics*, 3rd ed. (New York: Worth, 1997).

22. Irving Kristol, *Neoconservatism: The Autobiography of an Idea* (New York: Free Press, 1995).

23. David A. Stockman, *The Triumph of Politics: Why the Reagan Revolution Failed* (New York: Harper & Row, 1986), p. 10.

24. Lou Cannon, *President Reagan: The Role of a Lifetime* (New York: PublicAffairs—orig. Simon and Schuster, 2000), p. 69.

25. Transcript of first Bush-Gore presidential debate, October 3, 2000, www.newsmax.com/articles/?a=2000/10/3/214311, last accessed March 13, 2007.

26. Floyd Norris, "Speaking of Recession," *New York Times*, December 10, 2000, section 4, p. 2.

27. Sebastian Mallaby, "Goodbye to Reaganomics," *Washington Post*, February 19, 2001, p. A33.

28. See Matthew D. Shapiro and Joel Slemrod, "Did the 2001 Tax Rebate Stimulate Spending? Evidence from Taxpayer Surveys," in *Tax Policy and the Economy*, vol. 17, ed. James M. Poterba (Cambridge: MIT Press, 2003), pp. 83–109, available at www-personal.umich.edu/~shapiro/Shapiro-Slemrod-TPE-PostConferenceDraft.pdf, last accessed March 13, 2007; see also Matthew D. Shapiro and Joel Slemrod, "Consumer Response to Tax Rebates," *American Economic Review* (March 2003): 381–396.

29. David E. Sanger, "President Asserts Shrunken Surplus May Curb Congress," *New York Times*, August 25, 2001, p. 1.

30. Matthew Benjamin, "You Gotta Have a Gimmick," *U.S. News & World Report*, May 26, 2003, p. 39.

31. In addition to tax-rate cuts, the smorgasbord included a gradual phasing out of the estate tax until its complete elimination in 2010, followed by a restoration of it in 2011 to its pre-2001 rules; beginning in 2007, a phasing out of limitations on the ability of high-income taxpayers to benefit from itemized deductions and personal exemptions; changes intended to reduce the so-called marriage penalty, which can cause some couples to pay more if they file jointly than if they were single and filing separately; higher contribution limits for Individual Retirement Accounts, 401(k)s, and other tax-favored retirement savings plans; new or expanded tax breaks for child-care and adoption costs, as well as education-related expenses; a temporary allowance for larger up-front corporate deductions for investment in new machinery and equipment; an expansion of tax breaks for small businesses; and a reduction to 15 percent of the tax rate on dividends and capital gains through 2008 (previously, dividends were taxed at regular income tax rates and the top long-term rate was 20 percent).

32. William G. Gale and Peter R. Orszag, "Economic Effects of Making the 2001 and 2003 Tax Cuts Permanent" (Urban-Brookings Tax Policy Center, Discussion Paper No. 17, October 2004, table 5), available at www.brookings.edu/views/papers/20040817galeorszag.pdf, last accessed March 13, 2007.

33. Joel Friedman and Katharine Richards, *Capital Gains and Dividend Tax Cuts: Data Make Clear That High Income Households Benefit the Most* (Center on Budget and Policy Priorities, January 30, 2006); available at www.cbpp.org/1-30-06tax2.htm, last accessed March 13, 2007.

34. Paul Krugman, "The Tax-Cut Con," *New York Times Magazine*, September 14, 2003, p. 54.

35. "The Non-Taxpaying Class," *Wall Street Journal*, November 20, 2002. See also "Lucky Duckies Again," *Wall Street Journal*, January 20, 2003; and "Even Luckier Duckies," *Wall Street Journal*, June 3, 2003.

36. Congressional Budget Office, *Effective Federal Tax Rates: 1997–2000*, August 2003, p. 2; available at www.cbo.gov/ftpdocs/45xx/doc4514/08-29-Report.pdf, last accessed March 13, 2007.

37. *Effective Federal Tax Rates*, p. 23.

38. Edmund L. Andrews, "Too Many Pennies from Heaven?" *New York Times*, February 16, 2003, section 3, p. 15.

39. Edmund L. Andrews, "A Salesman for Bush's Tax Plan Who Has Belittled Similar Ideas," *New York Times*, February 28, 2006, p. C1.

40. Gale and Orszag, "Economic Effects," p. 27.

41. Isaac Shapiro, Richard Kogan, and Aviva Aron-Dine, "How Robust Is the Current Economic Expansion?" (Center on Budget and Policy Priorities, January 19, 2007), www.cbpp.org/8-9-05bud.htm, last accessed March 13, 2007.

42. Gene Amromin, Paul Harrison, and Steven Sharpe, *How Did the 2003 Dividend Tax Cut Affect Stock Prices?* Federal Reserve Board, Washington, D.C., May 29, 2006, www.federalreserve.gov/pubs/feds/2005/200561/200561pap.pdf, last accessed March 13, 2007.

43. Karen Richardson, "Did the Dividend Tax Cut Work? Policy Change Didn't Boost Market's 'Aggregate' Value, Federal Reserve Report Says," *Wall Street Journal*, December 6, 2005, p. C3.

44. U.S. Census Bureau, *Income, Poverty, and Health Insurance Coverage in the United States: 2005*, August 2006, p. 31, available at www.census.gov/prod/2006pubs/p60-231.pdf, last accessed March 13, 2007.

45. Ibid., p. 46.

46. Greg Ip, "Snow Defends President's Handling of Economy," *Wall Street Journal*, March 20, 2006, p. A3.

47. Treasury Assistant Secretary Mark A. Warshawsky, "Ask the White House," May 18, 2006, available at www.whitehouse.gov/ask/20060518.html, last accessed March 13, 2007.

48. Shapiro, Kogan, and Aron-Dine, "How Robust Is the Current Economic Expansion?"

49. Ruth Carlitz and Richard Kogan, "CBO Data Show Tax Cuts Have Played Much Larger Role Than Domestic Spending Increases in Fueling the Deficit,"

January 31, 2005, available at www.cbpp.org/1-25-05bud.htm, last accessed March 13, 2007.

50. Carroll Doherty, *Do Deficits Matter Anymore? Apparently Not to the Public*, Pew Research Center, March 14, 2006, http://pewresearch.org/obdeck/?ObDeckID=10.

51. Sebastian Edwards, *Is the Current Account Deficit Sustainable? And if Not, How Costly Is Adjustment Likely to Be?* (National Bureau of Economic Research, August 2005), p. 10, available at www.anderson.ucla.edu/documents/areas/fac/gem/adjustment.pdf, last accessed March 13, 2007.

52. Edwards, *Is the Current Account Deficit Sustainable?* p. 40.

53. *Seven Signs of Fiscal Sense: An Analysis of the President's Fiscal Year 2007 Budget*, Concord Coalition, issue brief, February 27, 2006, p. 29, available at www.concordcoalition.org/issues/fedbudget/issue-briefs/060224-SevenSignsAnalysis.pdf, last accessed March 13, 2007.

54. Congressional Budget Office, *Analyzing the Economic and Budgetary Effects of a 10 Percent Cut in Income Tax Rates*, December 1, 2005, available at www.cbo.gov/ftpdocs/69xx/doc6908/12-01-10PercentTaxCut.pdf, last accessed March 13, 2007.

55. Data from the Department of the Treasury and Office of Management and Budget are available at http://a257.g.akamaitech.net/7/257/2422/15feb20061000/www.gpoaccess.gov/eop/2006/B79.xls, last accessed March 13, 2007.

56. See William A. Niskanen, *"Starve the Beast" Does Not Work*, Cato Policy Report, March/April 2004, p. 2, www.cato.org/pubs/policy_report/v26n2/cpr-26n2-2.pdf, last accessed March 13, 2007.

57. Data from the Department of the Treasury and Office of Management and Budget are available at http://a257.g.akamaitech.net/7/257/2422/15feb20061000/www.gpoaccess.gov/eop/2006/B79.xls, last accessed March 13, 2007.

58. Robert L. Bartley, *The Seven Fat Years and How to Do It Again* (New York: Free Press, 1992).

59. Ibid., p. 53.

60. Benjamin M. Friedman, "The Morning After," *New York Review of Books*, August 13, 1992.

5. Rocky Mountain Lows

1. *State TABOR Proposals—2006 Legislative Session*, Center on Budget and Policy Priorities, November 1, 2006, www.cbpp.org/6-1-05tabor.pdf, last accessed March 14, 2007.

2. Daniel Franklin and A. G. Newmyer III, "Is Grover Over?" *Washington Monthly* (March, 2005), www.washingtonmonthly.com/features/2005/0503.franklin1.html, last accessed March 14, 2007.

3. John J. Miller, "America's Best Governor: For Republicans, a Rocky Mountain High—Bill Owens," *National Review* (September 2, 2002), www.findarticles.com/p/articles/mi_m1282/is_16_54/ai_90570238, last accessed March 14, 2007.

4. George F. Will, "Riding High in Colorado," *Washington Post*, October 19, 2003, p. B07.

5. John Cassidy, "The Ringleader: How Grover Norquist Keeps the Conservative Movement Together," *New Yorker* (August 1, 2005), p. 42.

6. Cara DeGette, "Douglas Edward Bruce: Colorado Dreamin'," *Colorado Springs Independent*, August 24, 1994, www.csindy.com/csindy/10thann/1994-08-24-cover.html, last accessed March 14, 2007.

7. This section summarizing the history of Douglas Bruce's TABOR efforts draws from Daniel A. Smith's "Populist Entrepreneur: Douglas Bruce and the Tax and Government Limitation Moment in Colorado, 1986–1992," *Great Plains Research* 6 (Fall 1996): 269–294.

8. Ibid, p. 286.

9. Ibid, p. 287.

10. John Gunther, *Inside USA* (New York: Harper and Brothers, 1947).

11. Peter Schrag, *Paradise Lost: California's Experience, America's Future* (Berkeley: University of California Press, 1998, 2004).

12. David H. Bradley, Nicholas Johnson, and Iris J. Lav, *The Flawed "Population Plus Inflation" Formula: Why TABOR's Growth Formula Doesn't Work*, Center on Budget and Policy Priorities, January 13, 2005, www.cbpp.org/1-13-05sfp3.htm, last accessed March 14, 2007.

13. Nicholas Johnson, Carol Hedges, and Jim Zelenski, *Colorado's Fiscal Problems Have Been Severe and Are Likely to Continue*, Center on Budget and Policy Priorities, March 17, 2004, p. 9.

14. Kyle Henley, "State Budget Squeeze Tough on Lawmakers," *Colorado Springs Gazette*, February 29, 2004, www.findarticles.com/p/article/mi_qn4191/is_20040299/ai_n10031050, last accessed March 14, 2007.

15. David Bradley and Karen Lyons, *A Formula for Decline: Lessons from Colorado for States Considering TABOR*, Center on Budget and Policy Priorities, October 19, 2005, www.cbpp.org/10-19-05sfp.htm, last accessed March 14, 2007.

16. Ibid.

17. *TABOR Issue Brief*, Bell Policy Center, March 10, 2005, www.thebell.org/pdf/TB05Medicaid.pdf, last accessed March 14, 2007.

18. Carol Dreck, "Special Delivery: Colorado Ranks Sixth Worst in the Nation for Low Birthweight Babies," *Denver Post*, April 18, 1999, p. E-01.

19. David Bradley, *Fiction and Fact: A Response to the Tax Foundation's Distortion of Colorado's TABOR* Center on Budget and Policy Priorities, May 2, 2005, www.cbpp.org/5-2-05sfp.htm, last accessed March 14, 2007.

20. Jim Hughes, "Panel OKs Medicaid Bill for Prenatal Care," *Denver Post*, January 20, 2005, p. B2.

21. M. Lynsey Morris, the associate director for federal affairs at the March of Dimes (presentation to Association of Maternal and Child Health Programs, 2005 Annual Conference, February 19–23, 2005), www.cademedia.com/archives/mchb/amchp2005/transcripts/d2a.htm, last accessed March 14, 2007.

22. *Colorado Childhood Immunization Rates: Policy and Practice* (Colorado Health Institute, May 2005), www.coloradohealthinstitute.org/Documents/Childhood_Immunization_Full_Report.pdf, last accessed March 14, 2007.

23. Karen Auge, "No Longer Last, Colorado Is 44th in Vaccinating Children," *Denver Post*, July 27, 2005, p. B-02.

24. *Colorado Childhood Immunization*, pp. 17, 18, 35, 54.

25. Marsha Austin, "State Leading Nation in Whooping-Cough Cases," *Denver Post*, October 7, 2005, p. A-01.

26. *Colorado Childhood Immunization*, p. 19.

27. *Sky High Health Care Costs in the Mile High City* (a report prepared for Colorado for Health Care by the Project for Strategic Health Care Purchasing, September 2005), p. 11.

28. Marsha Austin, "Cutting Benefits to Poor Assailed," *Denver Post*, May 4, 2003, p. K-01.

29. Barbara O'Brien and Al Meiklejohn, "Amendment 23: Rescue Failing Public Education," *Denver Post*, October 22, 2000, p. K-01.

30. Allison Sherry, "School Repairs Languish," *Denver Post*, August 1, 2004, p. A-01.

31. Paul Teske, "State School Spending Near Bottom of Class," *Denver Post*, April 17, 2005, p. E-01.

32. Bradley and Lyons, *A Formula for Decline*.

33. Allison Sherry and Karen Rouse, "A Shortage of Substitutes," *Denver Post*, April 1, 2005, p. B-01.

34. Bradley and Lyons, *A Formula for Decline*.

35. Dan Haley, "The High Cost of Higher Ed," *Denver Post*, July 17, 2005, p. E-01.

36. Spiros Protopsaltis, *No College for You! Colorado's Higher Education System at the Breaking Point* (Bell Policy Center, Summer 2005), pp. 11, 17.

37. Dave Curtin, "State's Colleges Decry Finances," *Denver Post*, December 20, 2004, p. A-01.

38. "CU—Still a Public University?" *Denver Post*, p. E-06.

39. Chris Frates, "Colorado Voters May Decide on Funding for Colleges," *Denver Post*, February 15, 2004, p. B-01.

40. Kim Rueben and Kelly Rader, *State and Local Tax Revenues* (Tax Policy Center, March 28, 2005), www.urban.org/UploadedPDF/1000754_Tax_Facts_3-28-05.pdf, last accessed March 14, 2007.

41. Chris Atkins, *An Analysis of Misleading Attacks on Colorado's Taxpayer's Bill of Rights* (Tax Foundation, March 25, 2005), p. 1, www.taxfoundation.org/news/printer/316.html, last accessed March 14, 2007.

42. David Bradley, *Fiction and Fact: A Response to the Tax Foundation's Distortion of Colorado's TABOR* (Center on Budget and Policy Priorities, May 2, 2005), p. 2, www.cbpp.org/5-2-05sfp.htm, last accessed March 14, 2007.

43. Atkins, *An Analysis of Misleading Attacks*, p. 3.

44. Bradley, *Fiction and Fact*, pp. 4–6.

45. Atkins, *An Analysis of Misleading Attacks*, p. 4.

46. Bradley, *Fiction and Fact*, p. 6.

47. Atkins, *An Analysis of Misleading Attacks*, p. 4.

48. Bradley, *Fiction and Fact*, pp. 8–9.

49. *SCHIP Annual Report*, 2003, State of Colorado, www.cms.hhs.gov/schip/annual-reports/2003/charco03.pdf, last accessed March 14, 2007.

50. Atkins, *An Analysis of Misleading Attacks*, p. 4.

51. Bradley, *Fiction and Fact*, pp. 9–10.

52. Geoffrey F. Segal, George Passantino, Adam B. Summers, Lisa Snell, and Tarren R. Bragdon, *Priority Colorado: Balancing the Budget while Preserving TABOR and Colorado's Quality of Life* (Independence Institute, Issue Paper #4-2005, February 2005), pp. 1–2, www.i2i.org/articles/IP_4_2005.pdf, last accessed March 14, 2007.

53. Ibid., pp. 17–18.

54. *JBC Staff Comments Related to "Priority Colorado" Report*, Colorado General Assembly Joint Budget Committee, February 21, 2005, www.state.co.us/gov_dir/leg_dir/jbc/prioritycoloradoreport.pdf, last accessed March 14, 2007.

55. Joe Kovacs, "Rush Limbaugh Thinks Arnold Is Conservative," *WorldNet Daily*, August 21, 2003, www.worldnetdaily.com/news/printer-friendly.asp?ARTICLE_ID=34199, last accessed March 14, 2007.

56. Lee Green, "Don't Be a 'Girlie Man,'" *Los Angeles Times Magazine*, April 17, 2005, p. 12.

57. Lawrence Kudlow, "Terminating Any Doubt," *National Review Online*, August 21, 2003, www.nationalreview.com/kudlow/kudlow082103.asp, last accessed March 14, 2007.

58. Major Garrett, "No Tax Pledge Becomes Test for Schwarzenegger," Foxnews.com, August 27, 2003.

59. Stephen J. Carroll, Cathy Krop, Jeremy Arkes, Peter A. Morrison, and Ann Flanagan, *California's K-12 Public Schools: How Are They Doing?* (RAND, 2005), p. xxxvi, www.rand.org/pubs/monographs/2004/RAND_MG186.pdf, last accessed March 14, 2007.

60. Ibid., pp. xxvii–xxx, 99–100, 133.

61. Peter Schrag, "Too Many Restrictions Keep California in Political Gridlock," *Sacramento Bee*, July 13, 2005.

62. Mark Z. Barabak, "From Ashes of 2005 Defeat, Gov. Rises to New Role," *Los Angeles Times*, November 8, 2006.

63. George F. Will, "Taxes and Colorado's 'Apostate,'" *Washington Post*, October 2, 2006, p. B07.

6. Sophisticated Sabotage

1. Stuart Shapiro, "Unequal Partners: Cost-Benefit Analysis and Executive Review of Regulations," *Environmental Law Reporter* (July 2005), www.policy.rutgers.edu/faculty/shapiro/elr%20article.pdf, last accessed March 14, 2007.

2. Cass R. Sunstein, *Risk and Reason: Safety, Law, and the Environment* (Cambridge, U.K.: Cambridge University Press, 2002), p. 18.

3. See, for example, Edith Stokey and Richard Zeckhauser, *A Primer for Policy Analysis* (New York: W. W. Norton, 1978).

4. John F. Morrall III, "Saving Lives: A Review of the Record" (AEI-Brookings Joint Center for Regulatory Studies, Working Paper 03-6, July 2003), www.aei-brookings .org/admin/authorpdfs/page.php?id=275, last accessed March 14, 2007.

5. See Lisa Heinzerling, "Regulatory Costs of Mythic Proportions," *Yale Law Journal* 107 (1998), www.law.georgetown.edu/faculty/Heinzerling/Articles/Regula- tory_Costs_Yale_LJ.pdf, last accessed March 14, 2007, and Richard W. Parker, "Is Government Regulation Irrational? A Reply to Morrall and Hahn" (University of Connecticut School of Law Working Paper Series, 2004), http://lsr.nellco.org/cgi/ viewcontent.cgi?article=1030&context=uconn/ucwps, last accessed March 14, 2007.

6. Steve Weinberg, "Mr. Bottom Line," *OnEarth Magazine* (Spring 2003), www.nrdc.org/onearth/03spr/graham1.asp, last accessed March 14, 2007.

7. Ibid.

8. Ibid.

9. Ibid.

10. John D. Graham, *Comparing Opportunities to Reduce Heath Risks: Toxin Control, Medicine, and Injury Prevention* (National Center for Policy Analysis, June 1995), www.ncpa.org/studies/s192/s192.html, last accessed March 14, 2007.

11. Susan E. Dudley, *Primer on Regulation* (The Mercatus Policy Series: Policy Resource no. 1, November 2005), www.mercatus.org/repository/docLib/20060510 _Primer_on_Regulation_Dudley_Dec_2005_Final_as_Posted.pdf, last accessed March 14, 2007.

12. Philip K. Howard, *The Death of Common Sense: How Law Is Suffocating America* (New York: Random House, 1994).

13. See *Myths and Consequences: Paying for the Use of Myths and Distortions by Anti-Regulatory Zealots*, Citizens for Sensible Safeguards, 1994.

14. See Nina A. Burleigh, "Breaking the Rules," *ABA Journal* (May 1995).

15. U.S. Office of Management and Budget, Office of Information and Regula- tory Affairs, *Informing Regulatory Decisions: 2004 Draft Report to Congress on the Costs and Benefits of Federal Regulations and Unfunded Mandates on State, Local, and Tribal Entities*, pp. 5–6, www.whitehouse.gov/omb/inforeg/draft_2004 _cbreport.pdf, last accessed March 14, 2007.

16. Thomas O. McGarity, Sidney Shapiro, and David Bollier, *Sophisticated Sabotage: The Intellectual Games Used to Subvert Responsible Regulation* (Washing- ton, D.C.: Environmental Law Institute, 2004), p. 6.

17. Eban Goodstein, "Polluted Data," *American Prospect*, November 1, 1997, www.prospect.org/web/page.ww?section=root&name=ViewPrint&articleId=4757, last accessed March 14, 2007.

18. Jocelyn Kaiser, "How Much Are Human Lives and Health Worth?" *Science* 299, no. 5614, (March 21, 2003), p. 1836.

19. Thomas O. McGarity, "Professor Sunstein's Fuzzy Math," *Georgetown Law Journal* (July 2002), www.findarticles.com/p/articles/mi_qa3805/is_200207/ ai_n9105571/print, last accessed March 14, 2007.

20. Stephen Breyer, *Breaking the Vicious Circle: Toward Effective Risk Regula- tion* (Cambridge: Harvard University Press, 1993), p. 47.

21. See the March 11, 2002, letter from Joan Claybrook, president of Public Citizen, to John D. Graham, www.citizen.org/congress/regulations/bush_admin/articles.cfm?ID=7270, last accessed March 14, 2007.

22. The August 6, 2003, decision is available here: www.autosafety.org/TPMSRuling.pdf, last accessed March 14, 2007.

23. Rick Weiss, " 'Data Quality' Law Is Nemesis of Regulation," *Washington Post*, August 16, 2004, p. A01, www.washingtonpost.com/wp-dyn/articles/A3733-2004Aug15.html. See also Chris Mooney, *The Republican War on Science* (New York: Basic Books, 2005), pp. 102–120.

24. Stuart Shapiro, "An Evaluation of the Bush Administration Reforms to the Regulatory Process," July 27, 2005 (*Presidential Studies Quarterly*, forthcoming).

25. Andrew C. Revkin, "Law Revises Standards for Scientific Study," *New York Times*, March 21, 2002, p. 30.

26. *The Reality of the Data Quality Act's First Year: A Correction of OMB's Report to Congress* (OMB Watch, July 2004), p. 7, www.ombwatch.org/info/dataqualityreport.pdf, last accessed March 15, 2007.

27. See, for example, John Graham, "The 'Smart Regulation' Agenda: Progress and Challenges" (luncheon remarks to the AEI-Brookings Joint Center for Regulatory Studies, November 7, 2005), www.aei-brookings.org/admin/authorpdfs/page.php?id=1210, last accessed March 15, 2007.

28. *The Bush Regulatory Record: A Pattern of Failure* (OMB Watch, September 2004), pp. 4–5, www.ombwatch.org/regs/2004/patternoffailure/finalreport.pdf, last accessed March 15, 2007.

29. Ibid., p. 7.

30. *Polluters Breathe Easier: EPA Environmental Court Actions Decline* (Environmental Integrity Project, October 12, 2004), www.environmentalintegrity.org/pub260.cfm, last accessed March 15, 2007.

31. Seth Borenstein, "Pollution Citations Plummet under Bush," *Philadelphia Inquirer*, December 9, 2003, p. A01.

32. Environmental Protection Agency, *FY 2004 End-of-Year Enforcement and Compliance Five-Year Trends*, www.epa.gov/compliance/resources/reports/endofyear/eoy2004/fy045yeartrend.pdf, last accessed March 15, 2007.

33. Chris Bowman, "EPA Pumps Up Its Record," *Sacramento Bee*, July 6, 2003, p. A1.

34. *Federal Pollution Enforcement Declines: Details by Statute* (TRAC Report, 2004), http://trac.syr.edu/tracreports/environ/87/, last accessed March 15, 2007.

35. EPA Office of Inspector General, *New Source Review Rule Change Harms EPA's Ability to Enforce against Coal-Fired Electric Utilities*, September 30, 2004, www.epa.gov/oig/reports/2004/20040930-2004-P-00034.pdf, last accessed March 15, 2007.

36. Seth Borenstein, "Environment Worsened under Bush in Many Key Areas, Data Show," Knight Ridder, October 13, 2004, www.commondreams.org/headlines04/1013-12.htm, last accessed March 15, 2007.

7. "It Hasn't Worked Like We Thought it Would in Theory"

1. See, for example, Milton Friedman, "The Promise of Vouchers," *Wall Street Journal*, December 5, 2005, p. A20. Friedman's arguments for school vouchers were first published in Robert A. Solo, ed., *Economics and the Public Interest* (Rutgers University Press, 1958), and then again in his collection of essays *Capitalism and Freedom* (Chicago: University of Chicago Press, 1962).

2. Sarah Carr, "Gut Instinct Guides Parents' Choices," *Milwaukee Journal Sentinel*, June 14, 2005, p. 1, www.jsonline.com/story/index.aspx?id=333502, last accessed March 15, 2007.

3. The Bradleys were brothers who created what became the Allen-Bradley Company, a Milwaukee-based manufacturer of electronic and radio components. Lynde died in 1942. Harry and his partner at the helm of the firm, Fred Loock, shared a deep disdain for both communism and the federal government and were charter members of the John Birch Society, based in nearby Appleton, Wisconsin; the Birch Society founder Robert Welch frequently spoke at Allen-Bradley sales meetings. Harry Bradley died in 1965 and Loock in 1973. In 1985, Rockwell International bought Allen-Bradley for $1.65 billion, of which $290 million was devoted to converting the sleepy $14 million Allen-Bradley Foundation, which mainly supported local causes such as museums and universities, into a much larger institution renamed after the two brothers. The Bradley Foundation's board decided to shift its mission to conservative political causes because, as chairman "Tiny" Rader put it, "The principles Harry believed in gave us the strongest economy, the highest living standard, and the greatest individual freedom in the world. We felt it was our task to preserve those principles." Michael Joyce, who had been working as executive director of the Olin Foundation, was recruited to come to Milwaukee to engineer the foundation's makeover. See John Gurda, *The Bradley Legacy* (Milwaukee: The Lynde and Harry Bradley Foundation, 1992), and John J. Miller, *A Gift of Freedom* (San Francisco: Encounter Books, 2006).

4. Katherine M. Skiba, "Bradley Philanthropy: Group Commands Influence," *Milwaukee Journal Sentinel*, September 17, 1995, p. 1.

5. Phone interview with John Witte, February 2, 2006.

6. "Quality Counts '98: The Urban Challenge," *Education Week* (January 8, 1998), www.teachermag.net/sreports/qc98/intros/in-toc.htm.

7. John E. Chubb and Terry M. Moe, *Politics, Markets and America's Schools* (Washington, D.C.: Brookings Institution, 1990).

8. Jeffrey R. Henig, "Repackaging Choice," in *Rethinking School Choice: Limits of the Market Metaphor* (Princeton, N.J.: Princeton University Press, 1994), p. 87.

9. For example, Henig, in *Rethinking School Choice: Limits of the Market Metaphor* (Princeton, N.J.: Princeton University Press, 1994), raises several significant concerns about Chubb and Moe's analysis: (1) they convert small gains in the number of correctly answered test questions by private school students into "gains measured in years," which conveys a much higher degree of significance than is statistically the case (Henig cites John Witte's work on that point); (2) they focus on test score changes between the sophomore and senior years, though abundant research

shows that the early grades are much more important in establishing how students perform over time; (3) the data Chubb and Moe used are ill-suited to providing reliable information about private schools, their independent effect, or choice per se; the number of private schools included is small (only 111, all but 27 Catholic schools) and doesn't allow reliable estimates of the performance of different types of schools; and (4) the data do not contain any direct measure of students' exercise of choice or the extent to which schools are forced to respond to market demands. It is assumed that all private schools are forced to compete for student customers, even though some elite private schools have long waiting lists and some parochial schools charge tuitions so low that they may lose money for each additional student they accept.

10. Bob Lowe, *The Hollow Promise of School Vouchers* (Rethinking Schools Online, 2002), www.rethinkingschools.org/special_reports/voucher_report/v_sosholw .shtml#5, last accessed March 15, 2007.

11. 1999–2000 Joint Legislative Audit Committee, *Milwaukee Parental Choice Program: An Evaluation*, February 2000, pp. 14, 17, www.legis.state.wi.us/lab/reports/ 00-2full.pdf, last accessed March 15, 2007.

12. Grant information is available from Media Transparency here: www .mediatransparency.org/grantsearchresults.php?searchString=Paul+E.+Peterson, last accessed March 15, 2007.

13. Bob Davis, "Studies on Private Education Result in a Public Clash of Egos," *Wall Street Journal*, October 11, 1996, p. A1.

14. Bruce Fuller, of the University of California at Berkeley, noted that Peterson's study "is based on less than 80 students who lasted four years in just three choice schools. Comparable data are not available on the other 2,900 children who spent less than four years or could not be tracked. Would we believe a scientist who claimed that smoking has no harmful health effects based on a study that simply tracked smokers who were alive?"

15. Cecilia E. Rouse, "Private School Vouchers and Student Achievement: An Evaluation of the Milwaukee Parental Choice Program," *Quarterly Journal of Economics* 113, no. 2 (1998): 553–602.

16. Steve Schultze, "Defending Choice Law Has Cost $372,000," *Milwaukee Journal Sentinel*, January 16, 1997, p. 10.

17. Robert G. Kaiser and Ira Chinoy, "How Scaife's Money Powered a Movement," *Washington Post*, May 2, 1999, p. A01.

18. Alan J. Borsuk, Sarah Carr, and Leonard Sykes Jr., "Inside School Choice: 15 Years of School Vouchers," *Milwaukee Journal Sentinel*, June 12–18, 2005. The entire series is available here: www.jsonline.com/news/choice/, last accessed March 15, 2007.

19. Caroline Minter Hoxby, "Rising Tide," in *Education Next* (Winter 2001), http://media.hoover.org/documents/ednext20014_68.pdf, last accessed March 15, 2007.

20. Indeed, a RAND study of charter schools found that Texas students attending them had lower-than-average test scores, before leaving the regular public schools—an observation that somewhat dispels concerns that voucher and charter schools would "cream" the best students from the public schools. See Kevin Booker, Ron Zimmer, and Richard Buddin, "The Effect of Charter Schools on School Peer

Composition" (RAND Working Paper, October 2005), www.ncspe.org/publications_files/RAND_WR306.pdf, last accessed March 15, 2007.

21. Jonathan Plucker et al., *Evaluation of the Cleveland Scholarship and Tutoring Program: Summary Report 1998–2004* (Center for Evaluation and Education Policy at Indiana University, February, 22, 2006), www.schoolchoiceinfo.org/data/research/200602_Clev_Summary.pdf, last accessed March 15, 2007.

22. The Center for Education Reform considers "strong" state laws to be ones that include these provisions: no cap on the number of charter schools allowed; multiple charter-granting agencies; no formal evidence of local support required before start-up; greater legal and fiscal autonomy; automatic waiver from state and district laws; exemption from collective bargaining and work rules; guarantee of full per-pupil funding, but no more and no special support for those schools serving poor students. For more generally on charter schools and accountability, see Amy Stuart Wells, ed., *Where Charter School Policy Fails: The Problems of Accountability and Equity* (New York: Teachers College Press, 2002).

23. *The Charter School Debate* (Brookings Institution Briefing, February 18, 2004), transcript available at www.brookings.edu/comm/events/20040218.pdf, last accessed March 15, 2007.

24. National Center for Education Statistics, *A Closer Look at Charter Schools Using Hierarchical Linear Modeling*, August 2006, http://nces.ed.gov/pubsearch/pubsinfo.asp?pubid=2006460, last accessed March 15, 2007.

25. Caroline M. Hoxby, *Achievement in Charter Schools and Regular Public Schools in the United States: Understanding the Differences* (National Bureau of Economic Research, December 2004), http://post.economics.harvard.edu/faculty/hoxby/papers/hoxbycharter_dec.pdf, last accessed March 15, 2007.

26. Joydeep Roy and Lawrence Mishel, "Advantage None: Re-Examining Hoxby's Finding of Charter School Benefits" (Economic Policy Institute Briefing Paper, April 15, 2005), www.epinet.org/content.cfm/bp158, last accessed March 15, 2007.

27. Christopher Lubienski and Sarah Theule Lubienski, *Charter, Private, Public School and Academic Achievement: New Evidence from NAEP Mathematics Data* (National Center for the Study of Privatization in Education, Teachers College, Columbia University, January 2006), www.ncspe.org/publications_files/OP111.pdf, last accessed March 15, 2007.

28. National Assessment of Education Progress, *Comparing Private Schools and Public Schools Using Hierarchical Linear Modeling*, U.S. Department of Education, July 2006, http://nces.ed.gov/pubsearch/pubsinfo.asp?pubid=2006461, last accessed March 15, 2007.

29. Paul E. Peterson and Elena Llaudet, "On the Public-Private School Achievement Debate," August 2, 2006, www.ksg.harvard.edu/pepg/pdf/Papers/PEPG06-02-PetersonLlaudet.pdf, last accessed March 15, 2007.

30. Christopher Lubienski and Sarah Theule Lubienski, "Review of 'On the Public-Private School Achievement Debate,'" Education Policy Studies Laboratory, Arizona State University, August 30, 2006, epsl.asu.edu/epru/ttreviews/EPSL-0608-207-EPRU.pdf, last accessed March 15, 2007.

31. U.S. Bureau of the Census, *A Half-Century of Learning: Historical Statistics on Educational Attainment in the United States, 1940 to 2000*, Table 1, Internet Release Date: April 6, 2006, www.census.gov/population/socdemo/education/phct41/table1.xls, last accessed March 15, 2007.

32. National Commission on Excellence in Education, *A Nation at Risk: The Imperative for Educational Reform*, U.S. Department of Education, April 1983, www.ed.gov/pubs/NatAtRisk/index.html, last accessed March 15, 2007.

33. Robert B. Schwartz and Marian A. Robinson, "Goals 2000 and the Standards Movement," *Brookings Paper on Education Policy, 2000* (Washington, D.C.: Brookings Institution Press, 2000), p. 173.

34. Martin Carnoy and Susanna Loeb, "Does External Accountability Affect Student Outcomes? A Cross-State Analysis," in *Redesigning Accountability Systems for Education* (New York: Teachers College Press, 2004), pp. 189–219.

35. Newt Gingrich, "Religion and Politics: The Legitimate Role" (Heritage Lecture #507, December 1, 1994), www.heritage.org/Research/PoliticalPhilosophy/HL507.cfm, last accessed March 15, 2007.

36. See, for example, Walt Haney, "The Myth of the Texas Miracle in Education," *Education Policy Analysis* 8, no. 41 (August 19, 2000), http://epaa.asu.edu/epaa/v8n41/, last accessed March 15, 2007.

37. James E. Ryan, "The Perverse Incentives of the No Child Left Behind Act," *New York University Law Review* 79, no. 3 (June 2004): 989, www.law.nyu.edu/journals/lawreview/issues/vol79/no3/NYU303.pdf, last accessed March 15, 2007.

38. David J. Hoff and Kathleen Kennedy Manzo, "Bush Claims about NCLB Questioned," *Education Week*, March 14, 2007, p. 1.

39. See Department of Education, *Fact Sheet on Title I, Part A*, August 2002, www.ed.gov/rschstat/eval/disadv/title1-factsheet.doc, last accessed March 15, 2007.

40. Sam Dillon, "States Are Relaxing Education Standards to Avoid Sanctions from Federal Law," *New York Times*, May 22, 2003, p. 29.

41. Lynn Olson, "A 'Proficient' Score Depends on Geography," *Education Week*, February 20, 2002, p. 1.

42. Diane Ravitch, "National Standards: '50 Standards for 50 States' Is a Formula for Incoherence and Obfuscation," *Education Week*, January 5, 2006.

43. Sam Dillon, "Students Ace State Tests, but Earn D's from U.S.," *New York Times*, November 26, 2005, p. 1.

44. Charles Clotfelter, Helen Ladd, Jacob Vigdor, and Roger Aliaga, "Do School-Based Accountability Systems Make It More Difficult to Retain and Attract High Quality Teachers?" *Journal of Policy Analysis and Management* 23, no. 2 (2004).

45. Thomas J. Kane and Douglas O. Staiger, *Unintended Consequences of Racial Subgroup Rules in No Child Left Behind? The Politics and Practice of School Accountability*, ed. Paul E. Peterson and Martin R. West (Washington, D.C.: Brookings Institution Press, 2003), pp. 152–176.

46. Amy Stuart Wells and Jennifer Jellison Holme, "No Accountability for Diversity: Standardized Tests and the Demise of Racially Mixed Schools" (paper presented at a conference on "The Resegregation of Southern Schools?" Chapel Hill,

N.C., August 30, 2002), www.civilrightsproject.harvard.edu/research/reseg02/wells_holme.pdf, last accessed March 15, 2007.

47. The number of people living in high-poverty neighborhoods—where the poverty rate is 40 percent or higher—declined by 24 percent, or 2.5 million people, in the 1990s. While the reasons for that significant drop-off are not entirely clear, most analysts agree that the strong wage growth among low-income workers in the late 1990s played an important role. See Paul A. Jargowsky, *Stunning Progress, Hidden Problems: The Dramatic Decline in Concentrated Poverty in the 1990s* (Brookings Institution, May 2003), www.brookings.edu/es/urban/publications/jargowskypoverty.pdf, last accessed March 15, 2007.

48. See, for example, National Center for Education Statistics, *Highlights from the Trends in International Mathematics and Science Study, 2003*, U.S. Department of Education, December 2004, http://nces.ed.gov/pubs2005/2005005.pdf, last accessed March 15, 2007; also, National Center for Education Statistics, *International Comparisons in Fourth-Grade Reading Literacy*, U.S. Department of Education, April 2003, http://nces.ed.gov/pubs2003/2003073.pdf, last accessed March 15, 2007.

49. National Center for Education Statistics, *Urban Schools: The Challenge of Location and Poverty*, U.S. Department of Education, July 1996, http://nces.ed.gov/pubsearch/pubsinfo.asp?pubid=96184, last accessed March 15, 2007.

50. Richard D. Kahlenberg, *Helping Children Move from Bad Schools to Good Ones* (Century Foundation, 2006), www.tcf.org/Publications/Education/kahlenbergsoa6-15-06.pdf, last accessed March 15, 2007.

51. Abigail Thernstrom and Stephan Thernstrom, *No Excuses: Closing the Racial Gap in Learning* (New York: Simon and Schuster, 2004).

52. Kahlenberg, *Helping Children Move.*

53. Jonathan Kozol, *The Shame of the Nation: The Restoration of Apartheid Schooling in America* (New York: Crown, 2006), pp. 226–233.

54. William H. Freivogel, "St. Louis: Desegregation and School Choice in the Land of Dred Scott," in *Divided We Fail: Coming Together through Public School Choice* (New York: Century Foundation Press, 2002), pp. 209–235.

55. Kahlenberg, *Helping Children Move.*

8. "Tough It Out"

1. Stan Liebowitz, *Why Health Care Costs Too Much* (Cato Institute, Policy Analysis No. 211, June 23, 1994), www.cato.org/pubs/pas/pa211.html, last accessed March 16, 2007.

2. Marilyn Werber Serafini, "The Father of HSAs," *National Journal* (February 7, 2004).

3. John C. Goodman and Devon M. Herrick, *Health Savings Accounts: Answering the Critics: Part II* (National Center for Policy Analysis, March 21, 2006), www.ncpa.org/pub/ba/ba545/, last accessed March 16, 2007.

4. Emmett B. Keeler, *Effects of Cost Sharing on Use of Medical Services and Health* (RAND Corporation, 1992), www.rand.org/pubs/reprints/2005/RP1114.pdf, last accessed March 16, 2007.

5. Joseph P. Newhouse, *Free for All? Lessons from the RAND Health Insurance Experiment* (Cambridge: Harvard University Press, 1993).

6. Kathleen Lohr et al., "Use of Medical Care in the RAND Health Insurance Experiment," *Medical Care* 24 (9, supplement), (September 1986): S1+.

7. Arnold S. Relman, *A Second Opinion: Rescuing America's Health Care* (New York: A Century Foundation Book, Public Affairs, 2007), pp. 102–103.

8. Didem Bernard and Jessica Banthin, *Out of Pocket Expenditures on Health Care and Health Insurance Premiums among the Nonelderly Population, 2003* (Medical Expenditure Panel Survey, Statistical Brief #121, March 2006), www.meps.ahrq .gov/mepsweb/data_files/publications/st121/stat121.pdf, last accessed March 16, 2007.

9. In addition to the original RAND study, other research has shown that greater cost sharing can negatively affect the health of patients by leading them to cut back on medical services. For example, one study found that increased patient cost sharing for prescription drugs in Canada led to a reduction in the use of essential drugs by 15 percent for the elderly and 22 percent for low-income patients. Adverse medical events increased by 117 percent for the elderly and 97 percent for those with low incomes. (See Robyn Tamblyn et al., "Adverse Events Associated with Prescription Drug Cost-Sharing among Poor and Elderly Persons," *Journal of the American Medical Association* 285, no. 4 [January 4, 2001]: 421–429.)

Another study found that after an employer increased cost sharing for prescription drugs, workers discontinued their use of such essential prescriptions as ACE inhibitors and statins by statistically significant levels. (See Haiden A. Huskamp et al., "The Effect of Incentive-Based Formularies on Prescription Drug Utilization and Spending," *New England Journal of Medicine* 349, no. 23 [December 4, 2003]: 2224–2232.)

The Medical Outcomes study, which kept track of 3,589 chronically ill patients for four years, concluded that cost sharing reduced the use of care for both minor and serious symptoms, although the self-reported health status of the individuals was not affected. (See Mitchell D. Wong et al., "Effects of Cost Sharing on Care Seeking and Health Status: Results from the Medical Outcomes Study," *American Journal of Public Health* 91, no. 11 [November 2001]: 1889–1894.)

Moreover, studies show decisively that a much more significant problem than overuse of particular health services is insufficient and inadequate medical care. Between 2003 and 2006, RAND published the results of an even more ambitious study analyzing the quality of health care in America. It found that, overall, the roughly 6,700 participants who agreed to provide access to their medical records received only about half of the recommended care. The study found that the gap between recommended care and the treatment that patients actually received was wide throughout the country, across the income spectrum, for both genders, irrespective of the patient's race, and whether or not patients had insurance. The nature of many of those shortcomings generally fell under the category of insufficient care. For example, participants received appropriate screening services just 52.2 percent of the time and 58.5 percent for follow-up care. The proportion of recommended care for chronic conditions was 56.1 percent. (See *The First National Report Card on the*

Quality of Health Care in America [The RAND Corp., 2006], highlights available at www.rand.org/pubs/research_briefs/2006/RAND_RB9053-2.pdf), last accessed March 16, 2007.

10. Atul Gawande, *Complications: A Surgeon's Notes on an Imperfect Science* (New York: Henry Holt, 2002), pp. 7, 236–237.

11. Douglas Holtz-Eakin, "Health Care Spending and the Uninsured," CBO Testimony before the Senate Committee on Health, Education, Labor, and Pensions, January 28, 2004, p. 9, www.cbo.gov/ftpdocs/49xx/doc4989/01-28-HealthTestimony .pdf, last accessed March 15, 2007.

12. Gerard F. Anderson et al., "Health Spending in the United States and the Rest of the Industrialized World," *Health Affairs* 24, no. 24 (July/August 2005): 903+.

13. See Charles R. Morris, *Too Much of a Good Thing: Why Health Care Spending Won't Make Us Sick* (New York: Century Foundation Press, 2000).

14. Malcolm Gladwell, "The Moral Hazard Myth," *New Yorker*, August 29, 2005, www.newyorker.com/fact/content/articles/050829fa_fact, last accessed March 16, 2007.

15. For a thorough overview, see Edwin Park, *Health Savings Accounts Unlikely to Significantly Reduce Health Care Spending* (Center on Budget and Policy Priorities, June 12, 2006), www.cbpp.org/6-12-06health.htm, last accessed March 16, 2007.

16. Linda Blumberg and Leonard E. Burman, "Most Households' Medical Expenses Exceed HSA Deductibles," *Tax Notes*, August 16, 2004, p. 759, www.urban.org//UploadedPDF/1000678_TaxFacts_081604.pdf, last accessed March 16, 2007.

17. Alan C. Monheit, "Persistence in Health Expenditures in the Short Run: Prevalence and Consequences," *Medical Care* 41 (July 2003 Supplement).

18. Bob Lyke, Chris Peterson, and Neela Ranade, *Health Savings Accounts*, Congressional Research Service, March 23, 2005, p. 29, www.belmont.edu/hr/pdf/ CRSReportforCongress.pdf, last accessed March 16, 2007.

19. "Financial Incentives Alone Unlikely to Curb Health Care Costs, Watson Wyatt Says," Watson Wyatt Worldwide press release, April 24, 2006, available at www.watsonwyatt.com/news/press.asp?ID=15974, last accessed March 16, 2007.

20. Christine Borger, Sheila Smith, Christopher Truffer, et al., "Health Spending Projections through 2015: Changes on the Horizon," *Health Affairs*, Web exclusive, February 22, 2006.

21. See, for example, Laurence Baker et al., "The Relationship between Technology Availability and Health Care Spending," Web exclusive, *Health Affairs*, November 5, 2003; also, Leif Wellington Haase, *A New Deal for Health: How to Cover Everyone and Get Medical Costs under Control* (Century Foundation, 2005), particularly pp. 13–14.

22. See Jason Furman, *Expansion in HSA Tax Breaks Is Larger—and More Problematic—Than Previously Understood* (Center on Budget and Policy Priorities, February 7, 2006), www.cbpp.org/2-4-06tax.htm, last accessed March 16, 2007.

23. For a comprehensive assessment as of June 2006, see Sara R. Collins, "Health Savings Accounts: Why They Won't Cure What Ails U.S. Health Care," the Commonwealth Fund, Invited Testimony, Committee on Ways and Means, U.S. House of Representatives, Hearing on Health Savings Accounts, June 28, 2006, www

.cmwf.org/usr_doc/Collins_WaysandMeans_Testimony__6-28-06.pdf, last accessed March 16, 2007.

24. Paul Fronstin and Sara R. Collins, *Early Experience with High-Deductible and Consumer-Driven Health Plans: Findings from the EBRI/Commonwealth Fund Consumerism in Health Care Survey* (EBRI/Commonwealth Fund, December 2005), www.cmwf.org/usr_doc/fronstin_consumerism_survey.pdf, last accessed March 16, 2007.

25. Ibid., pp. 17–18.

26. Ibid., pp. 18, 20, 23.

27. Sarah Rubinstein, "High-Deductible Shoppers Find HSA Plans May Cost More," *Wall Street Journal*, June 6, 2006.

28. Larry Lutey, Testimony before the House Committee on Ways and Means, June 28, 2006, http://waysandmeans.house.gov/hearings.asp?formmode=view&id =5068, last accessed March 16, 2007.

29. Almost all of the South Africa MSA boosterism comes from one source, Shaun Matisonn, who is the executive vice president of Discovery Health, one of the largest insurance administrators in South Africa. Matisonn has written briefs for the National Center for Policy Analysis and a chapter in a volume edited by Regina E. Herzlinger, *Consumer-Driven Health Care: Implications for Providers, Payers, and Policymakers* (New York: Jossey-Bass, 2004).

30. Timothy Stoltzfus Jost, *Consumer-Driven Health Care in South Africa: Lessons from Comparative Health Policy Studies*, draft manuscript from a forthcoming book.

31. South African Department of Health, *Inquiry in the Various Social Security Aspects of the South African Health Care System*, May 14, 2002, p. 123, www.doh .gov.za/docs/reports/2002/inquiry/medical.pdf, last accessed March 16, 2007.

32. World Health Organization, *Medical Savings Accounts: Lessons Learned from Limited International Experience*, 2002.

33. William C. Hsiao, "Behind the Ideology and Theory: What Is the Empirical Evidence for Medical Savings Accounts?" *Journal of Health Politics, Policy and Law* 26, no. 4 (August 2001), www.hsph.harvard.edu/phcf/Papers/Ideology%20and %20theory%20-%20Hsiao.pdf, last accessed March 16, 2007.

34. Hsiao, "Behind the Ideology."

35. Michael D. Barr, "Medical Savings Accounts in Singapore: A Critical Inquiry," *Journal of Health Politics, Policy and Law* 26, no. 4 (August 2001): 709–726.

36. Fred Brock, "Two Holes in the Medicare Drug Law," *New York Times*, January 11, 2004.

37. *Big Dollars, Little Sense: Rising Medicare Prescription Drug Prices* (Families USA, June 2006), www.familiesusa.org/assets/pdfs/Big-Dollars-Little-Sense.pdf, last accessed March 15, 2007.

38. Colin Baker, *Would Prescription Drug Importation Reduce U.S. Drug Spending?* Congressional Budget Office, April 29, 2004, www.cbo.gov/showdoc.cfm?index =5406&sequence=0, last accessed March 15, 2007.

39. Jonathan Cohn, "Shrug Coverage," *New Republic*, January 30, 2006, www .tnr.com/doc.mhtml?i=20060130&s=trb013006, last accessed March 15, 2007.

40. "Drug Plan Shows Pitfalls, Possibilities of Consumer-Driven Coverage," *National Journal's CongressDaily* (January 26, 2006).

41. President George W. Bush, speech on medical liability reform, Collinsville, Illinois, January 5, 2005, www.whitehouse.gov/news/releases/2005/01/20050105-4.html, last accessed March 15, 2007.

42. Tom Baker, *The Medical Malpractice Myth* (Chicago: University of Chicago Press, 2005).

43. Harvard Medical Practice Study, *Patients, Doctors, and Lawyers: Medical Injury, Malpractice Litigation, and Patient Compensation in New York: The Report of the Harvard Medical Practice Study to the State of New York* (Cambridge, Mass.: Harvard University Press, 1990).

44. Seth A. Seabury, Nicholas M. Pace, and Robert T. Reville, "Forty Years of Jury Verdicts," *Journal of Empirical Legal Studies* 1, no. 1 (March 2004): 1–25.

45. Baker, *The Medical Malpractice Myth*, pp. 148–152.

46. Congressional Budget Office, *The Effects of Tort Reform: Evidence from the States*, June 2004, www.cbo.gov/showdoc.cfm?index=5549&sequence=0, last accessed March 16, 2007.

47. See Haase's "A New Deal for Health" for trade-offs among different universal approaches.

48. Information about the institute and the program is available at its home page: www.ihi.org/ihi, last accessed March 16, 2007.

49. Karen Auge, "Data Get to Heart of Hospital Care," *Denver Post*, June 27, 2006, p. B-01.

50. Klein, "The Medical Malpractice Myth." *Slate*, July 11, 2006, www.slate.com/id/2145400/.

9. "A Sure Loser"

1. Indermit Gill, Truman Packard, and Juan Yermo, *Keeping the Promise of Social Security in Latin America* (World Bank and Stanford University Press, 2004), portions available at wbln1018.worldbank.org/LAC/LAC.nsf/ECADocbyUnid/146EBBA3371508E785256CBB005C29B4?Opendocument, last accessed March 15, 2007.

2. Stephen J. Kay, *State Capacity and Pensions* (report prepared for the LASA XXIV International Congress in Dallas, March 27–29, 2003), www.frbatlanta.org/filelegacydocs/StateCapacityandPensionsKay.pdf, last accessed March 15, 2007.

3. Larry Rohter, "Chile's Candidates Agree to Agree on Pension Woes," *New York Times*, January 10, 2006, p. 3.

4. Norma Cohen, "A Bloody Mess," *American Prospect*, January 11, 2005, www.prospect.org/web/printfriendly-view.ww?id=8997, last accessed March 19, 2007.

5. Cohen, "Bloody Mess."

6. Jackie Calmes, "How a Victorious Bush Fumbled Plan to Revamp Social Security: A Divided Republican Party, Strong Opposition Derails Push for Private Accounts," *Wall Street Journal*, October 20, 2005, p. A1.

7. See, for example, Robert M. Ball, "Meeting Social Security's Long-Range Shortfall" (Century Foundation, September 5, 2006), www.tcf.org/Publications/

RetirementSecurity/ballplan.pdf, last accessed March 19, 2007. Ball's plan has five main elements: (1) gradually raising the cap on earnings covered by Social Security so that 90 percent would be taxed and counted for benefits; (2) beginning in 2010, changing the estate tax to a dedicated Social Security tax; (3) investing a portion of the trust fund in equities; (4) adapting the more accurate consumer price index (the so-called chained index) recently developed by the Bureau of Labor Statistics in calculating cost of living increases in Social Security benefits; and (5) beginning in 2010, covering all new state and local employees under Social Security—the only significant category of workers who remain uncovered.

8. Because the privatization debate took place in 2005, this chapter uses the numbers from that year's Trustees report even though they have been subsequently updated (with only very minor changes). The 2005 Trustees report and a summary of it are available here: www.ssa.gov/OACT/TR/TR05/index.html, last accessed March 19, 2007.

9. Jason Furman and Robert Greenstein, *What the New Trustees' Report Shows about Social Security* (Center on Budget and Policy Priorities, March 24, 2005), www.cbpp.org/3-23-05socsec.pdf, last accessed March 19, 2007.

10. Jason Furman, William G. Gale, and Peter R. Orszag, *Would Borrowing $2 Trillion for Individual Accounts Eliminate $10 Trillion in Social Security Liabilities?* (Center on Budget and Policy Priorities, December 13, 2004), www.cbpp.org/12-13 -04socsec.htm, last accessed March 19, 2007.

11. Congressional Budget Office, *The Outlook for Social Security*, June 2004, chap. 1, www.cbo.gov/showdoc.cfm?index=5530&sequence=0, last accessed March 19, 2007; note that since the 2005 debate, CBO has issued new projections forecasting that the trust fund would become depleted in 2046.

12. Jason Furman, *The Impact of the President's Proposal on Social Security Solvency and the Budget* (Center on Budget and Policy Priorities, July 22, 2005), www.cbpp.org/5-10-05socsec.htm, last accessed March 19, 2007.

13. A common claim among privatization advocates is that all their plans would merely borrow now instead of borrowing later. Cato's Michael Tanner, for example, has said, "All we're asking Congress to do now is pay a little more up front, rather than pay a lot more later. We're not creating new costs. We're taking costs that exist but are simply kept off the books right now, we're putting them on the books to be honest about them, then we're moving them forward in time and paying them today rather than tomorrow. So I think the whole idea of this transition thing is a bit of a red herring." What's fishy, though, is Tanner's argument. His claim only begins to approach reality if no adjustments are ever made to actually strengthen Social Security's finances. But the seventy-five-year shortfall could be averted entirely through a combination of modest benefit cuts and tax increases without any borrowing whatsoever. In the process, federal debt would be substantially reduced rather than increased. For example, former Social Security commissioner Robert Ball's reform proposal would eradicate the shortfall while cutting the national debt by more than 28 percent of GDP by 2050, according to calculations by the Center on Budget and Policy Priorities. Under his plan, the government's annual interest payments would be $188 billion lower, in today's dollars, than they would otherwise be. In contrast, interest

payments would be $133 billion higher under the president's privatization proposal. (See James Horney and Richard Kogan, *Private Accounts Would Substantially Increase Federal Debt and Interest Payments* [Center on Budget and Policy Priorities, August 2, 2005], www.cbpp.org/7-27-05socsec-sum.htm, last accessed March 19, 2007.)

14. See Robert Barro, "Why Private Accounts Are Bad Public Policy," *Business Week*, April 4, 2005, www.businessweek.com/magazine/content/05_14/b3927030_mz007.htm, last accessed March 19, 2007; Gary Becker, "A Political Case for Social Security Reform," *Wall Street Journal*, February 15, 2005, www.opinionjournal.com/extra/?id=110006321, last accessed March 19, 2007; and John Geanakoplos, Olivia Mitchell, and Stephen Zeldes, *Would a Privatized Social Security System Really Pay a Higher Rate of Return?* [National Bureau of Economic Research Reprint No. 2206, 1998].

15. Much more detail about this subject is available in Jason Furman, *Would Private Accounts Provide a Higher Rate of Return Than Social Security?* (Center on Budget and Policy Priorities, June 2, 2005), www.cbpp.org/6-2-05socsec.htm, last accessed March 19, 2007.

16. Benefits cut under "progressive price indexing," an idea put forward by the president's Social Security commission, would have the effect over time of significantly reducing the share of past earnings that Social Security benefits would replace upon retirement. Instead of tying benefit levels to increases in average wages over the course of a worker's career, they would be linked to price inflation—which over time is lower than wage growth. The effect would be relatively modest at first, but decades from now, benefits for middle-income and upper-income workers would be much lower than they otherwise would be.

17. Jason Furman, *How Would the President's New Social Security Proposals Affect Middle Class Workers and Social Security Solvency?* (Center on Budget and Policy Priorities, revised May 10, 2005), www.cbpp.org/4-29-05socsec.htm, last accessed March 19, 2007. Note that the projections for Social Security are based on currently scheduled benefits. Assuming an alternative scenario in which guaranteed benefits would be cut to the level now projected after the trust fund becomes depleted is problematic because privatization proposals themselves don't cover a large share of the shortfall. The appropriate benchmark to use for measuring benefit changes under any proposal is what the public expects to receive—that is, the existing benefit structure.

18. *Social Security: Performance and Accountability Report for Fiscal Year 2005* (Baltimore: Social Security Administration, 2005), p. 9, www.socialsecurity.gov/finance/2005/FY_05_PAR.pdf, last accessed March 19, 2007.

19. David Stockman, *The Triumph of Politics* (New York: Harper and Row, 1986), p. 187.

20. Lou Cannon, *President Reagan: The Role of a Lifetime* (New York: PublicAffairs, 1991, 2000), p. 214.

21. Edward D. Berkowitz, *Robert Ball and the Politics of Social Security* (Madison: University of Wisconsin Press, 2003), pp. 303–304.

22. Michael A. Hiltzik, *The Plot against Social Security* (New York: Harper-Collins, 2005), p. 89.

23. President Ronald Reagan's remarks on signing the Social Security Amendments of 1983, April 20, 1983, www.ssa.gov/history/reaganstmts.html#1983, last accessed March 19, 2007.

24. President George W. Bush's remarks at West Virginia University in Parkersburg, West Virginia, April 5, 2005, www.whitehouse.gov/news/releases/2005/04/print/20050405-4.html, last accessed March 19, 2007.

25. Stuart Butler and Peter Germanis, "Achieving a 'Leninist' Strategy," *Cato Journal* 3, no. 2 (Fall 1983): 547+.

26. Nancy J. Altman, *The Battle for Social Security: From FDR's Vision to Bush's Gamble* (New York: John Wiley & Sons, 2005), p. 258.

27. Edmund L. Andrews, "Clamor Grows in the Privatization Debate," *New York Times*, December 17, 2004, p. 26.

28. See Joseph White, *False Alarm: Why the Greatest Threat to Social Security and Medicare Is the Campaign to "Save" Them* (Baltimore: A Century Foundation Book, Johns Hopkins University Press, 2001).

29. Eoghan W. Stafford, "Spotlight on Marty," *Harvard Crimson*, February 10, 2003, www.thecrimson.com/article.aspx?ref=270923, last accessed March 19, 2007; see also David Leonhardt, "Scholarly Mentor to Bush's Team," *New York Times*, December 1, 2002, section 3, p. 1.

30. U.S. Congressional Budget Office, letter from June E. O'Neill, director, to the Honorable Bill Archer analyzing a proposal by Professor Martin Feldstein to set up personal retirement accounts financed by tax credits, August 4, 1998, www.cbo.gov/showdoc.cfm?index=763&sequence=0, last accessed March 19, 2007.

31. Peter R. Orszag and Jonathan M. Orszag, *All That Glitters Is Not Gold: The Feldstein-Liebman Analysis of Reforming Social Security with Individual Accounts* (Center on Budget and Policy Priorities, April 26, 2000), www.cbpp.org/4-26-00socsec.pdf, last accessed March 19, 2007.

32. Martin Feldstein and Jeffrey Liebman, "The Distributional Effects of an Investment-Based Social Security System" (Working Paper 7492, National Bureau of Economic Research, January 2000).

33. Roger Lowenstein, "A Question of Numbers," *New York Times Magazine*, January 16, 2005, pp. 40+.

34. Milton Friedman, *Capitalism and Freedom* (Chicago: University of Chicago Press, 1962, reissued in 1982 with new preface), p. 182.

35. Barry Goldwater, *Conscience of a Conservative* (Shepherdsville, Ky.: Victor Publishing, 1960).

36. Letter to Dwight D. Eisenhower's brother Edgar Newton Eisenhower, November 8, 1954, www.eisenhowermemorial.org/presidential-papers/first-term/documents/1147.cfm, last accessed March 19, 2007.

37. Ron Suskind, *The Price of Loyalty: George W. Bush, the White House, and the Education of Paul O'Neill* (New York: Simon and Schuster, 2004), p. 156.

38. Available on the commission's Web site: www.csss.gov/, last accessed March 19, 2007.

39. Hiltzik, *The Plot against Social Security*, p. 198.

40. Deborah Pryce and Rick Santorum, *Saving Social Security: A Guide to Social Security Reform*, House and Senate Republican Conference, January 27, 2005, www.talkingpointsmemo.com/docs/gop.socsec.strategy.memo.pdf, last accessed March 19, 2007.

41. Michael Tanner, "One Wasted Year = $660 Billion," *New York Sun*, November 21, 2005; www.cato.org/pub_display.php?pub_id=5212, last accessed March 19, 2007.

42. See *Brad DeLong's Semi-Daily Journal*, May 22, 2006, http://delong.typepad.com/sdj/2006/05/greg_mankiw_cri.html, last accessed March 19, 2007.

10. America's *Real* Problem—and How to Overcome It

1. See Jacob S. Hacker, *The Great Risk Shift* (New York: Oxford University Press, 2006).

2. Mark Schmitt of the New America Foundation was, to my knowledge, the first to draw the important connections between security and opportunity. See, for example, this post on his blog: http://markschmitt.typepad.com/decembrist/2005/03/security_iis_io.html, last accessed March 19, 2007. See also Jacob S. Hacker, "Message of Truth: Security and Opportunity Go Hand-in-Hand," *The Democratic Strategist*, September 2006, www.thedemocraticstrategist.org/0609/hackerRT.php, last accessed March 19, 2007.

3. Ross Douthat and Reihan Salam, "The Buck Starts Here," *Weekly Standard*, October 9, 2006, www.theweeklystandard.com/Content/Public/Articles/000/000/012/762fiyke.asp?pg=1, last accessed March 19, 2007.

4. Jonathan Rauch, *Government's End: Why Washington Stopped Working* (New York: PublicAffairs, 1999), pp. 244–245.

5. Michael Lind, *Up from Conservatism: Why the Right Is Wrong for America* (New York: Free Press Paperbacks, 1996), p. 269.

INDEX